BY PHILIP S. FONER

The Life and Writings of Frederick Douglass (4 vols.)
History of the Labor Movement in the United States (4 vols.)
A History of Cuba and Its Relations with the United States (2 vols.)
The Complete Writings of Thomas Paine (2 vols.)
Business and Slavery: The New York Merchants and the Irrepressible Conflict
The Fur and Leather Workers Union
Jack London: American Rebel
Mark Twain: Social Critic
The Jews in American History: 1654-1865
The Autobiographies of the Haymarket Martyrs
The Case of Joe Hill
The Letters of Joe Hill
The Bolshevik Revolution: Its Impact on American Radicals, Liberals, and Labor
The Black Panthers Speak
Helen Keller: Her Socialist Years
The Basic Writings of Thomas Jefferson
The Selected Writings of George Washington
The Selected Writings of Abraham Lincoln
The Selected Writings of Franklin D. Roosevelt

W.E.B.
DU BOIS
SPEAKS

Speeches and Addresses
1920-1963

Edited by Dr. Philip S. Foner

With a tribute by
Dr. Kwame Nkrumah

PATHFINDER

New York   London   Montréal   Sydney

Copyright © 1970 by Philip S. Foner and Shirley Graham Du Bois
All rights reserved

ISBN 0-87348-126-7 paper; 0-87348-182-8 cloth
Library of Congress Catalog Card No. 78-108719
Manufactured in the United States of America

First edition, 1970
Seventh printing, January 1991

Acknowledgment is gratefully made to the following for
    permission to reprint the specified material:
Shirley Graham Du Bois for "The Revelation of Saint Orgne
    the Damned," copyright © 1939 by W.E.B. Du Bois.
University of Chicago Press for "Prospect of a World Without
    Race Conflict," from *American Journal of Sociology,* March 1944.
    Copyright © 1944 by University of Chicago Press.
National Association for the Advancement of Colored People
    for "An Appeal to the World" and "The Negro and Imperialism."
New Masses for "Bound by the Color Line."
Masses & Mainstream for "Behold the Land" and "I Take My Stand."
The estate of Daniel S. Gillmore for "The Nature of Intellectual Freedom."
Jewish Life for "The Negro and the Warsaw Ghetto."
Seven Sea Books, Berlin, for "What Is Wrong with the United States?"
Shirley Graham Du Bois for "Africa Awake!" and "Hail Humankind!"
Helen Alfred for "The Negro and Socialism."
*Freedomways: A Quarterly Review of the Negro Freedom
    Movement* for "Encyclopedia Africana."

Pathfinder
410 West Street, New York, NY 10014, U.S.A.

Pathfinder distributors around the world:
Australia (and Asia and the Pacific):
    Pathfinder, 19 Terry St., Surry Hills, Sydney, NSW 2010
Britain (and Europe, Africa, and the Middle East):
    Pathfinder, 47 The Cut, London, SE1 8LL
Canada:
    Pathfinder, 6566, boul. St-Laurent, Montréal, Québec, H2S 3C6
Iceland:
    Pathfinder, Klapparstíg 26, 2d floor, 121 Reykjavík
New Zealand:
    Pathfinder, 157a Symonds Street, Auckland
Sweden:
    Pathfinder, Vikingagatan 10, S-113 42, Stockholm
United States (and Caribbean and Latin America):
    Pathfinder, 410 West Street, New York, NY 10014

CONTENTS

PREFACE

In the first volume of *W. E. B. Du Bois Speaks*, we brought the career of this great black American to the period immediately after World War I and closed the volume with his platform for the future of Africa. This was read to a meeting sponsored by the NAACP while Dr. Du Bois himself was in France working to implement the terms of his platform at the Versailles Peace Congress.

In the present volume, Dr. Du Bois's speeches cover the years 1920 to his death in Ghana in 1963. In 1936, in an address at the Centennial Exposition of the Republic of Texas, Dr. Du Bois pointed out: "The Negro is the central thread of American history." The material in this volume offers us enormous insights into that "central thread." Certainly no one who wishes to understand Afro-American history from the turn of the twentieth century can achieve this without reading the penetrating concepts set forth in *W. E. B. Du Bois Speaks*. Moreover, since Dr. Du Bois constantly used the Negro's past to illuminate the problems America faced and the path which it must follow to solve them, the reader will also obtain an unusual understanding of the entire background of black Americans from Africa through a large portion of the twentieth century.

The present volume clearly reveals Dr. Du Bois's growing radicalism as he matured in his experience and thinking. Always interested in socialism, he became more and more convinced as events revealed the increasing evils of capitalism and imperialism, that only a socialist society held out hope for mankind and especially for Negro Americans and his beloved Africa. In 1958 he put it bluntly: " . . . it is clear that the salvation of American Negroes lies in socialism."

Present-day students who might wonder what America was like during the terrible years of McCarthyism may be able to understand when they read that at the time friends and admirers of this great black scholar sought to honor him on his ninetieth birthday in 1958, not a single American of distinction dared to sponsor the event. Dr. Du Bois had committed the sin of identifying himself with peace and socialism and of refusing to join the anti-Soviet, anti-Communist witch-hunters.

But contemporary students will also obtain inspiration from Dr. Du Bois's courage during those years, so tragic for American democracy, when his voice was heard repeatedly telling the American people: "No! Enough of this hysteria, this crazy foolishness!" That voice is still today, but the insights, the courage, and the confidence of W. E. B. Du Bois are still with us in the pages of these two volumes.

Shortly the letters of W. E. B. Du Bois, edited by Herbert Aptheker (who is also editing a multi-volume collection of Dr. Du Bois's writings), will be published by J. B. Lippincott Company, and Dr. Du Bois's brilliant editorials in *The Crisis*, edited by Henry Lee Moon, will be published by Simon and Schuster, Inc. These volumes, speeches, letters and editorials, will give us at last a thorough understanding of a man whose life comprised an important chapter in world history.

In preparing the present volume, I received much assistance from numerous organizations. I wish to thank the staffs of the libraries of Lincoln University, Pennsylvania, the Schomburg Branch of the New York Public Library, the Library of Congress, Talladega College Library, Fisk University Library, and Howard University Library. I also wish to thank the following for permission to reprint speeches of Dr. Du Bois: *Freedomways, National Guardian, Jewish Currents* (formerly *Jewish Life*), *The Worker, American Journal of Sociology, New Masses*, Helen Alfred, Encyclopedia Africana Secretariat, the National Association for the Advancement of Colored People, and the Estate of Daniel S. Gillmor. I am especially indebted to Mrs. Shirley Graham Du Bois for her cooperation in the undertaking.

Philip S. Foner
Lincoln University, Pennsylvania

1

ON BEING BLACK

While he was at Fisk, Du Bois declared publicly: "I am a Negro; and I glory in the name! I am proud of the black blood that flows in my veins. . . . [I] have come here . . . to join hands with my people." He joined hands in their humiliations too. But he always fought back, and in speeches to audiences throughout the years, he told what it meant to be black in the United States. In 1920, The New Republic *published "On Being Black" which was shortly to appear in Du Bois's book,* Darkwater.

My friend, who is pale and positive, said to me yesterday, as the tired sun was nodding: "You are too sensitive."

I admit, I am — sensitive, I am artificial. I cringe or am bumptious or immobile. I am intellectually dishonest, art-blind, and I lack humor.

"Why don't you stop all this," she retorts triumphantly.

You will not let us.

"There you go, again. You know that I — "

Wait! I answer. Wait!

I arise at seven. The milkman has neglected me. He pays little attention to colored districts. My white neighbor glares elaborately. I walk softly, lest I disturb him. The children jeer as I pass to work. The women in the streetcar withdraw their skirts or prefer to stand. The policeman is truculent. The elevator man hates to serve Negroes. My job is insecure because the white union wants it and does not want me. I try to lunch, but no place near will serve me. I go forty blocks to Marshall's, but the Committee of Fourteen closes Marshall's; they say that white women frequent it.

"Do all eating places discriminate?"

No, but how shall I know which do not — except —

I hurry home through crowds. They mutter or get angry. I go to a mass meeting. They stare. I go to a church. "We don't admit niggers!"

Or perhaps I leave the beaten track. I seek new work. "Our employees would not work with you; our customers would object."

I ask to help in social uplift.

"Why — er — we will write you."

I enter the free field of science. Every laboratory door is closed and no endowments are available.

I seek the universal mistress, Art; the studio door is locked.

I write literature. "We cannot publish stories of colored folk of that type." It's the only type I know.

This is my life. It makes me idiotic. It gives me artificial problems. I hesitate, I rush, I waver. In fine — I am sensitive!

My pale friend looks at me with disbelief and curling tongue.

"Do you mean to sit there and tell me that this is what happens to you each day?"

Certainly not, I answer low.

"Then you only fear it will happen?"

I fear!

"Well, haven't you the courage to rise above a — almost a craven fear?"

Quite — quite craven is my fear, I admit; but the terrible thing is — these things do happen!

"But you just said —"

They do happen. Not all each day — surely not. But now and then — now seldom; now, sudden; now after a week, now in a chain of awful minutes; not everywhere, but anywhere — in Boston, in Atlanta. That's the hell of it. Imagine spending your life looking for insults or for hiding places from them — shrinking (instinctively and despite desperate bolsterings of courage) from blows that are not always, but ever; not each day, but each week, each month, each year. Just, perhaps, as you have choked back the craven fear and cried, "I am and will be the master of my—"

"No more tickets downstairs; here's one to the smoking gallery."

You hesitate. You beat back your suspicions. After all, a cigarette with Charlie Chaplin—then a white man pushes by—

"Three in the orchestra."

"Yes, sir." And in he goes.

Suddenly your heart chills. You turn yourself away toward the golden twinkle of the purple night and hesitate again. What's the use? Why not always yield—always take what's offered—always bow to force, whether of cannons or dislike? Then the great fear surges in your soul, the real fear—the fear beside which other fears are vain imaginings; the fear lest right there and then you are losing your own soul; that you are losing your own soul and the soul of a people; that millions of unborn children, black and gold and mauve, are being there and then despoiled by you because you are a coward and dare not fight!

Suddenly that silly orchestra seat and the cavorting of a comedian with funny feet become matters of life, death, and immortality; you grasp the pillars of the universe and strain as you sway back to that befrilled ticket girl. You grip your soul for riot and murder. You choke and sputter, and she, seeing that you are about to make a "fuss," obeys her orders and throws the tickets at you in contempt. Then you slink to your seat and crouch in the darkness before the film, with every tissue burning! The miserable wave of reaction engulfs you. To think of compelling puppies to take your hard-earned money; fattening hogs to hate you and yours; forcing your way among cheap and tawdry idiots—God! What a night of pleasure!

*   *   *

Why do not those who are scarred in the world's battle and hurt by its hardness, travel to these places of beauty and drown themselves in the utter joy of life? I asked this once sitting in a southern home. Outside, the spring of a Georgia February was luring gold to the bushes and languor to the soft air. Around me sat color in human flesh — brown that crimsoned readily; dim soft-yellow that escaped description; cream-like duskiness that shadowed to rich tints of autumn leaves. And yet a suggested journey in the world brought no response.

"I should think you would like to travel," said the white one.

But no, the thought of a journey seemed to depress them.

Did you ever see a "Jim-Crow" waiting-room? There are always exceptions, as at Greensboro — but usually there is no heat in winter and no air in summer; with undisturbed loafers and train hands and broken, disreputable settees; to buy a ticket is torture; you stand and stand and wait and wait until every white person at the "other window" is waited on. Then the tired agent yells across, because all the tickets and money are over there —

"What d'y'e want? What? Where?"

The agent browbeats and contradicts you, hurries and confuses the ignorant, gives many persons the wrong change, compels some to purchase their tickets on the train at a higher price, and sends you and me out on the platform, burning with indignation and hatred!

The "Jim-Crow" car is up next the baggage car and engine. It stops out beyond the covering in the rain or sun or dust. Usually there is no step to help you climb on, and often the car is a smoker cut in two, and you must pass through the white smokers or else they pass through your part, with swagger and noise and stares. Your compartment is a half or a quarter or an eighth of the oldest car in service on the road. Unless it happens to be a through express, the plush is caked with dirt, the floor is grimy, and the windows dirty. An impertinent white newsboy occupies two seats at the end of the car and importunes you to the point of rage to buy cheap candy, Coca-Cola, and worthless, if not vulgar, books. He yells and swaggers, while a continued stream of white men saunters back and forth from the smoker, to buy and hear. The white train crew from the baggage car uses the "Jim-Crow" to lounge in and perform their toilet. The conductor appropriates two seats for himself and his papers and yells gruffly for your tickets almost before the train has started. It is best not to ask him for information even in the gentlest tones. His information is for white persons chiefly. It is difficult to get lunch or clean water. Lunchrooms either don't serve niggers or serve them at some dirty and ill-attended hole in the wall. As for toilet rooms — don't! If you have to change cars, be wary of junctions which are usually without accommodation and filled with quarrelsome white persons who hate a "darky dressed up." You are apt to have the company of a sheriff and a couple of meek or sullen black prisoners on part of your way and dirty colored section hands will pour in toward night and drive you to the smallest corner.

"No," said the little lady in the corner (she looked like an ivory cameo and her dress flowed on her like a caress) "We don't travel much."

Pessimism is cowardice. The man who cannot frankly acknowledge the "Jim-Crow" car as a fact and yet live and hope, is simply afraid either of himself or of the world. There is not in the world a more disgraceful denial of human brotherhood than the "Jim-Crow" car of the southern United States; but, too, just as true, there is nothing more beautiful in the universe than sunset and moonlight on Montego Bay in far Jamaica. And both things are true and both belong to this, our world, and neither can be denied.

*   *   *

High in the tower, where I sit above the loud complaining of the human sea, I know many souls that toss and whirl and pass, but none there are that intrigue me more than the Souls of White Folk.

Of them I am singularly clairvoyant. I see in and through them. I view them from unusual points of vantage. Not as a foreigner do I come, for I am native, not foreign, bone of their thought and flesh of their language. Mine is not the knowledge of the traveler or the colonial composite of dear memories, words and wonder. Nor yet is my knowledge that which servants have of masters, or mass of class, or capitalist of artisan. Rather I see the working of their entrails. I know their thoughts and they know that I know. This knowledge makes them now embarrassed, now furious! They deny my right to live and be and call me misbirth! My word is to them mere bitterness and my soul, pessimism. And yet as they preach and strut and shout and threaten, crouching as they clutch at rags of facts and fancies to hide their nakedness, they go twisting, flying by my tired eyes and I see them ever stripped — ugly, human.

The discovery of personal whiteness among the world's peoples is a very modern thing — a nineteenth and twentieth century matter, indeed. The ancient world would have laughed at such a distinction. The Middle-Age regarded skin color with mild curiosity; and even up into the eighteenth century we were hammering our national manikins into one, great, Universal Man, with fine frenzy which ignored color and race even more than birth. Today we have changed all that, and the world in a sudden, emotional conversion has discovered that it is white and by that token, wonderful!

*   *   *

As we saw the dead dimly through rifts of battlesmoke and heard faintly the cursings and accusations of blood brothers, we darker men said: This is not Europe gone mad; this is not aberration nor insanity; this is Europe; this seeming Terrible is the real soul of white culture — back of all culture — stripped and visible today. This is where the world has arrived — these dark and awful depths, and not the shining and ineffable heights of which it boasted. Here is wither the might and energy of modern humanity has really gone.

But may not the world cry back at us and ask: "What better thing have you to show? What have you done or would do better than this if you had today the world rule? Paint with all riot of hateful colors the thin skin of European culture — is it not better than any culture that arose in Africa or Asia?"

It is. Of this there is no doubt and never has been; but why is it better? Is it better because Europeans are better, nobler, greater, and more gifted than other folk? It is not. Europe has never produced and never will in our day bring forth a single human soul who cannot be matched and overmatched in every line of human endeavor by Asia and Africa. Run the gamut, if you will, and let us have the Europeans who in sober truth overmatch Nefertari, Mohammed, Rameses, and Askea, Confucius, Buddha, and Jesus Christ. If we could scan the calendar of thousands of lesser men, in like comparison, the result would be the same; but we cannot do this because of the deliberately educated ignorance of white schools by which they remember Napoleon and forget Sonni Ali.[1]

Why, then, is Europe great? Because of the foundations which the mighty past have furnished her to build upon: the iron trade of ancient, black Africa, the religion and empire-building of yellow Asia, the art and science of the "dago" Mediterranean shore, east, south, and west, as well as north. And where she has builded securely upon this great past and learned from it, she has gone forward to greater and more splendid human triumph; but where she has ignored this past and forgotten and sneered at it, she has shown the cloven hoof of poor, crucified humanity — she has played, like other empires gone, the world fool!

The New Republic, February 18, 1920, pp. 338-41

2

MARCUS GARVEY

In the bitter, tension-ridden years after World War I Marcus Garvey's Universal Negro Improvement Association won millions of followers, particularly among the black masses of the northern cities. Garvey led the greatest black nationalist movement in American history, and appealed to the black masses as no leader had ever before. While scholars disagree over the actual numbers of members Garvey recruited for the UNIA — estimates range from 500,000 to three million — there is no question that Garvey launched the first mass movement among black Americans, and that his influence has continued down to the present day.

The goals of the Universal Negro Improvement Association were to instill race pride, develop an independent black colony in Africa, and gain economic and political control of black communities in the United States. With these objectives, Dr. Du Bois, in the main, agreed, and in a number of speeches on Garvey, he described him as "a sincere, hardworking idealist," but also a "stubborn, domineering leader of the mass." He had "worthy industrial and commercial schemes," but was "an inexperienced businessman." While Garvey's "dream of Negro industry, commerce and the ultimate freedom of Africa were feasible," his "methods are bombastic, wasteful, illogical and ineffective and almost illegal." Du Bois also opposed Garvey on the question of social equality, criticizing him for being willing to accept the position that the United States belonged to the white race and the Negro should not fight for equality in American society. His most telling criticism

*consisted of a detailed recitation of the financing of the
Black Star Line which Garvey launched through the sale
of stock to blacks only.*

*Much of what Dr. Du Bois said about Garvey in his
speeches was published in* The Crisis *of December 1920
and January 1921 and is presented below.*

Marcus Garvey was born at St. Ann's Bay, Jamaica,
about 1885. He was educated at the public school and
then for a short time attended the Church of England
Grammar School, although he was a Roman Catholic
by religion. On leaving school he learned the printing
trade and followed it for many years. In Costa Rica
he was associated with Marclam Taylor in publishing
the *Bluefield's Messenger.* Later he was on the staff of
La Nacion. He then returned to Jamaica and worked
as a printer, being foreman of the printing department
of P. Benjamin's Manufacturing Company of Kingston.
Later he visited Europe and spent some time in England
and France and while abroad conceived his scheme of
organizing the Negro Improvement Society. This society
was launched August 1, 1914, in Jamaica, with these
general objects among others:

"To establish a Universal Confraternity among the race";
"to promote the spirit of race pride and love"; "to administer to and assist the needy"; "to strengthen the imperialism of independent African States"; "to conduct a worldwide commercial and industrial intercourse."

His first practical object was to be the establishment of
a farm school. Meetings were held and the Roman Catholic Bishop, the Mayor of Kingston, and many others
addressed them. Nevertheless the project did not succeed
and Mr. Garvey was soon in financial difficulties. He
therefore practically abandoned the Jamaica field and
came to the United States. In the United States his movement for many years languished until at last with the
increased migration from the West Indies during the war
he succeeded in establishing a strong nucleus in the Harlem district of New York City.

His program now enlarged and changed somewhat in

emphasis. He began especially to emphasize the commercial development of the Negroes and as an islander familiar with the necessities of ship traffic he planned the "Black Star Line." The public for a long time regarded this as simply a scheme of exploitation, when they were startled by hearing that Garvey had bought a ship. This boat was a former coasting vessel, thirty-two years old, but it was put into commission with a black crew and a black captain and was announced as the first of a fleet of vessels which would trade between the colored peoples of America, the West Indies and Africa. With this beginning, the popularity and reputation of Mr. Garvey and his association increased quickly.

In addition to the *Yarmouth* he is said to have purchased two small boats, the *Shadyside,* a small excursion steamer which made daily excursions up the Hudson, and a yacht which was designed to cruise among the West Indies and collect cargo in some central spot for the *Yarmouth.* He had first announced the Black Star Line as a five million dollar corporation, but in February 1920, he announced that it was going to be a ten million dollar corporation with shares selling at five dollars. To this he added in a few months the Negro Factories Corporation capitalized at one million dollars with two hundred thousand one-dollar shares, and finally he announced the subscription of five million dollars to free Liberia and Haiti from debt.

Early in 1920 he called a convention of Negroes to meet in New York City from the first to the thirty-first of August, "to outline a constructive plan and program for the uplifting of the Negroes and the redemption of Africa." He also took title to three apartment houses to be used as offices and purchased the foundation of an unfinished Baptist Church which he covered over and used for meetings, calling it "Liberty Hall." In August 1920, his convention met with representatives from various parts of the United States, several of the West Indian Islands and the Canal Zone and a few from Africa. The convention carried out its plan of a month's meetings and culminated with a mass meeting which filled Madison Square Garden. Finally the convention adopted a "Declaration of Independence" with sixty-six articles, a universal anthem and colors — red, black and green — and elected Mr. Garvey as "His Excellency, the Provisional President of Africa," together with a number of various other leaders from the various parts of the Negro world. This in brief is the history of the Garvey movement.

The question comes: (1) Is it an honest, sincere movement? (2) Are its industrial and commercial projects businesslike and effective? (3) Are its general objects plausible and capable of being carried out?

The central and dynamic force of the movement is Garvey. He has with singular success capitalized and made vocal the great and long-suffering grievances and spirit of protest among the West Indian peasantry. Hitherto the black peasantry of the West Indies has been almost leaderless. Its natural leaders, both mulatto and black, have crossed the color line and practically obliterated social distinction, and to some extent economic distinction, between them and the white English world on the Islands. This has left a peasantry with only the rudiments of education and with almost no economic chances, groveling at the bottom. Their distress and needs gave Garvey his vision.

It is a little difficult to characterize the man Garvey. He has been charged with dishonesty and graft, but he seems to me essentially an honest and sincere man with a tremendous vision, great dynamic force, stubborn determination and unselfish desire to serve; but also he has very serious defects of temperament and training: he is dictatorial, domineering, inordinately vain and very suspicious. He cannot get on with his fellow workers. His entourage has continually changed. [1] He has had endless lawsuits and some cases of fisticuffs with his subordinates and has even divorced the young wife whom he married with great fanfare of trumpets about a year ago. All these things militate against him and his reputation. Nevertheless I have not found the slightest proof that his objects were not sincere or that he was consciously diverting money to his own uses. The great difficulty with him is that he has absolutely no business sense, no flair for real organization and his general objects are so shot through with bombast and exaggeration that it is difficult to pin them down for careful examination.

On the other hand, Garvey is an extraordinary leader of

men. Thousands of people believe in him. He is able to stir them with singular eloquence and the general run of his thought is of a high plane. He has become to thousands of people a sort of religion. He allows and encourages all sorts of personal adulation, even printing in his paper the addresses of some of the delegates who hailed him as "His Majesty." He dons on state occasion a costume consisting of an academic cap and gown flounced in red and green!

Of Garvey's curious credulity and suspicions one example will suffice: in March 1919, he held a large mass meeting at Palace Casino which was presided over by Chandler Owen and addressed by himself and Phillip Randolph. Here he collected $204 in contributions on the plea that while in France, W. E. B. Du Bois had interfered with the work of his "High Commissioner" by "defeating" his articles in the French press and "repudiating" his statements as to lynching and injustice in America! The truth was that Mr. Du Bois never saw or heard of his "High Commissioner," never denied his nor anyone's statements of the wretched American conditions, did everything possible to arouse rather than quiet the French press and would have been delighted to welcome and cooperate with any colored fellow worker.

When it comes to Mr. Garvey's industrial and commercial enterprises there is more ground for doubt and misgiving than in the matter of his character. First of all, his enterprises are incorporated in Delaware, where the corporation laws are loose and where no financial statements are required.[2] So far as I can find, and I have searched with care, Mr. Garvey has never published a complete statement of the income and expenditures of the Negro Improvement Association or of the Black Star Line or of any of his enterprises, which really revealed his financial situation. A courteous letter of inquiry sent to him July 22, 1920, asking for such financial data as he was willing for the public to know, remains to this day unacknowledged and unanswered.

Now a refusal to publish a financial statement is no proof of dishonesty, but it *is* proof that either Garvey is ill-advised and unnecessarily courting suspicion, or that his industrial enterprises are not on a sound business basis;

otherwise he is too good an advertiser not to use a promising balance sheet for all it is worth.

There has been one balance sheet, published July 26, 1920, purporting to give the financial condition of the Black Star Line after one year of operation; neither profit or loss is shown, there is no way to tell the actual cash receipts or the true condition of the business. Nevertheless it does make some interesting revelations.

The total amount of stock subscribed for is $590,860. Of this $118,153.28 is not yet paid for, leaving the actual amount of paid-in capital charged against the corporation, $472,706.72. Against this stands only $355,214.59 of assets (viz.: $21,985.21 in cash deposits and loans receivable; $12,975.01 in furniture and equipment; $288,515.37 which is the alleged value of his boats; $26,000 in real estate and $5,739 of insurance paid in advance). To offset the assets he has $152,264.14 of other liabilities (accrued salaries, $1,539.30; notes and accounts payable, $129,224.84; mortgages due $21,500). In other words, his capital stock of $472,706.72 is after a year's business impaired to such extent that he has only $202,950.45 to show for it.

Even this does not reveal the precariousness of his actual business condition. Banks before the war in lending their credit refused to recognize any business as safe unless for every dollar of current liabilities there were two dollars of current assets. Today, since the war, they require *three* dollars of current assets to every *one* of current liabilities. The Black Star Line had on July 26, $16,485.21 in current assets and $130,764.14 in current liabilities, when recognition by any reputable bank called for $390,000 in current assets.

Moreover, another sinister admission appears in this statement: the cost of floating the Black Star Line to date has been $289,066.27. In other words, it has cost nearly $300,000 to collect a capital of less than half a million. Garvey has, in other words, spent more for advertisement than he has for his boats!

This is a serious situation, and even this does not tell the whole story: the real estate, furniture, etc., listed above, are probably valued correctly. But how about the boats? The *Yarmouth* is a wooden steamer of 1,452 gross tons, built in 1887. It is old and unseaworthy; it came near sinking a year ago and it has cost a great deal for repairs. It is said that it is now laid up for repairs with a large bill due. Without doubt the inexperienced purchasers of this vessel paid far more than it is worth, and it will soon be utterly worthless unless rebuilt at a very high cost. [3]

The cases of the *Kanawha* (or *Antonio Maceo*) and the *Shadyside* are puzzling. Neither of these boats is registered as belonging to the Black Star Line at all. The former is recorded as belonging to C. L. Dimon, and the latter to the North and East River Steamboat Company. Does the Black Star Line really own these boats, or is it buying them by installments, or only leasing them? We do not know the facts and have been unable to find out. Under the circumstances they look like dubious "assets."

The majority of the Black Star stock is apparently owned by the Universal Negro Improvement Association. There is no reason why this association, if it will and can, should not continue to pour money into its corporation. Let us therefore consider then Mr. Garvey's other resources.

Mr. Garvey's income consists of (*a*) dues from members of the U. N. I. Association; (*b*) shares in the Black Star Line and other enterprises, and (*c*) gifts and "loans" for specific objects. If the U. N. I. Association has "3,000,000 members" then the income from that source alone would be certainly over a million dollars a year. If, as is more likely, it has under 300,000 paying members, he may collect $150,000 annually from this source. Stock in the Black Star Line is still being sold. Garvey himself tells of one woman who had saved about four hundred dollars in gold: "She brought out all the gold and bought shares in the Black Star Line." Another man writes this touching letter from the Canal Zone: "I have sent twice to buy shares amounting to $125 (numbers of certificates 3752 and 9617). Now I am sending $35 for seven more shares. You might think I have money, but the truth, as I stated before, is that I have no money now. But if I'm to die of hunger it will be all right because I'm determined to do all that's in my power to better the conditions of my race." [4]

In addition to this he has asked for special contributions. In the spring of 1920 he demanded for his coming convention in August, "a fund of two million dollars ($2,000,000) to capitalize this, the greatest of all conventions." In October he acknowledged a total of something over $16,000 in small contributions. Immediately he announced "a constructive loan" of $2,000,000, which he is presumably still seeking to raise. [5]

From these sources of income Mr. Garvey has financed his enterprises and carried on a wide and determined propaganda, maintained a large staff of salaried officials, clerks and agents, and published a weekly newspaper. Notwithstanding this considerable income, there is no doubt that Garvey's expenditures are pressing hard on his income, and that his financial methods are so essentially unsound that unless he speedily revises them the investors will certainly get no dividends and worse may happen. [6] He is apparently using the familiar method of "kiting" — i.e., the money which comes in as investment in stock is being used in current expenses, especially in heavy overhead costs, for clerk hire, interest and display. Even his boats are being used for advertisement more than for business — lying in harbors as exhibits, taking excursion parties, etc. These methods have necessitated mortgages on property and continually new and more grandiose schemes to collect larger and larger amounts of ready cash. Meantime, lacking businessmen of experience, his actual business ventures have brought in few returns, involved heavy expense and threatened him continually with disaster or legal complication.

On the other hand, full credit must be given Garvey for a bold effort and some success. He has at least put vessels manned and owned by black men on the seas and they have carried passengers and cargoes. The difficulty is that he does not know the shipping business, he does not understand the investment of capital, and he has few trained and staunch assistants.

The present financial plight of an inexperienced and headstrong promoter may therefore decide the fate of the whole movement. This would be a calamity. Garvey is the beloved leader of tens of thousands of poor and bewildered people who have been cheated all their lives. His failure would mean a blow to their faith, and a loss of their little savings, which it would take generations to undo.

Moreover, shorn of its bombast and exaggeration, the main lines of the Garvey plan are perfectly feasible. What he is trying to say and do is this: American Negroes can, by accumulating and ministering their own capital, organize industry, join the black centers of the south Atlantic by commercial enterprise and in this way ultimately redeem Africa as a fit and free home for black men. This is true. It is *feasible*. It is, in a sense, practical; but it will take for its accomplishment long years of painstaking, self-sacrificing effort. It will call for every ounce of ability, knowledge, experience and devotion in the whole Negro race. It is not a task for one man or one organization, but for coordinate effort on the part of millions. The plan is not original with Garvey but he has popularized it, made it a living, vocal ideal and swept thousands with him with intense belief in the possible accomplishment of the ideal.

This is a great, human service; but when Garvey forges ahead and almost single-handed attempts to realize his dream in a few years, with large words and wild gestures, he grievously minimizes his task and endangers his cause.

To instance one illustrative fact: there is no doubt but what Garvey has sought to import to America and capitalize the antagonism between blacks and mulattoes in the West Indies. This has been the cause of the West Indian failures to gain headway against the whites. Yet Garvey imports it into a land where it has never had any substantial footing and where today, of all days, it is absolutely repudiated by every thinking Negro; Garvey capitalizes it, has sought to get the cooperation of men like R. R. Moton on this basis, and has aroused more bitter color enmity inside the race than has ever before existed. The whites are delighted at the prospect of a division of our solidifying phalanx, but their hopes are vain. American Negroes recognize no color line in or out of the race, and they will in the end punish the man who attempts to establish it.

Then too Garvey increases his difficulties in other directions. He is a British subject. He wants to trade in British territory. Why then does he needlessly antagonize and even insult Britain? He wants to unite all Negroes. Why then does he sneer at the work of the powerful group of his race in the United States where he finds asylum and sympathy? Particularly, why does he decry the excellent and rising business enterprises of Harlem — intimating that his schemes alone are honest and sound when the facts flatly contradict him? He proposes to settle his headquarters in Liberia — but has he asked permission of the Liberian government? Does he presume to usurp authority in a land which has successfully withstood England, France and the United States — but is expected tamely to submit to Marcus Garvey? How long does Mr. Garvey think that President King would permit his anti-English propaganda on Liberian soil, when the government is straining every nerve to escape the Lion's Paw?

And, finally, without arms, money, effective organization or base of operations, Mr. Garvey openly and wildly talks of "conquest" and of telling white Europeans in Africa to "get out!" and of becoming himself a black Napoleon! [7]

Suppose Mr. Garvey should drop from the clouds and concentrate on his industrial schemes as a practical first step toward his dreams: the first duty of a great commercial enterprise is to carry on effective commerce. A man who sees in industry the key to a situation, must establish sufficient businesslike industries. Here Mr. Garvey has failed lamentably.

The *Yarmouth,* for instance, has not been a commercial success. Stories have been published alleging its dirty condition and the inexcusable conduct of its captain and crew. To this Mr. Garvey may reply that it was no easy matter to get efficient persons to run his boats and to keep a schedule. This is certainly true, but if it is difficult to secure one black boat crew, how much more difficult is it going to be to "build and operate factories in the big industrial centers of the United States, Central America, the West Indies and Africa to manufacture every marketable commodity" and also "to purchase and build ships of larger tonnage for the African and South American trade" and also to raise "five million dollars to free Liberia" where "new buildings are to be erected, administrative buildings are to be built, colleges and universities are to be constructed" and finally to accomplish what Mr. Garvey calls the "conquest of Africa"?!

To sum up: Garvey is a sincere, hardworking idealist; he is also a stubborn, domineering leader of the mass; he has worthy industrial and commercial schemes but he is an inexperienced businessman. His dreams of Negro industry, commerce and the ultimate freedom of Africa are feasible; but his methods are bombastic, wasteful, illogical and ineffective and almost illegal. If he learns by experience, attracts strong and capable friends and helpers instead of making needless enemies; if he gives up secrecy and suspicion and substitutes open and frank reports as to his income and expenses, and above all if he is willing to be a co-worker and not a czar, he may yet in time succeed in at least starting some of his schemes toward accomplishment. But unless he does these things and does them quickly he cannot escape failure.

Let the followers of Mr. Garvey insist that he get down to bedrock business and make income and expense balance; let them gag Garvey's wilder words, and still preserve his wide power and influence. American Negro leaders are not jealous of Garvey—they are not envious of his success; they are simply afraid of his failure, for his failure would be theirs. He can have all the power and money that he can efficiently and honestly use, and if in addition he wants to prance down Broadway in a green shirt, let him—but do not let him foolishly overwhelm with bankruptcy and disaster one of the most interesting spiritual movements of the modern Negro world.

The Crisis, December 1920, pp. 58-60; January 1921, pp. 112-15.

3

THE AMENIA CONFERENCE:
AN HISTORIC NEGRO GATHERING

Late in 1915, Booker T. Washington died. Soon the idea spread among Negro leaders to bring together the followers of Washington and those who had rejected his ideology and attempt to achieve a unity in thought and action so that black Americans might speak as one voice. To this end a conference was called at Joel Spingarn's home in Amenia, N.Y., in 1916 to discuss the problems of the Negro people. The Amenia Conference brought together the most distinguished Negroes in the country, and for the first time in many years, the Negro leaders of the country expressed a unanimity of opinion.

Dr. Du Bois, a leading figure at the conference, spoke frequently on the events leading up to the gathering and the significance of the meeting. His speech was published in September 1925 as Number Eight of the Troutbeck Leaflets.

It was in August 1916, and the place was Troutbeck, near Amenia. I had no sooner seen the place than I knew it was mine. It was just a long, southerly extension of my own Berkshire Hills. There was the same slow, rocky uplift of land, the nestle of lake and the sturdy murmur of brooks and brown rivers. Afar off were blue and mysterious mountains, and there was a road that rose and dipped and wound and wandered and went on and on past farm and town to the great hard world beyond.

There was the village, small, important, complete, with shadows of old homes; with its broad street that was at once thoroughfare, entrance, and exit. There were the people who had always lived there and their fathers before them, and the people merely passing.

Out from the town lay the farm. I saw its great trees bending over the running brook with a sense of utter friendship and intimate memory, though in truth I had never seen it before. And then one could trudge from the more formal home and lawn, by lane and fence with rise and fall of land, until one came to the lake. The lake, dark and still, lay in the palm of a great, calm hand. The shores rose slowly on either side and had a certain sense of loneliness and calm beauty.

It was in 1916. There was war in Europe but a war far, far away. I had discussed it from time to time with a calm detachment. I had said: "A New Year, comrades! Come, let us sit here high in the Hills of Life and take counsel one with another. How goes the battle there below, down where dark waters foam, and dun dust fills the nostrils, and the hurry and sweat of humankind is everywhere? Evil, evil, yes, I know. Yonder is murder: so thick is the air with blood and groans that our pulses no longer quicken, our eyes and ears are full. Here, to homewards, is breathless gain and gambling and the steady, unchecked, almost unnoticed growth of human hate."

Our own battle in America, that war of colors which we who are black always sense as the principal thing in life, was forming in certain definite lines. Booker Washington was dead. He had died but the year before, 1915. I remember the morning that I heard of it. I knew that it ended an era and I wrote: "The death of Mr. Washington marks an epoch in the history of America. He was the greatest Negro leader since Frederick Douglass, and the most distinguished man, white or black, who has come out of the South since the Civil War. His fame was international and his influence far-reaching. Of the good that he accomplished there can be no doubt: he directed the attention of the Negro race in America to the pressing necessity of economic development; he emphasized technical education, and he did much to pave the way for an understanding between the white and darker races. On the other hand there can be no doubt of Mr. Washington's mistakes and shortcomings: he never adequately grasped the growing bond of politics and industry; he did not understand the deeper foundations of human training, and his basis of better understanding between white and black was founded on caste.

"We may then generously and with deep earnestness lay on the grave of Booker T. Washington testimony of our thankfulness for his undoubted help in the accumulation of Negro land and property, his establishment of Tuskegee and spreading of industrial education, and his compelling of the white South to think at least of the Negro as a possible man. On the other hand, in stern justice, we must lay on the soul of this man a heavy responsibility for the consummation of Negro disfranchisement, the decline of the Negro college and public school, and the firmer establishment of color caste in this land.

"What is done is done. This is not fit time for recrimination or complaint. Gravely and with bowed head let us receive what this great figure gave of good, silently rejecting all else. Firmly and unfalteringly let the Negro race in America, in bleeding Haiti, and throughout the world, close ranks and march steadily on, determined as never before to work and save and endure, but never to swerve from their great goal: the right to vote, the right to know, and the right to stand as men among men throughout the world."[1]

Already we had formed the National Association for the Advancement of Colored People, a precarious thing without money, with some influential members, but we were never quite sure whether their influence would stay with us if we "fought" for Negro rights. We started in tiny offices at 20 Vesey Street and then took larger ones at 26. Finally on the eve of the undreamed-of World War we had moved to 70 Fifth Avenue.

There have been many versions as to how this organization was born, all of them true and yet not the full truth. In a sense William English Walling founded it a hundred years after Lincoln's birth, because of his indignation at a lynching in Lincoln's birthplace. But in reality the thing was born long years before when, under the roar of Niagara Falls, there was formed the Niagara Movement by twenty-nine colored men. How they screamed at us and threatened! The *Outlook*, then at the zenith of its power, declared that we were ashamed of our race and jealous of Mr. Washington. The colored press unanimously condemned us and listed our failures. We were told that we were fighting the stars in their courses. Yet from that beginning of the Niagara Movement in 1905 down to the formation of the National Association for the Advancement of Colored People in 1909, we were welding the weapons, breasting the blows, stating the ideals, and preparing the membership for the larger, stronger organization. Seven of the twenty-nine went on the first Board of Directors of the NAACP, and the rest became leading members. [2]

There came six years of work. It is, perhaps, hard to say definitely just what we accomplished in these six years. It was perhaps a matter of spirit and getting ready, and yet we established *The Crisis* magazine and had it by 1916 almost self-supporting. We had branches of our organization throughout the country. We had begun to move upon the courts with test cases. We had held mass meetings through the country. We had stirred up Congress and we had attacked lynching.

We said in the Sixth Annual Report: "The National Association for the Advancement of Colored People was first called into being on the one hundredth anniversary of the birth of Abraham Lincoln. It conceives its mission to be the completion of the work which the great emancipator began. It proposes to make a group of 10,000,000 Americans free from the lingering shackles of past slavery: physically free from peonage, mentally free from ignorance, politically free from disfranchisement, and socially free from insult.

"We are impelled to recognize the pressing necessity of such a movement when we consider these facts:

"The lynching of 2,812 prisoners without trial in the last thirty years.

"The thousands of unaccused black folk who have in these years been done to death.

"The widespread use of crime and alleged crime as a source of public revenue.

"The defenseless position of colored women, continually threatened by laws to make their bodies indefensible and their children illegitimate.

"The total disfranchisement of three-fourths of the black voters.

"The new attack on property rights.

"The widespread and growing discrimination in the simplest matters of public decency and accommodation.

"All these things indicate not simply the suffering of a people, but greater than that, they show the impotence of American democracy. And so the National Association for the Advancement of Colored People appeals to the nation to accept the clear and simple settlement of the Negro problem, which consists in treating colored men as you would like to be treated if you were colored."

Our six years of organized work did not by any means satisfy us. We wanted a bigger, stronger organization, and especially we wanted to get rid of the all-too-true statement that we were asking for things that colored people did not want or at least did not want with any unity. The wall between the Washington camp and those who had opposed his policies was still there; and it occurred to J. E. Spingarn and his friends that up in the peace and quiet of Amenia and around this beautiful lake, colored men and women of all shades of opinion might sit down and rest and talk and agree on many things if not on all.

The conference, as Mr. Spingarn conceived it, was to be "under the auspices of the NAACP" but wholly independent of it, and the invitations definitely said this. They were issued by Mr. Spingarn personally, and the guests were assured that they would not be bound by any program of the NAACP. Thus the conference was intended primarily to bring about as large a degree as possible of unity of purpose among Negro leaders and to do this regardless of its effect upon any organization, although, of course, many of us hoped that some central organization and preferably the NAACP would eventually represent this new united purpose.

One can hardly realize today how difficult and intricate a matter it was to arrange such a conference, to say who should come and who should not, to gloss over hurts and enmities. I remember Mr. Spingarn's asking me with a speculative eye and tentative intonation if the editor of a certain paper ought not to be invited. Now that paper had had an exceedingly good time at my expense, and had said things about me and my beliefs with which I not only did not agree but which gave rise in my hot mind to convictions of deliberate misrepresentation. But after all the editor must come. He was important, and Mr. Spingarn was pleased to see that I agreed with him in this.

About two hundred invitations to white and colored people were actually issued, and in making up this list the advice of friends of Mr. Washington, like Major Moton and Mr. Emmett Scott and Mr. Fred Moore, was sought. There were messages of goodwill from many who could not attend: from Taft, Roosevelt, Hughes, Woodrow Wilson, and others. But all this selection of persons was the easier part of the thing. The guests had, of course, to be induced to come; fortunately it was possible to accomplish this, and sixty or more persons expressed their willingness to attend. We were going to make for ourselves a little village of tents, and there we had to be fed and amused, while a discreet program was carried out and careful hospitality extended. At this Joel and Amy and Arthur Spingarn and their friends worked long and assiduously, and the result was beautiful and satisfying.

I remember the morning when we arrived. It was misty with a northern chill in the air and a dampness all about. One felt cold and a bit lonely in those high grey uplands. There were only a few there at first, but they filtered in slowly, and with each came more of good cheer. At last we began to have a rollicking jolly time. Now and then, of course, there was just a little sense of stiffness and care in conversation when people met who for ten years had been saying hard things about each other; but not a false word was spoken. The hospitality of our hosts was perfect and the goodwill of all was evident.

There was a varied company. From the South came

Lucy Laney, John Hope, Henry A. Hunt, and R. R. Wright of Georgia; Emmett J. Scott of Alabama, former secretary of Booker Washington; J. C. Napier of Tennessee. From the West came Francis H. Warren of Detroit, Charles E. Bentley and George W. Ellis of Chicago, Mary B. Talbert of Buffalo, Charles W. Chesnutt of Cleveland, and B. S. Brown of Minnesota. Washington was represented by Mary Church Terrell, James A. Cobb, George W. Cook, Kelly Miller, L. M. Hershaw, Montgomery Gregory, Neval H. Thomas, and J. R. Hawkins. From Pennsylvania came Leslie Hill, L. J. Coppin, R. R. Wright, Jr., and W. Justin Carter. New York sent Fred Moore, Hutchins Bishop, James W. and J. Rosamond Johnson, Addie Hunton, W. L. Bulkley, William Pickens and Roy Nash, then secretary of the NAACP. Baltimore gave us Mason Hawkins and Ashbie Hawkins and Bishop Hurst. New England sent William H. Lewis, George W. Crawford, and Garnet Waller.

I doubt if ever before so small a conference of American Negroes had so many colored men of distinction who represented at the same time so complete a picture of all phases of Negro thought. Its very completeness in this respect was its salvation. If it had represented one party or clique it would have been less harmonious and unanimous, because someone would surely have essayed in sheer fairness to state the opinions of men who were not there and would have stated them necessarily without compromise and without consideration. As it was, we all learned what the majority of us knew. None of us held uncompromising and unchangeable views. It was after all a matter of emphasis. We all believed in thrift, we all wanted the Negro to vote, we all wanted the laws enforced, we all wanted assertion of our essential manhood; but how to get these things — there of course was infinite divergence of opinion.

But everybody had a chance to express this opinion, and at the same time the conference was not made up of sonorous oratory. The thing was too intimate and small. We were too near each other. We were talking to each other face to face, we knew each other pretty intimately, and there was present a pervading and saving sense of humor that laughed the poseur straight off the rostrum and that made for joke and repartee in the midst of serious argument. Of course and in fact let us confess here and now that one thing helped everything else: we were gloriously fed. There was a great tent with tables and chairs which became at will now dining room, now auditorium. Promptly at mealtime food appeared, miraculously steaming and perfectly cooked, out of the nothingness of the wide landscape. We ate hilariously in the open air with such views of the good green earth and the waving waters and the pale blue sky as all men ought often to see, yet few men do. And then filled and complacent we talked awhile of the thing which all of us call "The Problem," and after that and just as regularly we broke up and played good and hard. We swam and rowed and hiked and lingered in the forests and sat upon the hillsides and picked flowers and sang.

Our guests dropped by, the governor of the state, a member of Congress, a university president, an army officer, a distinguished grandson of William Lloyd Garrison, a Harlem real-estate man, businessmen, and politicians. We had the women there to complete the real conference, Mrs. Terrell, Mary B. Talbert, Mrs. Hunton, Lucy Laney, Dr. Morton Jones of Brooklyn; Inez Milholland, in the glory of her young womanhood dropped by, in this which was destined to be almost the last year of her magnificent life. Mrs. Spingarn strolled over now and then and looked at us quietly and thoughtfully.

The Amenia Conference in reality marked the end of an era and the beginning. As we said in our resolutions: "The Amenia Conference believes that its members have arrived at a virtual unanimity of opinion in regard to certain principles and that a more or less definite result may be expected from its deliberations. These principles and this practical result may be summarized as follows:

"1. The conference believes that all forms of education are desirable for the Negro and that every form of education should be encouraged and advanced.

"2. It believes that the Negro, in common with all other races, cannot achieve its highest development without complete political freedom.

"3. It believes that this development and this freedom cannot be furthered without organization and without a practical working understanding among the leaders of the colored race.

"4. It believes that antiquated subjects of controversy, ancient suspicions and factional alignments must be eliminated and forgotten if this organization of the race and this practical working understanding of its leaders are to be achieved.

"5. It realizes the peculiar difficulties which surround this problem in the South and the special need of understanding between leaders of the race who live in the South and those who live in the North. It has learned to understand and respect the good faith, methods and ideals of those who are working for the solution of this problem in various sections of the country.

"6. The conference pledges itself to the inviolable privacy of all its deliberations. These conclusions, however, and the amicable results of all the deliberations of the conference are fair subjects for discussion in the colored press and elsewhere.

"7. The conference feels that mutual understanding would be encouraged if the leaders of the race could meet annually for private and informal discussion under conditions similar to those which have prevailed at this conference."

It is a little difficult today to realize why it was necessary to say all this. There had been bitterness and real cause for bitterness in those years after the formation of the Niagara Movement and before the NAACP had come to the front. Men were angry and hurt. Booker Washington had been mobbed by Negroes in Boston, Monroe Trotter had been thrown in jail;[3] the lowest motives that one can conceive had been attributed to antagonists on either side — jealousy, envy, greed, cowardice, intolerance, and the like. Newspapers and magazine articles had seethed with threat, charge, and innuendo.

Then there had been numberless attempts at understanding which had failed. There was, for instance, that conference in Carnegie Hall when Andrew Carnegie through Booker T. Washington financed a general meeting of Negro leaders.[4] It was a much larger conference than

that at Amenia but its spirit was different. It was a conference carefully manipulated. There was no confidence
there and no complete revelation. It savored more of
armed truce than of understanding. Those of us who
represented the opposition were conscious of being forced
and influenced against our will. Lyman Abbott of the
Outlook came and talked with us benevolently. Andrew
Carnegie himself came. Numbers of rich and powerful
whites looked in upon us and admonished us to be good,
and then the opposition between the wings flamed in bitter
speech and charge. Men spoke with double tongues saying
one thing and meaning another.

And finally there came compromise and an attempt at
constructive effort which somehow no one felt was real.
I had proposed a Committee of Twelve to guide the Negro
race, but when the committee was finally constituted I
found that it predominately represented only one wing
of the controversy and that it was financed indirectly
by Andrew Carnegie, and so I indignantly withdrew and
the Committee of Twelve never functioned but died leaving
only a few pamphlets which Hugh Brown edited. There
were other efforts, but it needed time and understanding,
and when the Amenia Conference came the time was ripe.

We talked of many matters at Amenia — of education,
politics, organization, and the situation in the South. First
of all we spoke of the former subjects of controversy;
then we made the deliberations private, and to this day
there is no record of what various persons said; and
finally we declared for annual meetings of the conference,
and then we got to the main subjects of controversy.

If the world had not gone crazy directly after the Amenia
Conference and indeed at the very time of its meeting
had not been much more widely insane than most of us
realized, it is probable that the aftermath of this conference
would have been even greater than we can now see. It
happened because of the war that there was but the one
conference held at Amenia. While we were there the world
was fighting and had fought two long years. In another
year America was destined to join the war and the Negro
race was to be torn and shaken in its very heart by new

and tremendous problems. The old order was going and a new race situation was to be developed.

Of all this the Amenia Conference was a symbol. It not only marked the end of the old things and the old thoughts and the old ways of attacking the race problem, but in addition to this it was the beginning of the new things. Probably on account of our meeting the Negro race was more united and more ready to meet the problems of the world than it could possibly have been without these beautiful days of understanding. It was a "close ranks!"[5] before the great struggle that issued in the new world. How appropriate that so tremendous a thing should have taken place in the midst of so much quiet and beauty there at Troutbeck, which John Burroughs knew and loved throughout his life, a place of poets and fishermen, of dreamers and farmers, a place far apart and away from the bustle of the world and the centers of activity. It was all peculiarly appropriate, and those who in the future write the history of the way in which the American Negro became a man must not forget this event and landmark in 1916.

Troutbeck Leaflets, Number Eight, Amenia, New York, September 1925.

4

THE NEGRO CITIZEN

Dr. Du Bois delivered this speech to the Interracial Conference at Washington, D. C., December 19, 1928.

What we know about the civil and political rights of Negroes in the United States; what significance this knowledge has for social organizations whose purpose it is to improve conditions; and what further study by universities and research organizations is called for, is the subject of this paper.

Our general knowledge may thus be summarized: there is a system of color caste in the United States based on legal and customary race distinctions and discriminations, having to do with separation in travel, in schools, in public accommodations, in residence and in family relations. There is discrimination in the kind and amount of public-school education and in civil rights of various sorts and in courts, jails and fines. There is disfranchisement of voters by means of various tests, including restrictions as to registration, and as to voting in primaries; and including the right of summary administrative decisions; and finally there is lynching and mob violence.

Over against this there are the war amendments of the Constitution and various civil-right laws of the states and the decisions of the courts in these matters.

The results of these discriminations have been pretty carefully studied in the case of education and lynching, but have received little systematic study in the matter of voting and civil rights.

I doubt if it would be worthwhile to examine and expatiate on the general and pretty well-known facts of Negro citizenship and caste. I, therefore, pass to the matter of the significance of this general knowledge for social organizations whose purpose is to improve conditions.

Here we are confronted not simply by lack of exact data but by a clear disposition not to investigate or even to discuss. I know of no organization that has ever proposed to study Negro suffrage.

I distinctly remember when this recoiling from the facts covered other fields. There was a time when social studies, having to do primarily with the health, physique and growth of the Negro population, were of pressing importance because of the widespread assumption that the Negro was not adapted to the American climate or to conditions of life under freedom and that he was bound sooner or later to die out.

It was necessary, therefore, to test by such scientific measurements as were available these assumptions. Yet for a long time universities and social organizations refused to touch the matter and philanthropists refused funds and encouragement when Atlanta University attempted its wretchedly restricted pioneer work. Times changed. Today, tests and measurements have gone so far that there is no further question of the survival of the Negro race in America and the physical studies connected with him are no different and demand no different technique or organization from the general physical studies carried on in the nation. The real question narrows down to matters of sanitation, hospitals and income. What has Negro suffrage to do with these?

Again, between the years 1890 and 1910, the right of the American Negro to modern education had to be established and proven. It was assumed that the ability of the Negro to assimilate a college education was at least questionable; and it was dogmatically stated that the economic future of the Negro in America was such that all that he needed was industrial training to make him a contented laborer and servant; that this class of people did not need political power and could not use it; but that on the contrary their disfranchisement would free the South so that it could divide its vote on pressing political matters; and that the South could be depended upon to guard the rights of this working caste.

The fight was bitter and long drawn-out. Those of us who insisted that in modern industrial life no laboring class could maintain itself without educational leadership and political power were assailed, put out of court, accused of jealousy, and of an overwhelming desire to promote miscegenation.

Today finds the educational part of our contention answered by facts. We have twelve thousand college students, where we had less than one thousand in 1900, and we are graduating today annually 1,500 Bachelors of Art, when in 1900 we sent out less than 150. It is admitted now without serious question that the American Negro can use modern education for his group development, in economic and spiritual life.

There is, however, still the feeling that the present problems of Negro education are problems of charity, goodwill, self-sacrifice and double taxation and not problems which depend primarily for their final solution upon political power.

So, too, in the matter of housing, recreation and crime, we seem to assume that a knowledge of the facts of discrimination and of the needs of the colored public are sufficient, with faith, hope and charity, to bring ultimate betterment; and that in presenting demands to the government of city, state and nation, we have only to prove that Negro poverty, disease and crime hurt white citizens in order to induce the lawmakers elected by white citizens to do justice to black citizens.

In the matter of occupation and income the need of political power in any laboring class is conceded by every social student; for the American Negro or his friends to dream that he can sustain himself as a peasant proprietor, an artisan or day laborer, and secure recognition from his organized voting white fellow worker and a decent wage from his employer, without a vote, is extraordinary. It is a conceded impossibility in every modern land.

We can point with some pride to what has been accomplished in the courts in breaking down caste and establishing Negro citizenship, and in the abolition of mob law and lynching. But we are still uncertain in estimating the cause and effects of such actions.

I have heard a number of plausible and attractive explanations of the decline of lynching from 226 in 1896 to eleven in 1928. Some attribute it to prayer, and others to interracial resolutions; but I see it differently. I see lynching increase and decrease indifferently, until in 1919 a nationwide agitation was begun by the NAACP, backed by statistics, advertisements and meetings.[1] The curve of mob murder fell lazily. Then suddenly in a single year it dropped 75 percent. I study the occurrences of that year, 1922. And that study leads me to believe that the effective check to lynching was the organized political power of northern Negroes that put the Dyer Anti-Lynching Bill through the House of Representatives January 26, 1922, by a vote of 230 to 119.

The bill was forced through a Senate committee and reported to the Senate with a majority pledged to its passage. The only way that the South accomplished its defeat was by refusing to allow the government of the United States to function. Knowing that such high-handed measures were going a bit too far, the South promised to stop lynching and it has pretty nearly kept its word. And yet consider the cost: there has not been in Poland or in Haiti, in Russia or in the Balkans, a more open, impudent, and shameless holding up of democracy than the senators of the Bourbon South, holding office on the disfranchised Negro vote, accomplished in November 1922.[2]

The success which we have had before the courts in abolishing the hereditary right to vote which the "Grandfather" clauses bestowed on white southerners; the fight against segregation in residence and its spread in schools; the fight against the white primary and numerous civil-rights cases have not simply been brought to successful issue because of our present small but increasing political power, but are without significance unless they point to fuller political power.

I do not for a moment argue that political power will

immediately abolish color caste, make ignorant men intelligent or bad men good. We have caste and discrimination in the North with the vote, and social progress in some parts of the South without it. But there is this vast difference: in states like New York where we are beginning to learn the meaning and use of the ballot we are building a firm and unshakable basis of permanent freedom. While every advance in the South unprotected by political power is based on chance and changing personalities and may at any time be vetoed by a hostile voting group, I maintain that political power is the beginning of all permanent reform and the only hope for maintaining gains.

There is today a surprisingly large number of intelligent and sincere people, both white and black, who really believe that the Negro problem in the United States can ultimately be solved without our being compelled to face and settle the question of the Negro vote.

Nearly all of our social studies apparently come to this conclusion, either openly or by assumption, and do not say, as they ought to say, and as everyone knows in the long run they must say, that granted impulse by philanthropy, help by enlightened public opinion, and the aid of time, no permanent improvement in the economic and social condition of Negroes is going to be made so long as they are deprived of political power to support and defend it.

Nowhere else in the world is there any suggestion that a modern laboring class can permanently better itself without political power. It may be a question, it certainly is a question, as to just how labor is going to use this power ultimately so as to raise its economic and social status. But there is no question, but that such power must be had and today the world over it is being used.

With all the research that has gone on formerly, and especially in the last few years with regard to the American Negro, with singular equanimity, nothing has been said or done with regard to the Negro vote. I am, therefore, stressing in this paper the significance and the danger of this omission and I am seeking to say that of all the questions that are before us today that of political power on the part of the American Negro occupies, to my mind, the key position, and is the question which peculiarly tests the good faith of the American people, the honesty of philanthropy in America toward the Negro, and the sincerity of the National Interracial Conference.

I listened yesterday with mounting astonishment to a discussion of school betterment in the South. I am convinced that in no other civilized country in the world could such a discussion have taken place. The crucial problem was that of raising local funds for schools and of having the national government supplement those funds in the poorer states: and the essential point in the whole matter was surely the selection of local officials who would spend the money as the local voting population wished; would raise funds by local taxation fairly placed on local wealth and would expend national monies equitably. In any other land the first point of the debate would have been the question of the selection of such proper officials and of the democratic control of their actions.

That question in the debate to which I listened was never raised. It was assumed that, although there were to be separate schools for Negroes, Negroes were to have no voice in the selection of local officials, no control of their own taxation, no vote on expenditure; and that despite this through philanthropy and goodwill you were going to get and maintain a decent and adequate school system for them.

If the present rulers of Russia had heard this debate they would have gone into gales of laughter; and if any government had attempted to carry on a debate on these lines in the English Parliament, the German Reichstag or the French Chamber of Deputies, the government would have been thrown out forthwith. Every Englishman, Frenchman and German would have said, without qualification, that education today cannot be carried on as a matter of philanthropy and goodwill: that it is the duty of the state and that back of the state must stand some effective democratic control.

Most nations would have made this control the ballot in the hands of all adult citizens and even Italy and Russia and Turkey would affirm that this is the ideal toward which they consistently and steadily march.

It is of extraordinary significance that in an intelligent and openhearted assembly, such a clear and obvious point was either not thought of or worse yet, the members did not have the courage to make it.

In the question of the lack of public funds for growing expense in education one cannot assume that Americans do not know what the public thought of the world in the most progressive countries is doing, in insisting that wealth bear a greater burden of taxation and that poverty be exempt. The United States is the one great country of the world where wealth is escaping taxation and where the burden of public contributions that falls upon the farmer, the small householder, the laborer and particularly the black laborer is crushing in its incidence; and yet how little is said of drafting by universal suffrage sufficient wealth for the public good to pay every reasonable expense and of putting the people, black and white, back of such draft.

I hold this truth to be self-evident, that a disfranchised working class in modern industrial civilization is worse than helpless. It is a menace, not simply to itself, but to every other group in the community. It will be diseased; it will be criminal; it will be ignorant; it will be the plaything of mobs, and it will be insulted by caste restrictions.

So far we are upon old ground. This argument has been urged many times in the past. It has failed to impress the people of the United States simply because so many folk do not care about the future of American Negroes. They once almost hoped that the problem would be settled by the Negroes dying out or migrating, or bowing in dumb submission to any kind of treatment that the people of the United States decided to give them.

But today, the matter is changed, and it is changed because those Americans who have any ability to see and think are beginning slowly to realize that when democracy fails for one group in the United States, it fails for the nation; and when it fails for the United States it fails for the world. A disfranchised group compels the disfranchisement of other groups. The white-primary system in the South is simply a system which compels the white man to disfranchise himself in order to take the vote away from the Negro.

The present extraordinary political psychology of the Negro in the South; namely that the voluntary disfranchisement of intelligent and thrifty black men is helping to solve the Negro problem, is simply putting into the hands of scoundrels and grafters, white and black, the meager remains of those political rights which 200,000 black Civil War soldiers fought to gain.

All this has led to extraordinary results. In the past we have deplored disfranchisement in the South because of its effect on the Negro. But it is not simply that the Negro remains a slave as long as he is disfranchised, but that southern white laborers are dragged inevitably down to the Negro's position, and that the decent white South is not only deprived of decent government, but of all real voice in both local and national government. It is as true today as it ever was that the nation cannot exist half slave and half free.

Today, in the South, politicians have every incentive to cut down the number of voters, black and white. The Republican organization, in nine cases out of ten, becomes simply the tail to the Democratic kite. Party government disappears. Political power is vested in the hands of a clique of professional politicians, white and black, and there is nothing that has been done in dirty politics by Tammany in New York, by Thompson in Chicago, or Vare in Philadelphia, that you cannot find duplicated by the political oligarchies which rule the southern South.

Political ignorance in the South has grown by leaps and bounds. The mass of people in the South today have no knowledge as to how they are governed or by whom. Elections have nothing to do with broad policies and social development but are matters of the selection of friends to lucrative offices and punishment of personal enemies. Local administration is a purposely disguised system of intrigue which not even an expert could unravel.

Today, a small group of western congressmen, to the dismay of East and South, are investigating the sale of offices by black Republicans in the South; but offices from the highest to the lowest have been regularly sold by white Republicans and white Democrats in the South and are being sold today.

And yet, of all this, there must be no criticism, no exposure, no real investigation, no political revolt, because the decent white South lacks the moral courage to expose and punish rascals even though they are white and to stand up for democracy even if it includes black folk.

I yield to no man in my admiration for what the new young South is doing in liberalizing race relations and humanizing thought, but I maintain that until the liberal white South has the guts to stand up for democracy regardless of race there will be no solution of the Negro problem and no solution of the problem of popular government in America. You cannot build bricks of molasses.

Nor is this all. Because of the rotten boroughs of the South, real democratic government is impossible in the North. The Democratic Party cannot become a liberal body because the bulk of its support depends upon disfranchisement, caste and race hate in the South. It depends on minimizing participation in politics by all people, black and white, and stifling of discussion. It is the only part of the nation where the woman suffrage amendment is largely ignored and yet the white women do not dare to open their mouths to protest.

So long as this party holds this grip on 114 electoral votes despite argument, with no reference to dominant political questions and with no reference to the way in which votes are actually cast, this party cannot be displaced by a third party. With no third-party corrective for a discredited minority, democratic government becomes simply impossible without something resembling revolution.

When in 1912 Roosevelt tried to appeal to liberal thought in the United States against the reactionary Republicans and the bourbon Democrats, he only succeeded in putting the Democrats in power. When La Follette tried to do the same thing in 1924, he simply scared the country into larger reaction, since they realized that they had to choose between bourbon democracy and organized privilege.

In 1928, we had an extraordinary spectacle. It is too well known for me to comment. I only remind the reader that the right of southern white men to vote as they wished on public questions was openly and vehemently denied and the right of dominant political cliques holding their power by disfranchising four million white and black voters, to make their own election returns as to the vote cast, without state or national investigation or inquiry, was successfully maintained. This is the only modern nation in the world which does not control its own elections.

How is all this going to be remedied? How are we going to restore normal democracy in the United States? It is not a question of the millennium; of being able through democratic government to do everything immediately. But it is a question, and a grave and insistent question, whether the United States of America is going to maintain or surrender democracy as the fundamental starting point of permanent human uplift. If democracy is still our cornerstone, must it be smashed because of twelve million Negroes? Better cut their throats quickly and build on.

On the other hand, if democracy fails in the United States, and fails because of our attitude toward a darker people, what about democracy in the world, and particularly in India, in China, in Japan and in Egypt? We have got a chance today, and an unrivaled chance, again to rescue and guide the world, as we did at the end of the eighteenth century. And we have the same kind of dilemma.

In those days when we started to build a nation of equal citizens, Negro slavery could have been abolished; its abolition was begun even in the South; but the respectable people, the smug people, sat down before it and organized the American Colonization Society,[3] which was the interracial movement of that day; and instead of fighting evil they were content to congratulate themselves on the good already accomplished. In the long run, they did less than nothing.

So today it is fortunate that people can sit down at interracial conferences and find so much to congratulate themselves about in the improved relation between races, and the increased knowledge which they have of each other. But all of this is going to be of no avail in the crisis approaching unless we take advantage of the present desire for knowledge and willingness to study and willingness to listen, and attack the main problem which is and has been the question of political power for the Negro citizens of the United States.

I do not for a moment minimize the difficulty of inaugurating in a land but a generation removed from slavery, of universal suffrage which includes children of slaves. It is extraordinarily difficult and calls for patience and tolerance. But my point is that the sooner we face the goal the quicker we will reach it. We are not going to make democracy in the South possible by admitting its impossibility and refusing to study and discuss the facts. Let us first of all say, and broadcast the fact, that all Americans of adult age and sufficient character and intelligence must vote and that any interference with or postponement of this realization is a danger to every other American— a danger to be attacked now and continuously and with dogged determination with a clear avowal of intention by every open-minded man.

What then is called for? Facts. A foundation of actual fact concerning the political situation of Negroes; their voting, their representation in local, state and national government; their taxation, their party affiliation and subservience to political machines; the economic nexus between political power and occupation and income.

This study beginning with Negroes should extend to whites. We must lift the curtain from democracy and view it in the open. We must insist that politics is no secret, shameful thing known only to ward heelers and political bosses, and to the corporations who buy and sell them. Here is the greatest and most insistent field of scientific investigation open to the social reformer.

The Crisis, vol. XXXVI, May 1929, pp.154-56, 171-73.

5

THE DENIAL OF ECONOMIC
JUSTICE TO NEGROES

In 1918, Dr. Du Bois wrote in The Crisis: *"I am among the few colored men who have tried conscientiously to bring about understanding and cooperation between American Negroes and the labor unions." He pointed out that he regularly carried on the title page of the magazine the union label, even though he was well aware that no black workers were permitted to participate in printing* The Crisis, *being systematically excluded from membership in the International Typographical Union. Still, he had entertained the hope that ultimately the organized white workers would see that their best interests lay in uniting with the unorganized Negro workers. But he had reluctantly come to the conclusion "that in the present union movement as represented by the American Federation of Labor, there is absolutely no hope of justice for an American of Negro descent." Earlier, as we have seen, Dr. Du Bois had reached the conclusion that the Socialist Party also held out no hope for the Negro.*

Invited in February 1929, to speak at the Forum on Current Events at the Rand School, a socialist educational center in New York City, Dr. Du Bois reemphasized his conviction that both the organized white workers and the socialists were guilty of betraying the cause of the Negro, and warned that neither could really achieve any basic advances unless they changed their policies. Even though he addressed an audience composed of trade unionists and socialists, Du Bois, as was typical of him, made no effort to soften his criticism of both elements.

The denial of economic justice to Negroes by white laborers is beginning to make justice to white labor impossible. Not only is the Negro vote growing, but any successful appeal to the labor vote, North or South, must be based upon the breaking down of the artificial power which the white employing South has gained by disfranchising of white and black laborers. The effect of this disfranchisement in the United States upon the labor vote is exactly the same as the similar system in the German Reichstag before the war, and in England before the Reform Bills.

So long as states like South Carolina, Georgia, Alabama and Mississippi can be absolutely manipulated by the political power of reactionary capitalists and big landholders, just so long the chance of any third party, labor or socialist, is practically nil. This has been manifested in the last three elections, and the appeal for justice which the black laborer is making today is not simply an appeal for charity; it is an appeal to white workmen to stop cutting off their own noses to spite their faces.

The sooner the Socialist Party braves the artificially encouraged race prejudice of white laborers in the South and comes out in speech and platform for democracy despite color, and for economic justice despite race prejudice, the sooner will the Socialist Party begin to grow on solid foundations. This can only be done against the suggestion of a great many socialists. One has only to search the utterances of the platforms of the Socialist Party concerning the Negro laborer to find that from 1872 to 1924 the Negro's plight in the United States was never once specifically mentioned. In 1928, for the first time a stand was taken against the disfranchisement of the Negroes but the theme was not developed and it was not shown how the disfranchisement of half the laboring class of the South carries with it the practical disfranchisement of the other half: and nullifies to a large extent the political power of the laboring man in the North.[1]

The first impulse of a socialist is to express surprise that the Socialist Party in America has so little support from American Negroes. They attribute this to the stupidity and backwardness of an undeveloped people who are not acquainted with the modern labor movement. This, however, is snap judgment. It would be well for those who wish for the widest success of the labor movement in the United States and for the advance of the movement toward the socialization of wealth and income to consider very carefully the historical relations of the labor movement in the United States and the American Negro.

The labor movement was imported into the United States by immigrant laborers, and these laborers from the earliest times found the Negro slave and freedmen as a competitor and tool in the hands of the capitalist. Instead, however, of taking the part of the Negro and helping him toward physical and economic freedom, the American labor movement from the beginning has tried to achieve freedom at the expense of the Negro. The Civil War was an attempt of white laborers in the United States to get western land and higher wages by confining Negroes to slavery and the South. This meant that the Negro before and after emancipation, in self-defense was propelled toward the employing class and the employing class was quick to take advantage of this.

The white employers, North and South, literally gave the Negroes work when white men refused to work with him; when he "scabbed" for bread and butter the employers defended him against mob violence of white laborers; they gave him educational institutions when white labor would have left him in ignorance; and even when the full-fledged socialist movement came, the socialists were afraid to make a direct appeal to the Negro vote because such an appeal would have militated against their chances of attracting white labor, North and South.

So long, therefore, as the logic of the socialist appeal was simply justice to black workers, it played a comparatively small part. Everybody is in favor of justice so long as it costs them no effort. But today matters are changing. The Negro today is growing in intelligence. His political power is growing. He is going to use it in no sentimental way. If American socialism cannot stand for the American Negro, the American Negro will not stand for American socialism. If the Negro more and more recognizes that his salvation, not only in the United States, but in the West Indies and Africa, lies in the public ownership of wealth and the socialization of income, and if, in addition to that, frankly and wholeheartedly, the Socialist Party stands for the rights of men in America without regard to race and color, Negroes must gradually see in the Socialist Party of America their next political step.

The New Leader, February 9, 1929.

6

SHALL THE NEGRO
BE ENCOURAGED TO SEEK
CULTURAL EQUALITY?

On March 17, 1929, the Chicago Forum sponsored a debate on the topic, "Shall the Negro Be Encouraged to Seek Cultural Equality?" Dr. Du Bois spoke for the affirmative and Lothrop Stoddard, the racist, white-supremacist, pro-Nordic ideologist, author of the fear-inspiring The Rising Tide of Color, *upheld the negative.*

We may well ask in the beginning: just what does one mean by "equality"? And what is "cultural" equality? We might even ask, just what are "Negroes"?—and, how are you going to "encourage" anyone to seek this sort of equality?

I am going to take the broad commonsense view of what these words mean. By equality, I do not mean absolute identity or similarity of gift, but gifts of essentially equal values to human culture. By culture, I mean that organized tide which men call civilization. And persons are encouraged to seek cultural equality by the taking down of bars and doing away with discriminations— by abolishing all efforts that directly or indirectly impede people in attaining a certain goal.

If you were not familiar with the race problem in the United States or in the modern world, you would ask: Why should you not encourage Negroes or anybody else in the wide world to seek cultural equality? Is not this the aim of civilization? Is it not the ideal for which all men yearn? What could you conceive as better than a world in which all citizens were not only encouraged to cultural equality but accomplished their aim? Would not this be the best conceivable sort of world?

And yet you who know America, know perfectly well that large numbers of people have always denied to the Negro even the chance to try to reach such a goal. This denial has taken two forms or perhaps two degrees of emphasis on the same thesis. In early days Americans said frankly: the Negro should not be encouraged to seek cultural equality because he cannot reach it; he is not really human in the sense that other people are human. One does not encourage dogs to do the things that men do, not because one has anything against dogs, but because dogs are not men and cannot act like men. And the same way (although perhaps the analogy is overdrawn), Americans do not encourage Negroes to share modern culture because they cannot share it; we would simply make them unhappy if we let them try to reach to things which they can never reach.

Some years ago that was a logical statement and a statement difficult to answer. But in the last generation things have happened, and they have happened fast. We have had since emancipation a bounding forward of these millions of dark people in America. It does not make any difference how far you may wish to minimize what Negroes have done or what judgment you have as to its lasting value, there is no doubt about the work that has been done by these millions of emancipated slaves and their descendants in America. It is one of the wonderful accomplishments of this generation. It has few parallels in human history.

Some people might assume that this rise of the American Negro from slavery to freedom, from squalor, poverty, and ignorance to thrift and intelligence and the beginnings of wealth, would bring unstinted applause. Negroes themselves expected this. They looked eagerly forward to this day when you cannot write a history or statement of American civilization and leave the black man out, as proof of their equality and manhood and they expected their advance, incomplete or imperfect though it remains, nevertheless, to be greeted with applause.

On the contrary, all Negroes know that with all the generous praise given us there has been no phase of the advance that has not been looked on with a strong undercurrent of apprehension. America has feared the coming forward of these black men; it has looked upon it as a sort of threat—and if you should ask just why that is so, white Americans would state the thesis which they have stated before but with some modification; they would say that the coming forward of these people does not prove that they can make as great a gift to culture as the white people have made; but whether they can or not, they must not be allowed to come forward because it threatens civilization! If you ask how this can possibly be—how the advance of one-tenth of a nation can be a threat to the rest— you have various kinds of answers.

In the first place some seem to regard culture as a quantitative sort of thing; there is a certain amount of culture in the world; if you divide it up among all people you have that much less for other people. Of course everybody knows that the quantitative theory of civilization does not hold, that the analogy is not perfect, and yet the reason we use it is because we do regard civilization today in terms of the number of our physical possessions. We are buried beneath our material wealth, and if we think, say, of motor cars, we conclude that if black people have motor cars, there are so many less for the white people to occupy. And so on. We go through the whole catalog of what a material age calls civilization, and think that if it is distributed to certain people, other people are not going to have as much.

Discarding this quantitative analogy we fall back to the other argument. After all, it is not the things which people have that makes the major part of civilization—the real civilization; real culture depends on quality and not quantity; it is not, therefore, so much a matter of distribution of goods—of distribution of quantity as of contamination of quality in goods and deeds.

And there we have brought back into the modern world the theory which the world has held and heard again and again—a few people have the chance to get unusual advancement; they have the chance to learn; they have leisure to think; they have food and shelter and encouragement;

they push forward in the world, and then, after they have reached certain heights, suddenly they are overcome with admiration for themselves; suddenly it is suggested to them that they are wonderful and unusual people; that the universe was made particularly and especially for them; that never before have human beings attained such height and mastery—and finally we have the theory of the Chosen People!

The theory is as old as human culture is old, and yet today it comes back to us in the new dress of the belief that everything that has been done in modern times has been done by the Nordic people; that they are the people who are the salt of the earth; that if anything is done to change their type of civilization, then civilization fails and falls; that what we have got to be afraid of is the coming forward of a mass of black people without real gift, without real knowledge of what culture is, who are going to spoil the divine gifts of the Nordics.

To a theory of this sort, the world—the overwhelming majority of human beings who are not Nordic—have a right to two replies:

First, your theory is unproven. There is no scientific proof that modern culture is of Nordic origin or that Nordic brains and physique are of better intrinsic quality than Mediterranean, Indian, Chinese or Negro. In fact, the proofs of essential human equality of gift are overwhelming.

But, if Nordics believe in their own superiority; if they wish voluntarily to work by themselves and for the development and encouragement of their own gifts; if they prefer not to mingle their blood with other races, or contaminate their culture with foreign strains, nothing is to hinder them from carrying out this program except themselves.

Nobody is going to make Nordics marry outside of their group unless they want to marry outside. They can keep their group closed if they wish. Of course, civilization is by the definition of the term, civilization for all mankind; but nobody is going to withhold applause if you make your contribution to the world.

Of course, civilization is the rightful heritage of all and

cannot be monopolized and confined to one group. A group organization to increase and forward culture is legitimate and will bring its reward in universal recognition and applause.

But this has never been the Nordic program. Their program is the subjection and rulership of the world for the benefit of the Nordics. They have overrun the earth and brought not simply modern civilization and technique, but with it exploitation, slavery and degradation to the majority of men. They have broken down native family life, desecrated homes of weaker peoples and spread their bastards over every corner of land and sea. They have been responsible for more intermixture of races than any other people, ancient or modern, and they have inflicted this miscegenation on helpless, unwilling slaves by force, fraud and insult; and this is the folk that today has the impudence to turn on the darker races when they demand a share of civilization, and cry: "You shall not marry our daughters!"

The blunt, crude reply is: Who in hell asked to marry your daughters? If this race problem must be reduced to a matter of sex, what we demand is the right to protect the decency of our own daughters.

But the insistent demand of the Darker World is far wider and deeper than this. The black and brown and yellow men demand the right to be men. They demand the right to have the artificial barriers placed in their path torn down and destroyed; they demand a voice in their own government; the organization of industry for the benefit of colored workers and not merely for white owners and masters; they demand education on the broadest and highest lines and they demand as human beings social contact with other human beings on a basis of perfect equality.

That is what they call civilization. That is what we American Negroes demand and the demand is so reasonable and logical that to deny it is not simply to hurt and hinder them, it is to fly in the face of your own white civilization.

Think of what has been done in the name of "white supremacy" right here in the United States; the Middle

West today is politically helpless because in order to deprive black Americans of the right to vote, they allowed the South to cast two votes — the vote of the white man and of the disfranchised Negro. The double political power of these rotten boroughs of the South makes democratic government in the United States a farce.

You decry lawlessness. Where do you get the lawlessness of Chicago and of the United States? You began it when as a nation you disregarded the Thirteenth, Fourteenth and Fifteenth Amendments and then are vastly surprised when you cannot enforce the Eighteenth. [1] You have organized your life so as not to carry out the laws which you yourselves made and you have the heritage of lawlessness to pay for it.

You have created here in the United States, which today pretends to the moral leadership of the world, a situation where on the last night of the old year you can slowly and publicly burn a human being alive for the amusement of Americans who represent some of the purest strains of Nordic blood in that great place, Mississippi, which has done so much for the civilization of the world!

Not simply in these things have you attacked your own civilization. You have made it almost impossible for America to think logically.

I said to you a while ago that I might ask you what Negroes were. I come back to that question. I stand here gladly as the representative of the Negro race, and yet I know and you know that I can equally stand here as a representative of the Nordic race. Wherever it seems necessary to deny me any privilege, then I am a Negro, and whenever I do anything that is worth doing, suddenly I become preponderately white. The United States measured soldiers in the great war and came to wonderful conclusions concerning their intelligence, but the conclusions they came to were conclusions for the Negro race, and they knew perfectly well the men they were measuring were not Negroes, but that perhaps 70 percent of them had white blood. It is impossible by any scientific measurement to divide men into races, and even to prove there are separate races, and yet we talk about races, and prescribe races and measure races; and because we are not talking logically when we talk about races, so we cannot talk logically about anything else—the tariff, farm relief, unemployment, credit, wages or capital.

The matter of our logic is not merely so important as that of our ethics and religion. Here you are, a great white nation with a magnificent Plan of Salvation. You have an ethical code far beyond anything the world ever knew—if you do not believe it, listen to what you preach to the darker peoples. You are followers of the Golden Rule and of the meek and lowly Jesus. Yet you do not try to follow out your own religion because you know when your religion comes up against the race problem that religion has nothing absolutely to do with your attitude toward Negroes. The attacks that white people themselves have made upon their own moral structure are worse for civilization than anything that any body of Negroes could ever do.

Therefore, you stand today before the Great Alternative. Are you going to allow the colored people in the United States and the colored races in the world to go forward toward the goals of civilization free and unhampered, or are you going to organize to see that these people are kept in the places where you think they ought to stay? Here is a great decision, a decision which the white world has got to face.

The temptation to hold these colored people back is tremendous, because it is not merely a matter of academic wish or of wanton prejudice, but it is the kernel of the organization of modern life. You have got the colored people working for you all through the world. You have got your investments so made that they depend upon colored labor in Asia, Africa, in the southern states of the United States, and in the islands of the sea. Your income and your power depends upon that organization being kept intact. If it is overthrown, if these black laborers get higher wages, if they begin to understand what life may be, if they increase in knowledge, self-assertion and power, it means the overthrow of the whole system of exploitation which is at the bottom of modern white civilization. What now is your decision?

Suppose you turn to the other side. Suppose you say,

despite anything that the darker races, including the
Negroes in the United States may ask, we are going to
sit tight and keep them where they belong. Then the question is, can you do it?

In the first place, have you the ability to do it? It is
going to call for ability. It is going to call for brains
and genius of the highest order, and looking back upon
the history of what you have done with the colored world,
you have no right to preen yourselves on what you are
going to do in the future. A few years ago you fell out
among yourselves, not because of any quarrel you had
with each other, but on the question as to how you are
going to divide among yourselves territory and raw materials belonging to colored people. The World War was
a matter of jealousy in the division of the spoils of Asia
and Africa, and by it you nearly ruined civilization. Have
you the genius and the brains to carry out further an
organization of men by which the white people of the
world are going to sit on top of it, using it mainly for
their own advantage and make the rest of the world serve?

If you have the ability to do this, there then comes the
next question: have you the force? Have you the physical
force and the machines to do it? Oh, you can do it in the
United States. You outnumber us ten to one. You can
sweep us off the face of the earth. You can starve us to
death or make us wish we had starved to death in the
face of your insults. But, remember, you are standing
before the whole world, with hundreds of darker millions
watching. No matter what happens to us, these colored
people of the world are not going to take forever the kind
of treatment they have been taking. They have got beyond
that. They have come to the place where they know what
civilization is, and if you are going to keep them in their
place, you are going to do it by brute force. Have you
got the force, and is it likely that you are going to get it?

*Report of Debate Conducted by the Chicago Forum, March
17, 1929*, Pamphlet, n.p., n.d., pp. 3-9.

7

EDUCATION AND WORK

*In a commencement address at Howard University,
June 6, 1930, Dr. Du Bois told the graduating students
the history of the ideological battle among Negroes early
in the twentieth century over different types of education
best suited to the welfare of black Americans, and summarized his views a quarter of a century later on education and the role of the Negro college.*

Between the time that I was graduated from college and
the day of my first experience at earning a living, there
was arising in this land, and more especially within the
Negro group, a controversy concerning the type of education which American Negroes needed. You, who are graduating today, have heard but echoes of this controversy
and more or less vague theories of its meaning and its
outcome. Perhaps it has been explained away to you and
interpreted as mere misunderstanding and personal bias.
If so, the day of calm review and inquiry is at hand.
And I suppose that, of persons living, few can realize
better than I just what that controversy meant and what
the outcome is. I want then today in the short time allotted me, to state, as plainly as I may, the problem of
college and industrial education for American Negroes,
as it arose in the past; and then to restate it as it appears
to me in its present aspect.

First of all, let me insist that the former controversy was
no mere misunderstanding; there was real difference of
opinion, rooted in deep sincerity on every side and fought

out with a tenacity and depth of feeling due to its great importance and fateful meaning.

It was, in its larger aspects, a problem such as in all ages human beings of all races and nations have faced; but it was new in 1895 as all time is new; it was con-centered and made vivid and present because of the immediate and pressing question of the education of a vast group of the children of former slaves. It was the ever new and age-young problem of youth, for there had arisen in the South a Joseph which knew not Pharaoh — a black man who was not born in slavery. What was he to become? Whither was his face set? How should he be trained and educated? His fathers were slaves, for the most part, ignorant and poverty-stricken; emancipated in the main without land, tools, nor capital — the sport of war, the despair of economists, the grave perplexity of science. Their children had been born in the midst of controversy, of internecine hatred, and in all the economic dislocation that follows war and civil war. In a peculiar way and under circumstances seldom duplicated, the whole program of popular education became epitomized in the case of these young black folk.

Before men thought or greatly cared, in the midst of the very blood and dust of battle, an educational system for the freedmen had been begun; and with a logic that seemed, at first, quite natural. The night school for adults had become the day school for children. The Negro day school had called for normal teaching and the small New England college had been transplanted and perched on hill and river in Raleigh and Atlanta, Nashville and New Orleans, and half a dozen other towns. This new Negro college was conceived of as the very foundation stone of Negro training.

But, meantime, any formal education for slaves or the children of slaves not only awakened widespread and deep-seated doubt, fear and hostility in the South, but it posed, for statesmen and thinkers, the whole question as to what the education of Negroes was really aiming at, and indeed, what was the aim of educating any working class. If it was doubtful as to how far the social and economic classes of any modern state could be essentially transformed and changed by popular education, how much more tremendous was the problem of educating a race whose ability to assimilate modern training was in grave question and whose place in the nation and the world, even granted they could be educated, was a matter of baffling social philosophy. Was the nation making an effort to parallel white civilization in the South with a black civilization? Or was it trying to displace the dominant white master class with new black masters or was it seeking the difficult but surely more reasonable and practical effort of furnishing a trained set of free black laborers who might carry on in place of the violently disrupted slave system? Surely, most men said, this economic and industrial problem of the New South was the first—the central, the insistent problem of the day.

There can be no doubt of the real dilemma that thus faced the nation, the northern philanthropist and the black man. The argument for the New England college, which at first seemed to need no apology, grew and developed. The matter of man's earning a living, said the college, is and must be important, but surely it can never be so important as the man himself. Thus the economic adaptation of the Negro to the South must in education be subordinated to the great necessity of teaching life and culture. The South, and more especially the Negro, needed and must have trained and educated leadership if civilization was to survive. More than most, here were land and people who needed to learn the meaning of life. They needed the preparation of gifted persons for the profession of teaching, and for other professions which would in time grow. The object of education was not to make men carpenters, but to make carpenters men.

On the other hand, those practical men who looked at the South after the war said: this is an industrial and business age. We are on the threshold of an economic expansion such as the world never saw before. Whatever human civilization has been or may become, today it is industry. The South because of slavery has lagged behind the world. It must catch up. Its prime necessity after the hate and holocaust of war is a trained reliable laboring class. Assume if you will that Negroes are men with every human capacity, nevertheless, as a flat fact, no rising group of peasants can begin at the top. If poverty and starvation are to be warded off, the children of the freedmen must not be taught to despise the humble work, which the mass of the Negro race must for untold years pursue. The transition period between slavery and freedom is a dangerous and critical one. Fill the heads of these children with Latin and Greek and highfalutin' notions of rights and political power, and hell will be to pay.

On the other hand, in the South, here is land and fertile land, in vast quantities, to be had at nominal prices. Here are employers who must have skilled and faithful labor, and have it now. There is in the near future an industrial development coming which will bring the South abreast with the new economic development of the nation and the world. Freedom must accelerate this development which slavery so long retarded. Here then is no time for a philosophy of economic or class revolution and race hatred. There must be friendship and goodwill between employer and employee, between black and white. They have common interests, and the matter of their future relations in politics and society can well be left for future generations and different times to solve. "Cast down your buckets where you are," cried Booker T. Washington; "In all things that are purely social we can be as separate as the fingers, yet one hand in all things essential to mutual progress."[1]

What was needed, then, was that the Negro first should be made the intelligent laborer, the trained farmer, the skilled artisan of the South. Once he had accomplished this step in the economic world and the ladder was set for his climbing, his future would be assured, and assured on an economic foundation which would be immovable. All else in his development, if he proved himself capable of development, even to the highest, would inevitably follow. Let us have, therefore, not colleges but schools to teach the technique of industry and to make men learn by doing.

These were the opposing arguments. They were real arguments. They were set forth by earnest men, white and black, philanthropist and teacher, statesman and seer. The controversy waxed bitter. The disputants came to rival organizations, to severe social pressure, to anger and even to blows. Newspapers were aligned for and against; employment and promotion depended often on a Negro's attitude toward industrial education. The Negro race and their friends were split in twain by the intensity of their feeling and men were labeled and earmarked by their allegiance to one school of thought or to the other.

Today, all this is past; by the majority of the older of my hearers, it is practically forgotten. By the younger, it appears merely as a vague legend. Thirty-five years, a full generation and more, have elapsed. The increase in Negro education by all measurements has been a little less than marvelous. In 1895, there were not more than 1,000 Negro students of full college grade in the United States. Today, there are over 19,000 in college and nearly 150,000 in high schools. In 1895, 60 percent of American Negroes, ten years of age or over, were illiterate. Today, perhaps three-fourths can read and write. The increase of Negro students in industrial and land-grant colleges has been equally large. The latter have over 16,000 students and the increasing support of the government of the states; while the great industrial schools, especially Hampton and Tuskegee, are the best endowed institutions for the education of black folk in the world.

What then has become of this controversy as to college and industrial education for Negroes? Has it been duly settled, and if it has, how has it been settled? Has it been transmuted into a new program, and if so, what is that program? In other words, what is the present norm of Negro education, represented at once by Howard University, Fisk, and Atlanta on one hand, and by Hampton Institute, Tuskegee, and the land-grant colleges on the other?

I answer once for all, the problem has not been settled. The questions raised in those days of controversy still stand in all their validity and all their pressing insistence on an answer. They have not been answered. They must be answered, and the men and women of this audience and like audiences throughout the land are the ones from whom the world demands final reply. Answers have been offered; and the present status of the problem has enormously changed, for human problems never stand still. But I must insist that the fundamental problem is still here.

Let us see. The Negro college has done a great work. It has given us leadership and intelligent leadership. Doubtless, without these colleges the American Negro would scarcely have attained his present position. The chief thing that distinguishes the American Negro group from the Negro groups in the West Indies, and in South America, and the mother group in Africa, is the number of men that we have trained in modern education, able to cope with the white world on its own ground and in its own thought, method and language.

On the other hand, there cannot be the slightest doubt but that the Negro college, its teachers, students and graduates, have not yet comprehended the age in which they live: the tremendous organization of industry, commerce, capital, and credit which today forms a superorganization dominating and ruling the universe, subordinating to its ends government, democracy, religion, education and social philosophy; and for the purpose of forcing into the places of power in this organization American black men either to guide or help reform it, either to increase its efficiency or make it a machine to improve our wellbeing, rather than the merciless mechanism which enslaves us; for this the Negro college has today neither program nor intelligent comprehension.

On the contrary, there is no doubt but that college and university training among us has had largely the exact effect that was predicted; it has turned an increasing number of our people not simply away from manual labor and industry, not simply away from business and economic reform, into a few well-paid professions, but it has turned our attention from any disposition to study or solve our economic problem. A disproportionate number of our college-trained students are crowding into teaching and medicine and beginning to swarm into other professions, and to form at the threshold of these better-paid jobs a white-collar proletariat, depending for their support on an economic foundation which does not yet exist.

Moreover, and perhaps for this very reason, the ideals of colored college-bred men have not in the last thirty years been raised an iota. Rather in the main, they have been lowered. The average Negro undergraduate has swallowed hook, line and sinker, the dead bait of the white undergraduate, who, born in an industrial machine, does not have to think, and does not think. Our college man today, is, on the average, a man untouched by real culture. He deliberately surrenders to selfish and even silly ideals, swarming into semi-professional athletics and Greek-letter societies, and affecting to despise scholarship and the hard grind of study and research. The greatest meetings of the Negro college year like those of the white college year have become vulgar exhibitions of liquor, extravagance, and fur coats. We have in our colleges a growing mass of stupidity and indifference.

I am not counseling perfection; as desperately human groups, we must expect our share of mediocrity. But as hitherto a thick and thin defender of the college, it seems to me that we are getting into our Negro colleges considerably more than our share of plain fools.

Acquiring as we do in college no guidance to a broad economic comprehension and a sure industrial foundation, and simultaneously a tendency to live beyond our means, and spend for show, we are graduating young men and women with an intense and overwhelming appetite for wealth and no reasonable way of gratifying it, no philosophy for counteracting it.

Trained more and more to enjoy sexual freedom as undergraduates, we refuse as graduates to found and support even moderate families, because we cannot afford them; and we are beginning to sneer at group organization and race leadership as mere futile gestures.

Why is this? What is wrong with our colleges? The method of the modern college has been proven by a hundred centuries of human experience: the imparting of knowledge by the old to the young; the instilling of the conclusions of experience, "line upon line and precept upon precept." But, of course, with this general and theoretical method must go a definite and detailed object suited to the present age, the present group, the present set of problems. It is not then in its method but in its practical objects that the Negro college has failed. It is handing on knowledge and experience but what knowledge and for what end? Are we to stick to the old habit of wasting time on Latin, Greek, Hebrew and eschatology, or are we to remember that, after all, the object of the Negro college is to place in American life a trained black man who can do what the world today wants done; who can help the world know what it ought to want done and thus by doing the world's work well may invent better work for a better world? This brings us right back to the object of the industrial school.

Negro industrial training in the United States has accomplishments of which it has a right to be proud; but it too has not solved its problem. Its main accomplishment has been an indirect matter of psychology. It has helped bridge the transition period between Negro slavery and freedom. It has taught thousands of white people in the South to accept Negro education, not simply as a necessary evil, but as a possible social good. It has brought state support to a dozen higher institutions of learning, and to some extent, to a system of public schools. On the other hand, it has tempered and rationalized the inner emancipation of American Negroes. It made the Negro patient when impatience would have killed him. If it has not made working with the hands popular, it has at least removed from it much of the stigma of social degradation. It has made many Negroes seek the friendship of their white fellow citizens, even at the cost of insult and caste. And thus through a wide strip of our country it has brought peace and not a sword.

But this has all been its indirect by-product, rather than its direct teaching. In its direct teaching, the kind of success which it has achieved differs from the success of the college. In the case of the industrial school, the practical object was absolutely right and still is right: that is, the desire of placing in American life a trained black man who could earn a decent living and make the living the foundation stone of his own culture and of the civilization of his group. This was the avowed object of the industrial school. How much has it done toward this? It has established some skilled farmers and among the masses some better farming methods. It has trained and placed some skilled artisans; it has given great impetus to the domestic arts and household economy; it has encouraged Negro business enterprise. And yet we have but to remember these matters to make it patent to all that the results have been pitifully small compared with the need. Our Negro farm population is decreasing; our Negro artisans are not gaining proportionately in industry and Negro business faces today a baffling crisis. Our success in household arts is due not to our effective teaching so much as to the medieval minds of our women who have not yet entered the machine age. Most of them seem still to think that washing clothes, scrubbing steps and paring potatoes were among the Ten Commandments.

Why now has the industrial school with all its partial success failed absolutely in its main object when that object of training Negroes for remunerative occupation is more imperative today than thirty-five years ago?

The reason is clear: if the college has failed because with the right general method it has lacked definite objects appropriate to the age and race, the industrial school has failed because with a definite object it lacked appropriate method to gain it. In other words, the lack of success of the industrial education of Negroes has come not because of the absence of desperate and devoted effort, but because of changes in the world which the industrial school did not foresee, and, which even if it had foreseen, it could not have prevented, and to which it has not the ability to adapt itself.

It is easy to illustrate this. The industrial school assumed that the technique of industry in 1895, even if not absolutely fixed and permanent, was at least permanent enough for training children into its pursuit and for use as a basis of broader education. Therefore, school work for farming, carpentry, bricklaying, plastering and painting, metal work and blacksmithing, shoemaking, sewing and cooking was introduced and taught.

But, meantime, what has happened to these vocations and trades? Machines and new industrial organizations have remade the economic world and ousted these trades either from their old technique or their economic significance. The planing mill does today much of the work of the carpenter and the carpenter is being reduced rapidly to the plane of a mere laborer. The building trades are undergoing all kinds of reconstruction, from the machine-made steel skyscraper, to the cement house cast in molds and the mass-made mail-order bungalow. Painting and masonry still survive, but the machine is after them; while printing and sewing are done increasingly by elaborate machines. Metal is being shaped by stamping mills. Nothing of shoemaking is left for the hands save mending, and in most cases, it is cheaper to buy a new shoe than to have an old one cobbled.

When it comes to the farm, a worldwide combination of circumstances is driving the farmer to the wall. Expensive machinery demands increasingly larger capital; excessive taxation of growing land values is eliminating the small owner; monopolized and manipulated markets and carriers make profits of the individual farmer small or nil; and the foreign competition of farms worked by serfs at starvation wages and backed by worldwide aggregations of capital — all this is driving farmers, black and white, from the soil and making the problem of their future existence one of the great problems of the modern world.

The industrial school, therefore, found itself in the peculiar position of teaching a technique of industry in certain lines just at the time when that technique was changing into something different, and when the new technique was a matter which the Negro school could not teach. In fact, with the costly machine, with mass production and organized distribution, the teaching of technique becomes increasingly difficult. Any person of average intelligence can take part in the making of a modern automobile, and he is paid, not for his technical training, but for his endurance and steady application.

There were many lines of factory work, like the spinning and weaving of cotton and wool, which the Negro could have successfully been set to learning, but they involved vast expenditures of capital which no school could control, and organized business at that time decreed that only white folk could work in factories. And that decree still stands. New branches of industry, new techniques are continually opening — like automobile repairing, electrical installments, and engineering — but these call for changing curricula and adjustments puzzling for a scnool and a set course of study.

In the attempt to put the Negro into business, so that from the inner seats of power by means of capital and credit he could control industry, we have fallen between two stools, this work being apparently neither the program of the college nor of the industrial school. The college treated it with the most approved academic detachment, while the industrial school fatuously assumed as permanent a business organization which began to change with the nineteenth century, and bids fair to disappear with the twentieth. In 1895 we were preaching individual thrift and saving; the small retail store and the partnership for business and the conduct of industry. Today, we are faced by great aggregations of capital and worldwide credit, which monopolize raw material, carriage and manufacture, distribute their products through cartels, mergers and chain stores, and are in process of eliminating the individual trader, the small manufacturer, and the little job. In this new organization of business the colored man meets two difficulties: first, he is not trained to take part in it; and, secondly, if he gets training, he finds it almost impossible to gain a foothold. Schools cannot teach as an art and trade that which is a philosophy, a government of men, an organization of civilization. They can impart a mass of knowledge about it, but this is the duty of the college of liberal arts and not the shop work of the trade school.

Thus the industrial school increasingly faces a blank wall and its astonishing answer today to the puzzle is slowly but surely to transform the industrial school into a college. The most revolutionary development in Negro education for a quarter-century is illustrated by the fact that Hampton today is one of the largest of Negro colleges and that her trade teaching seems bound to disappear within a few years. Tuskegee is a high school and college, with an unsolved program of the future of its trade schools. And the land-grant colleges, built to foster agriculture and industry, are becoming just like other colleges. And all this, as I said, is not the fault of the industrial school, it comes from this tremendous transformation of business, capital and industry in the twentieth century, which few men clearly foresaw and which only a minority of men or of teachers of men today fully comprehend.

In one respect, however, the Negro industrial school was seriously at fault. It set its face toward the employer and the capitalist and the man of wealth. It looked upon the worker as one to be adapted to the demands of those who conducted industry. Both in its general program and in its classroom, it neglected almost entirely the modern labor movement. It had little or nothing to teach concerning the rise of trade unions; their present condition, and their future development. It had no conception of any future democracy in industry. That is, the very vehicle which was to train Negroes for modern industry neglected in its teaching the most important part of modern industrial development: namely, the relation of the worker to modern industry and to the modern state.

The reason for this neglect is clear. The Negro industrial school was the gift of capital and wealth. Organized labor was the enemy of the black man in skilled industry. Organized labor in the United States was and is the chief obstacle to keep black folk from earning a living by its determined policy of excluding them from unions just as long as possible and compelling them to become "scabs" in order to live. The political power of southern white labor disfranchised Negroes, and helped build a caste system. How was the Negro industrial school easily to recognize, in this devil of its present degradation, the angel of its future enlightenment? How natural it was to look to white capital and not to labor for the emancipation of the black world—how natural and yet how insanely futile!

Here then are the successes and the failures of both Negro college and industrial school, and we can clearly see that the problem still stands unsolved: how are we going to place the black American on a sure foundation in the modern state? The modern state is primarily business and industry. Its industrial problems must be settled before its cultural problems can really and successfully be attacked. The world must eat before it can think. The Negro has not found a solid foundation in that state as yet. He is mainly the unskilled laborer; the casual employee; the man hired last and fired first; the man who must subsist upon the lowest wage and consequently share an undue burden of poverty, crime, insanity and ignorance. The only alleviation of his economic position has come from what little the industrial school could teach during the revolution of technique and from what the college took up as part of its mission in vocational training for professions.

For the college had to become a trainer of men for vocations. This is as true of the white college as of the colored college. They both tended to change their college curricula into prevocational preparation for a professional career. But the effort of the Negro college here was halfhearted. There persisted the feeling that the college had finished its work when it placed a man of culture in the world, despite the fact that our graduates who are men of culture are exceptional, and if placed in the world without ability to earn a living, what little culture they have does not long survive.

Thus, at the end of the first third of the twentieth century, while both college and industrial school can point to something accomplished, neither has reached its main objective, and they are in process of uniting to become one stream of Negro education with their great problem of object and method unsolved. The industrial school has done but little to impart the higher technique of the industrial process or of the business organization and it has done almost nothing toward putting the Negro workingman in touch with the great labor movement of the white world.

On the other hand, the Negro college has not succeeded in establishing that great and guiding ideal of group development and leadership within a dominating and expanding culture or in establishing the cultural life as the leading motif of the educated Negro. Its vocational work has been confined to the so-called learned professions, with only a scant beginning of the imparting of the higher technique of industry and science.

The result which I have outlined is not wholly unexpected. Perhaps we can now say that it was impossible fully to avoid this situation. We have a right to congratulate ourselves that we have come to a place of such stability and such intelligence as now to be ready to grapple with our economic problem. The fact of the matter is, we have up to this time been swept on and into the great maelstrom of the white civilization surrounding us. We have been inevitably made part of that vast modern organization of life where social and political control rests in the hands of those few white folk who control wealth, determine credit and divide income. We are in a system of culture where disparity of income is such that respect for labor as labor cannot endure; where the emphasis and outlook is not what a man does but what he is able to get for doing it; where wealth despises work and the object of wealth is to escape work, and where the ideal is power without toil.

So long as a lawyer can look forward to an income of $100,000 a year while a maid servant is well paid with $1,000, just so long the lawyer is going to be one hundred times more respectable than the servant and the servant is going to be called by her first name. So long as the determination of a person's income is not only beyond democratic control and public knowledge, but is a matter of autocratic power and secret manipulation, just so long the application of logic and ethics to wealth, industry and income is going to be a difficult if not insoluble problem.

In the modern world only one country is making a frontal attack upon this problem and that is Russia. Other countries are visualizing it and considering it, making some tentative and halfhearted effort but they have not yet attacked the system as a whole, and for the most part they declare the present system inevitable and eternal and incapable of more than minor and stinted improvement.

In the midst of such a world organization we come looking for economic stability and independence. Of course, our
situation is baffling and contradictory. And it is made all
the more difficult for us because we are by blood and descent and popular opinion an integral part of that vast
majority of mankind which is the victim and not the bene-
ficiary of present conditions, which is today working at
starvation wages and on a level of brute toil and without
voice in its own government or education in its ignorance,
for the benefit, the enormous profit, and the dazzling luxury of the white rulers of the world.

Here lies the problem and it is the problem of the combined Negro college and vocational school. Without the
intellectual leadership of college-bred men, we could not
hitherto have held our own in modern American civilization, but must have sunk to the place of the helpless proletariat of the West Indies and of South Africa. But, on the
other hand, for what has the college saved us? It has
saved us for that very economic defeat which the industrial
school was established to ward off and which still stands
demanding solution. The industrial school acted as bridge
and buffer to lead us out of the bitterness of Reconstruction
to the toleration of today. But it did not place our feet
upon the sound economic foundation which makes our
survival in America or in the modern world certain or
probable; and the reason that it did not do this was as
much the fault of the college as of the trade school. The
industrial school without the college was as helpless yesterday as the college is today helpless without systematic
training for modern industry.

Both college and industrial school have made extraordinary and complementary mistakes in their teaching
force: the industrial school secured usually as teacher a
man of affairs and technical knowledge, without culture
or general knowledge. The college took too often as teacher a man of books and brains with no contact with or
first-hand knowledge of real everyday life and ordinary
human beings, and this was true whether he taught sociology, literature or science. Both types of teacher failed.

What then is the unescapable task of the united college
and vocational school? It is without shadow of doubt a

new broad and widely efficient vocational guidance and
education for men and women of ability, selected by the
most careful tests and supported by a broad system of
free scholarships. Our educational institutions must gradu-
ate to the world men fitted to take their place in real life
by their knowledge, spirit, and ability to do what the world
wants done. This vocational guidance must have for its
object the training of men who can think clearly and function normally as physical beings; who have a knowledge
of what human life on earth has been, and what it is now;
and a knowledge of the constitution of the known universe.
All that, and in addition to that, a training which will
enable them to take some definite and intelligent part in
the production of goods and in the furnishing of human
services and in the democratic distribution of income so
as to build civilization, encourage initiative, reward effort
and support life. Just as the Negro college course with vision, knowledge and ideal must move toward vocational
training, so the industrial courses must ascend from mere
hand technique to engineering and industrial planning and
the application of scientific and technical knowledge to
problems of work and wage.

This higher training and vocational guidance must turn
out young men and women who are willing not only to
do the work of the world today but to provide for the
future world. Here then is the job before us. It is in a sense
the same kind of duty that lies before the educated white
man but it has an essential and important difference. If
we make a place for ourselves in the industrial and business world today, this will be done because of our ability
to establish a self-supporting organization sufficiently independent of the white organization to insure its stability
and our economic survival and eventual incorporation
into world industry. Ours is the double and dynamic function of tuning in with a machine in action so as neither
to wreck the machine nor be crushed or maimed by it.
Many think this is impossible. But if it is impossible, our
future economic survival is impossible.

Let there be no misunderstanding about this, no easy-
going optimism. We are not going to share modern civilization just by deserving recognition. We are going to

force ourselves in by organized far-seeing effort—by out-thinking and outflanking the owners of the world today who are too drunk with their own arrogance and power successfully to oppose us if we think and learn and do.

It is not the province of this paper to tell in detail just how this problem will be settled. Indeed, I could not tell you if I would. I merely stress the problem and emphasize the possibility of the solution. A generation ago those who doubted our survival said that no alien and separate nation could hope to survive within another nation; that we must be absorbed or perish. Times have changed. To-day it is rapidly becoming true that only within some great and all-inclusive empire or league can separate nations and groups find freedom and protection and economic scope for development. The small separate nation is becoming increasingly impossible and the League of Nations as well as Briand's proposed League of Europe shout this from the housetops. And just as loudly, the inevitable disintegration of the British Empire shows the impossibility of world-embracing centralized autocracy. This means that the possibility of our development and survival is clear, but clear only as brains and devotion and skilled knowledge point the way.

We need then, first, training as human beings in general knowledge and experience; then technical training to guide and do a specific part of the world's work. The broader training should be the heritage and due of all but today it is curtailed by poverty. The technical training of men must be directed by vocational guidance which finds fitness and ability. Then actual and detailed technical training will be done by a combination of school, laboratory and apprenticeship, according to the nature of the work and the changing technique.

The teachers of such a stream of students must be of a high order. College teachers cannot follow the medieval tradition of detached withdrawal from the world. The professor of mathematics in a college has to be more than a counting machine, or proctor of examinations; he must be a living man, acquainted with real human beings, and alive to the relation of his branch of knowledge to the technical problem of living and earning a living.

The teacher in a Negro college has got to be something far more than a master of a branch of human knowledge. He has got to be able to impart his knowledge to human beings whose place in the world is today precarious and critical and the possibilities and advancement of that human being in the world where he is to live and earn a living is of just as much importance in the teaching process as the content of the knowledge taught.

The man who teaches blacksmithing must be more than a blacksmith. He must be a man of education and culture, acquainted with the whole present technique and business organization of the modern world, and acquainted too with human beings and their possibilities. Such a man is difficult to procure. Because industrial schools did not have in the past such teachers for their classes and could not get them, their whole program suffered unmerited criticism. The teachers, then, cannot be pedants or dilettantes, they cannot be mere technicians and higher artisans, they have got to be social statesmen and statesmen of high order. The student body of such schools has got to be selected for something more than numbers. We must eliminate those who are here because their parents wish to be rid of them or for the social prestige or for passing the time or for getting as quickly as possible into a position to make money to throw away; and we must concentrate upon young men and women of ability and vision and will.

Today there is but one rivalry between culture and vocation, college training and trade and professional training, and that is the rivalry of time. Someday every human being will have college training. Today some must stop with the grades, and some with high school, and only a few reach college. It is of the utmost importance, then, and the essential condition of our survival and advance that those chosen for college be our best and not simply our richest or most idle.

But even this growth must be led; it must be guided by ideals. We have lost something, brothers, wandering in strange lands. We have lost our ideals. We have come to a generation which seeks advance without ideals — discovery without stars. It cannot be done. Certain great landmarks and guiding facts must stand eternally before us; and at the risk of moralizing, I must end by emphasizing this matter of the ideals of Negro students and graduates.

The ideal of *poverty*. This is the direct antithesis of the present American ideal of wealth. We cannot all be wealthy. We should not all be wealthy. In an ideal industrial organization no person should have an income which he does not personally need; nor wield a power solely for his own whim. If civilization is to turn out millionaires it will also turn out beggars and prostitutes either at home or among the lesser breeds without the law. A simple healthy life on limited income is the only reasonable ideal of civilized folk.

The ideal of *work* — not idleness, not dawdling, but hard continuous effort at something worth doing, by a man supremely interested in doing it, who knows how it ought to be done and is willing to take infinite pains doing it.

The ideal of *knowledge* — not guesswork, not mere careless theory; not inherited religious dogma clung to because of fear and inertia and in spite of logic, but critically tested and laboriously gathered fact martialed under scientific law and feeding rather than choking the glorious world of fancy and imagination, of poetry and art, of beauty and deep culture.

Finally, and especially, the ideal of *sacrifice*. I almost hesitate to mention this — so much sentimental twaddle has been written of it. When I say sacrifice, I mean sacrifice. I mean a real and definite surrender of personal ease and satisfaction. I embellish it with no theological fairy tales of a rewarding God or a milk-and-honey heaven. I am not trying to scare you into the duty of sacrifice by the fires of a mythical hell. I am repeating the stark fact of survival of life and culture on this earth:

> *"Entbehren sollst du — sollst entbehren."*
> Thou shalt forego, shalt do without.

The insistent problem of human happiness is still with us. We American Negroes are not a happy people. We feel perhaps as never before the sting and bitterness of our struggle. Our little victories won here and there serve but to reveal the shame of our continuing semislavery and social caste. We are torn asunder within our own group because of the rasping pressure of the struggle without. We are as a race not simply dissatisfied, we are embodied dissatisfaction.

To increase abiding satisfaction for the mass of our people, and for all people, someone must sacrifice something of his own happiness. This is a duty only to those who recognize it as a duty. The larger the number ready to sacrifice, the smaller the total sacrifice necessary. No man of education and culture and training who proposes to face his problem and solve it can hope for entire happiness. It is silly to tell intelligent human beings: Be good and you will be happy. The truth is today, be good, be decent, be honorable and self-sacrificing and you will not always be happy. You will often be desperately unhappy. You may even be crucified, dead and buried, and the third day you will be just as dead as the first. But with the death of your happiness may easily come increased happiness and satisfaction and fulfillment for other people — strangers, unborn babes, uncreated worlds. If this is not sufficient incentive, never try it — remain hogs.

The present census will show that the American Negro of the educated class and even of the middle industrial class is reproducing himself at an even slower rate than the corresponding classes of whites. To raise a small family today is a sacrifice. It is not romance and adventure. It is giving up something of life and pleasure for a future generation.

If, therefore, real sacrifice for others in your lifework appeals to you, here it is. Here is the chance to build an industrial organization on a basis of logic and ethics, such as is almost wholly lacking in the modern world. It is a tremendous task, and it is the task equally and at once of Howard and Tuskegee, of Hampton and Fisk, of the college and of the industrial school. Our real schools must become centers of this vast crusade. With the faculty and the student body girding themselves for this new and greater education, the major part of the responsibility will still fall upon those who have already done their schoolwork; and that means upon the alumni who, like you, have become graduates of an institution of learning.

Unless the vision comes to you and comes quickly, of the educational and economic problem before the American Negro, that problem will not be solved. You not only enter, therefore, today the worshipful company of that vast body of men upon whom a great center of learning, with ancient ceremony and colorful trappings, has put the accolade of intellectual knighthood, but men who have become the unselfish thinkers and planners of a group of people in whose hands lies the economic and social destiny of the darker peoples of the world, and by that token of the world itself.

Finally, no one may fail to stress before any audience, or on any occasion and on any errand bent, the overshadowing and all-inclusive ideal of *beauty* — "fair face of Beauty, all too fair to see" — fitness, rhythm, perfection of adaptation of ends to means. It is hard to mention this intelligently without maudlin sentiment and clouded words. May I speak then in parable?

Last night I saw the zeppelin sailing in silver across the new moon. Brilliant, enormous, lovely, it symbolized the civilization over which it hung. It rode serene above miles of death; like a needle it threaded together clouds and seas, stars and continents. Within its womb were caged eternal and palpitating forces of the universe, and yet without quiver it faced the utter ends of space. Across the city, mute, dominant, magnificent, imponderable — it flew.

And what it did, men and women of Howard, you may do — you must do or die. The zeppelin is neither miracle nor stroke of genius. It is unremittent toil and experiment and thought and infinite adaptation in the face of every discouragement and failure, in the face of death itself.

I thought as I saw it flying there, of an angel flying low — an angel of steel and silk and of grim and awful human aim. I remembered the word of our own poet, great, but little known:

> I thought I saw an angel flying low.
> I thought I saw the flicker of a wing
> Above the mulberry trees; but not again.
> Bethesda sleeps . . . .

The golden days are gone. Why do we wait
So long upon the marble steps, blood
Falling from our open wounds? and why
Do our black faces search the empty sky?
Is there something we have forgotten?
    Some precious thing
We have lost, wandering in strange lands? . . .

There was a day, I remember now,
I beat my breast and cried, "Wash me God,
Wash me with a wave of wind upon
The barley; O quiet One, draw near, draw near!
Walk upon the hills with lovely feet
And in the waterfall stand and speak."

Howard University Bulletin, vol. IX, January 1901, pp. 5-22.

8

A NEGRO NATION
WITHIN THE NATION

*Although Dr. Du Bois favored and fought for integration
and full equality throughout most of his life, there were
distinct periods when he believed that black Americans
could only achieve dignity and meaningful freedom through
their own organizations and without too much association with or dependence upon the white community. One
purpose for this program was the development of "race
pride" which Dr. Du Bois always held of prime importance. While he was attacked as condemning the Negro
to a segregated way of life, he actually believed that only
through control over their own economic and political
life could black Americans achieve equality in American
society. In a real sense, Dr. Du Bois projected what later
became to be known as Black Power. This he set forth
in speeches, articles, and editorials, and it was a major
issue in Dr. Du Bois's resignation from the NAACP on
June 26, 1934, after which he spoke widely on the need
for voluntary segregation. "A Negro Nation Within the
Nation" was the theme of many of these speeches, and
was published in* Current History *of June 1935.*

No more critical situation ever faced the Negroes of
America than that of today—not in 1830, nor in 1861,
nor in 1867. More than ever the appeal of the Negro
for elementary justice falls on deaf ears.

Three-fourths of us are disfranchised; yet no writer
on democratic reform, no third-party movement says a
word about Negroes. The Bull Moose crusade in 1912
refused to notice them;[1] the La Follette uprising in 1924

was hardly aware of them;[2] the Socialists still keep them in the background. Negro children are systematically denied education; when the National Educational Association asks for federal aid to education it permits discrimination to be perpetuated by the present local authorities. Once or twice a month Negroes convicted of no crime are openly and publicly lynched, and even burned; yet a National Crime Convention is brought to perfunctory and unwilling notice of this only by mass picketing and all but illegal agitation. When a man with every qualification is refused a position simply because his great-grandfather was black there is not a ripple of comment or protest.

Long before the depression Negroes in the South were losing "Negro" jobs, those assigned them by common custom — poorly paid and largely undesirable toil, but nevertheless life-supporting. New techniques, new enterprises, mass production, impersonal ownership and control have been largely displacing the skilled white and Negro worker in tobacco manufacturing, in iron and steel, in lumbering and mining, and in transportation. Negroes are now restricted more and more to common labor and domestic service of the lowest paid and worst kind. In textile, chemical and other manufactures Negroes were from the first nearly excluded, and just as slavery kept the poor white out of profitable agriculture, so freedom prevents the poor Negro from finding a place in manufacturing. The worldwide decline in agriculture has moreover carried the mass of black farmers, despite heroic endeavor among the few, down to the level of landless tenants and peons.

The World War and its wild aftermath seemed for a moment to open a new door; two million black workers rushed North to work in iron and steel, make automobiles and pack meat, build houses and do the heavy toil in factories. They met first the closed trade union which excluded them from the best-paid jobs and pushed them into the low-wage gutter, denied them homes and mobbed them. Then they met the depression.

Since 1929 Negro workers, like white workers, have lost their jobs, have had mortgages foreclosed on their farms and homes, have used up their small savings. But, in the case of the Negro worker, everything has been worse in larger or smaller degree; the loss has been greater and more permanent. Technological displacement, which began before the depression, has been accelerated, while unemployment and falling wages struck black men sooner, went to lower levels and will last longer.

Negro public schools in the rural South have often disappeared, while southern city schools are crowded to suffocation. The Booker Washington High School in Atlanta, built for 1,000 pupils, has 3,000 attending in double daily sessions. Above all, federal and state relief holds out little promise for the Negro. It is but human that the unemployed white man and the starving white child should be relieved first by local authorities who regard them as fellowmen, but often regard Negroes as subhuman. While the white worker has sometimes been given more than relief and been helped to his feet, the black worker has often been pauperized by being just kept from starvation. There are some plans for national rehabilitation and the rebuilding of the whole industrial system. Such plans should provide for the Negro's future relations to American industry and culture, but those provisions the country is not only unprepared to make but refuses to consider.

In the Tennessee Valley beneath the Norris Dam, where do Negroes come in? And what shall be their industrial place? In the attempt to rebuild agriculture the southern landholder will in all probability be put on his feet, but the black tenant has been pushed to the edge of despair. In the matter of housing, no comprehensive scheme for Negro homes has been thought out and only two or three local projects planned. Nor can broad plans be made until the nation or the community decides where it wants or will permit Negroes to live. Negroes are largely excluded from subsistence homesteads because Negroes protested against segregation, and whites, anxious for cheap local labor, also protested.

The colored people of America are coming to face the fact quite calmly that most white Americans do not like them, and are planning neither for their survival, nor for their definite future if it involves free, self-assertive modern manhood. This does not mean all Americans. A saving few are worried about the Negro problem; a still larger group are not ill-disposed, but they fear prevailing public opinion. The great mass of Americans are, however, merely representatives of average humanity. They muddle along with their own affairs and scarcely can be expected to take seriously the affairs of strangers or people whom they partly fear and partly despise.

For many years it was the theory of most Negro leaders that this attitude was the insensibility of ignorance and inexperience, that white America did not know of or realize the continuing plight of the Negro. Accordingly, for the last two decades, we have striven by book and periodical, by speech and appeal, by various dramatic methods of agitation, to put the essential facts before the American people. Today there can be no doubt that Americans know the facts; and yet they remain for the most part indifferent and unmoved.

The main weakness of the Negro's position is that since emancipation he has never had an adequate economic foundation. Thaddeus Stevens recognized this and sought to transform the emancipated freedmen into peasant proprietors.[3] If he had succeeded, he would have changed the economic history of the United States and perhaps saved the American farmer from his present plight. But to furnish 50,000,000 acres of good land to the Negroes would have cost more money than the North was willing to pay, and was regarded by the South as highway robbery.

The whole attempt to furnish land and capital for the freedmen fell through, and no comprehensive economic plan was advanced until the advent of Booker T. Washington. He had a vision of building a new economic foundation for Negroes by incorporating them into white industry. He wanted to make them skilled workers by industrial education and expected small capitalists to rise out of their ranks. Unfortunately, he assumed that the economic development of America in the twentieth century would resemble that of the nineteenth century, with free industrial opportunity, cheap land and unlimited resources under the control of small competitive capitalists. He lived to see industry more and more concentrated, land monopoly extended and industrial technique changed by wide introduction of machinery.

As a result, technology advanced more rapidly than Hampton or Tuskegee could adjust their curricula. The chance of an artisan's becoming a capitalist grew slimmer, even for white Americans, while the whole relation of labor to capital became less a matter of technical skill than of basic organization and aim.

Those of us who in that day opposed Booker Washington's plans did not foresee exactly the kind of change that was coming, but we were convinced that the Negro could succeed in industry and in life only if he had intelligent leadership and far-reaching ideals. The object of education, we declared, was not "to make men artisans but to make artisans men." The Negroes in America needed leadership so that, when change and crisis came, they could guide themselves to safety.

The educated group among American Negroes is still small, but it is large enough to begin planning for preservation through economic advancement. The first definite movement of this younger group was toward direct alliance of the Negro with the labor movement. But white labor today as in the past refuses to respond to these overtures.

For a hundred years, beginning in the thirties and forties of the nineteenth century, the white laborers of Ohio, Pennsylvania and New York beat, murdered and drove away fellow workers because they were black and had to work for what they could get. Seventy years ago in New York, the center of the new American labor movement, white laborers hanged black ones to lamp posts instead of helping to free them from the worst of modern slavery.[4] In Chicago and St. Louis, New Orleans and San Francisco, black men still carry the scars of the bitter hatred of white laborers for them. Today it is white labor that keeps Negroes out of decent low-cost housing, that confines the protection of the best unions to "white" men, that often will not sit in the same hall with black folk who already have joined the labor movement. White labor has to hate scabs; but it hates black scabs not because they are scabs but because they are black. It mobs white scabs to force them into labor fellowship. It mobs black scabs to starve and kill them. In the present fight of the American Federation of Labor against company unions it is attacking the only unions that Negroes can join.

Thus the Negro's fight to enter organized industry has made little headway. No Negro, no matter what his ability, can be a member of any of the railway unions. He cannot be an engineer, fireman, conductor, switchman, brakeman or yardman. If he organizes separately, he may, as in the case of the Negro Firemen's Union, be assaulted and even killed by white firemen. As in the case of the Pullman Porters' Union, he may receive empty recognition without any voice or collective help. The older group of Negro leaders recognize this and simply say it is a matter of continued striving to break down these barriers.

Such facts are, however, slowly forcing Negro thought into new channels. The interests of labor are considered rather than those of capital. No greater welcome is expected from the labor monopolist who mans armies and navies to keep Chinese, Japanese and Negroes in their places than from the captains of industry who spend large sums of money to make laborers think that the most worthless white man is better than any colored man. The Negro must prove his necessity to the labor movement and that it is a disastrous error to leave him out of the foundation of the new industrial state. He must settle beyond cavil the question of his economic efficiency as a worker, a manager and controller of capital.

The dilemma of these younger thinkers gives men like James Weldon Johnson[5] a chance to insist that the older methods are still the best; that we can survive only by being integrated into the nation, and that we must consequently fight segregation now and always and force our way by appeal, agitation and law. This group, however, does not seem to recognize the fundamental economic bases of social growth and the changes that face American industry. Greater democratic control of production and distribution is bound to replace existing autocratic and monopolistic methods.

In this broader and more intelligent democracy we can hope for progressive softening of the asperities and anomalies of race prejudice, but we cannot hope for its early and complete disappearance. Above all, the doubt, deep-planted in the American mind, as to the Negro's ability and efficiency as worker, artisan and administrator will fade but slowly. Thus, with increased democratic control of industry and capital, the place of the Negro will be increasingly a matter of human choice, of willingness to recognize ability across the barriers of race, of putting fit Negroes in places of power and authority by public opinion. At present, on the railroads, in manufacturing, in the telephone, telegraph and radio business, and in the larger divisions of trade, it is only under exceptional circumstances that any Negro no matter what his ability, gets an opportunity for position and power. Only in those lines where individual enterprise still counts, as in some of the professions, in a few of the trades, in a few branches of retail business and in artistic careers, can the Negro expect a narrow opening.

Negroes and other colored folk nevertheless, exist in larger and growing numbers. Slavery, prostitution to white men, theft of their labor and goods have not killed them and cannot kill them. They are growing in intelligence and dissatisfaction. They occupy strategic positions, within nations and beside nations, amid valuable raw material and on the highways of future expansion. They will survive, but on what terms and conditions? On this point a new school of Negro thought is arising. It believes in the ultimate uniting of mankind and in a unified American nation, with economic classes and racial barriers leveled, but it believes this is an ideal and is to be realized only by such intensified class and race consciousness as will bring irresistible force rather than mere humanitarian appeals to bear on the motives and actions of men.

The peculiar position of Negroes in America offers an opportunity. Negroes today cast probably 2,000,000 votes in a total of 40,000,000, and their vote will increase. This gives them, particularly in northern cities, and at critical times, a chance to hold a very considerable balance of power, and the mere threat of this being used intelligently and with determination may often mean much. The consuming power of 2,800,000 Negro families has recently been estimated at $166,000,000 a month—a tremendous power when intelligently directed. Their manpower as laborers probably equals that of Mexico or Yugoslavia. Their illiteracy is much lower than that of Spain or Italy. Their estimated per capita wealth about equals that of Japan.

For a nation with this start in culture and efficiency to

sit down and await the salvation of a white God is idiotic. With the use of their political power, their power as consumers, and their brainpower, added to that chance of personal appeal which proximity and neighborhood always give to human beings, Negroes can develop in the United States an economic nation within a nation, able to work through inner cooperation, to found its own institutions, to educate its genius, and at the same time, without mob violence or extremes of race hatred, to keep in helpful touch and cooperate with the mass of the nation. This has happened more often than most people realize, in the case of groups not so obviously separated from the mass of people as are American Negroes. It must happen in our case, or there is no hope for the Negro in America.

Any movement toward such a program is today hindered by the absurd Negro philosophy of Scatter, Suppress, Wait, Escape. There are even many of our educated young leaders who think that because the Negro problem is not in evidence where there are few or no Negroes, this indicates a way out! They think that the problem of race can be settled by ignoring it and suppressing all reference to it. They think that we have only to wait in silence for the white people to settle the problem for us; and finally and predominantly, they think that the problem of twelve million Negro people, mostly poor, ignorant workers, is going to be settled by having their more educated and wealthy classes gradually and continually escape from their race into the mass of the American people, leaving the rest to sink, suffer and die.

Proponents of this program claim, with much reason, that the plight of the masses is not the fault of the emerging classes. For the slavery and exploitation that reduced Negroes to their present level or at any rate hindered them from rising, the white world is to blame. Since the age-long process of raising a group is through the escape of its upper class into welcome fellowship with risen peoples, the Negro intelligentsia would submerge itself if it bent its back to the task of lifting the mass of people. There is logic in this answer, but futile logic.

If the leading Negro classes cannot assume and bear the uplift of their own proletariat, they are doomed for all time. It is not a case of ethics; it is a plain case of necessity. The method by which this may be done is, first, for the American Negro to achieve a new economic solidarity.

There exists today a chance for the Negroes to organize a cooperative state within their own group. By letting Negro farmers feed Negro artisans, and Negro technicians guide Negro home industries, and Negro thinkers plan this integration of cooperation, while Negro artists dramatize and beautify the struggle, economic independence can be achieved. To doubt that this is possible is to doubt the essential humanity and the quality of brains of the American Negro.

No sooner is this proposed than a great fear sweeps over older Negroes. They cry "No segregation"— no further yielding to prejudice and race separation. Yet any planning for the benefit of American Negroes on the part of a Negro intelligentsia is going to involve organized and deliberate self-segregation. There are plenty of people in the United States who would be only too willing to use such a plan as a way to increase existing legal and customary segregation between the races. This threat which many Negroes see is no mere mirage. What of it? It must be faced.

If the economic and cultural salvation of the American Negro calls for an increase in segregation and prejudice, then that must come. American Negroes must plan for their economic future and the social survival of their fellows in the firm belief that this means in a real sense the survival of colored folk in the world and the building of a full humanity instead of a petty white tyranny. Control of their own education, which is the logical and inevitable end of separate schools, would not be an unmixed ill; it might prove a supreme good. Negro schools once meant poor schools. They need not today; they must not tomorrow. Separate Negro sections will increase race antagonism, but they will also increase economic cooperation, organized self-defense and necessary self-confidence.

The immediate reaction of most white and colored people to this suggestion will be that the thing cannot be done without extreme results. Negro thinkers have from time to time emphasized the fact that no nation within a nation can be built because of the attitude of the dominant major-

ity, and because all legal and police power is out of Negro
hands, and because large-scale industries, like steel and
utilities, are organized on a national basis. White folk, on
the other hand, simply say that, granting certain obvious
exceptions, the American Negro has not the ability to
engineer so delicate a social operation calling for such self-
restraint, careful organization and sagacious leadership.

In reply, it may be said that this matter of a nation within
a nation[6] has already been partially accomplished in the
organization of the Negro church, the Negro school and the
Negro retail business, and, despite all the justly due criticism, the result has been astonishing. The great majority of
American Negroes are divided not only for religious but
for a large number of social purposes into self-supporting
economic units, self-governed, self-directed. The greatest
difficulty is that these organizations have no logical and
reasonable standards and do not attract the finest, most
vigorous and best educated Negroes. When all these things
are taken into consideration it becomes clearer to more and
more American Negroes that, through voluntary and increased segregation, by careful autonomy and planned economic organization, they may build so strong and efficient
a unit that twelve million men can no longer be refused
fellowship and equality in the United States.

Current History, vol. XLII, June 1935, pp. 265-69.

9

WHAT THE NEGRO HAS DONE FOR THE UNITED STATES AND TEXAS

The year 1936 marked the one-hundredth anniversary of the establishment of the Republic of Texas in 1836, and part of the Centennial Exposition was a Hall of Negro Life. To open the hall, Dr. Du Bois delivered an address on the contributions of the Negro to the United States and Texas which was a brilliant brief analysis of American Negro History. The speech was later published as a pamphlet by the Texas Centennial Commission.

The meaning of America is the possibilities of the common man. It is a refutation of that widespread assumption that the real makers of the world must always be a small group of exceptional men, while most men are incapable of assisting civilization or achieving culture. The United States of America proves, if it proves anything, that the number of men who may be educated and may achieve is much larger than the world has hitherto assumed, and that out of the ranks of the lowly, up from peasants, laborers, and servants, can come effective participation in and support for a great and impressive civilization. And that what has thus been done in the past can be accomplished to an even larger degree in the future as opportunity is opened to the masses of men.

This is clearly shown in the history of the Negro race in America and this pamphlet is an attempt to tell in small space the nature of the contribution which the Negro has made to civilization in the United States.

1. Negro Labor and Exploration

The most revealing commentary upon our modern attitude toward life is that we still regard hard human toil not as a contribution to civilization, but rather as an evil or even a degradation. In fact, labor is the beginning of civilization. As culture progresses much of the necessary hard toil can be transferred from the backs of human beings to beasts of burden, forces of nature, and to the machine. But the necessity of human labor can never be wholly done away with and the harder and more unlovely labor is at particular periods, the greater the contribution and sacrifice of those who do it.

The greatest gift of the Negro to America was this gift of toil. It was the prime reason for his presence in this country. The problem of America in the fifteenth and sixteenth centuries was the problem of manual labor. It was settled by importing white bond servants from Europe, and black servants from Africa, and compelling the American Indians to work. Indian slavery failed to play any great part because the small number of Indians in the West Indies were rapidly killed off by the unaccustomed toil, and those on the continent long retained unimpaired a group organization for self-defense.

The supply of white labor was limited by the labor demands of Europe and by law. On the other hand, the systematic development of the black slave trade was facilitated by religion and by deliberately instigated intertribal wars in Africa and led to a vast and continuous supply of black labor. Differentiation, therefore, in the status of labor was based increasingly upon the cost of importing laborers and consequently upon race and color. The white laboring class became increasingly free, and the black laboring class became predominantly enslaved.

The result of this labor was an economic organization by which the middle classes of the world were supplied with a cheap, sweetening material derived from sugarcane; a cheap luxury, tobacco; and finally and above all, a cheap and universal material for clothing, cotton. These were things that all men wanted who had anything to offer in labor or materials for the satisfaction of their wants. The cost of raising them was primarily a labor cost since land in America at that time was almost limitless in fertility and extent. World commerce, therefore, changed from a trade chiefly in luxuries for the rich, and became a supply of necessities for the middle class, with an enormously widened basis of demand. The slave trade became the beginning of modern international commerce. Invention was stimulated; the well-being of European workers increased; economic and political revolution followed to which America fell heir. New immigrants poured in; new conceptions of religion, government, and work arose. And at the bottom of this industrial and commercial pyramid, and industry's efficient foundation stone, was the toil of the increasing millions of black slaves in America.

As the value of this new raw material, especially sugar and cotton, increased, it became increasingly difficult to maintain a double legal and social standard among the laborers whose exploitation made this investment of capital profitable. The rise of white laborers in political power and more insistent demand for high wages and better conditions of work had to result in breaking the fetters of black slaves who were their competitors and kept down wages.

The number of Negroes and of persons of Negro descent increased rapidly from 1,002,037 in 1800 to 8,833,994 in 1900, and 11,891,143 in 1930. Emancipation placed a population of nearly 5,000,000 black people in the field of work gradually to be transformed from a slave to a free labor basis. The Negro worker today is an indispensable part of American industry, furnishing nearly 12 percent of all American breadwinners; one-third of all servants, one-fifth of all farmers, one-tenth of those employed in transportation and communication, 8 percent of the miners and 7 percent of those in the professions.

The Negro in America has not been simply an unskilled laborer; even in slavery days, there were considerable numbers of Negro artisans. Today, semiskilled and skilled Negro labor forms a large part of the black labor force. There have also been highly skilled mechanics and inventors, including men like Rillieux, who revolutionized the method of refining sugar; Matzeliger, who invented the machine for lasting shoes on which is based the monopoly of the United Shoe Company today; Elijah McCoy, the pioneer inventor of automatic lubrication, and Granville Woods, who patented fifty devices relating to electricity.

American Negroes from the beginning helped in the exploration of the country. There is widespread evidence of Negroes in America in the sixteenth century as servants, traders, and explorers. Negroes may have been instrumental in establishing the city of Mexico, and certainly Menendez had a company of trained Negro artisans and agriculturists when he founded St. Augustine in 1565. Perhaps the most romantic story of a Negro explorer is that of Stephen Dorantes, or as he is usually called, "Estevanico." As the slave of a Spaniard, Dorantes, he guided and rescued the three white survivors of the Narvaez Expedition of 1527, and led the expedition on the first overland journey from Florida to Mexico, passing through what is now the state of Texas. In Mexico, Estevanico became the servant of the viceroy of Mexico, and was sent on a journey to the Northwest to discover the Seven Cities of Cibola. He entered what is now Arizona in 1539, and was eventually killed by the Indians. He was thus the first person from the Old World to set foot on the southwestern part of the United States.

Negroes were with nearly all the Spanish explorers in Florida, Texas, Arizona, New Mexico, and Kansas. One was with the Lewis and Clark Expedition in 1804 and another with Fremont in his California expedition in 1843. And among the early settlers of California were many Negroes and mulattoes. Beside this, it is interesting to remember that the only living human being today who has actually set foot on the North Pole is Matthew Henson, the Negro assistant of Commodore Peary.

2. Negro Music

"Little of beauty has America given the world save the rude grandeur God himself stamped on her bosom; the human spirit in this new world has expressed itself in vigor and ingenuity rather than in beauty. And so by fateful chance the Negro folk song—the rhythmic cry of the slave—stands today not simply as the sole American music, but as the most beautiful expression of human experience born this side the seas."

For many years, Negro music in the United States received little attention. Then these songs became the basis of many current tunes and were caricatured by minstrels. Stephen Foster and others built up folk songs on Negro themes. During the Civil War, the first serious study of Negro American music was made and the Fisk Jubilee Singers after the war carried the music of these songs around the world. Today it is recognized as real and beautiful folk music and on it as a basis has been evolved a body of modern music of growing importance, including the work of Dvorak, Dett, Rosamond Johnson, and Coleridge-Taylor. New Negro composers are today bringing a new and higher development based on the themes of Negro folk songs: William Dawson, Shirley Graham, William Still, and others have had their music played by the best American orchestras before great audiences.

Work songs, including the "blues" and "mellows," have been evolved and the Negro dance and ragtime orchestration has spread all over the world. This music is American and not directly African, although traces of African music may be found in its rhythm and scales. It has utilized and modified the music of white folk; but it is mainly a production of Negroes on American soil. There can be no doubt of the greatness of the musical contribution which the Negroes have thus made and of its essential and fundamental Negro character.

3. Negro Literature, Science, and Art

From the earliest times, the presence of black men in America has inspired American writers, and the Negro forms a central theme in white American literature.

Beside this, there is a distinct and continuous line of development in a literature written by Negroes. In this must be included the folk tales of Joel Chandler Harris, which though set down by a white man, were clearly of Negro invention and origin. There have been other interesting collections of Negro folklore. The first colored writer of national importance was Phillis Wheatley, whose poems appeared in 1773, and who received flattering notice from George Washington and leading Englishmen. There came, then, a series of biographies, from the first bishop of the African Methodist Church down to Booker T. Washington. Many of the slave narratives and biographies were methods of appeal and propaganda. There were various essays and protests, like that of Paul Cuffe, and especially the first full-voiced, almost hysterical appeal of David Walker in 1829.[1]

In 1840 came stronger writers, like Garnett and William Wells Brown, and especially Douglass's epoch-making autobiography.[2] During the Civil War, there were additional slave narratives, histories and travels, and after the war, amid a flood of lesser works, we may notice Still's *Underground Railroad*, Simmons's biographical dictionary, and Williams's two-volume *History of the Negro Race*. Since the beginning of the twentieth century, we have had the work of Chesnutt, Fauset, Fisher, and Hurston, the novelists; Dunbar, Cullen, McKay, Weldon Johnson, and Hughes, the poets; and many other writers of distinction.

On the dramatic stage, Negroes have found entrance with difficulty. The first great Negro actor was Ira Aldridge, who had to go to Europe to find his opportunity, but was there honored and decorated by the kings of four countries. In the United States, there arose comedians, like Bert Williams, and actors like Gilpin, Robeson, and Richard Harrison. Negroes have done creditable work in painting and sculpture. Henry O. Tanner is recognized as the leading American painter resident in Europe; Edmonia Lewis worked during the Civil War; Meta Warrick Fuller during the World War; and Elizabeth Prophet stands high today among American sculptors of any color.

The work of Negroes in science has been handicapped by their difficulties in securing entrance into laboratories and institutions of research. And yet, we have had Benjamin Banneker, who was a pioneer among American scientists, and helped lay out the city of Washington;

Carver, the chemist; Just, the biologist, Fuller, the psychiatrist, and Hinton in syphilology.

Between 1874 and 1930, 116 Negroes have been elected to the Phi Beta Kappa in white northern colleges; ninety-seven Negroes were mentioned in *Who's Who in America, 1929-1930*; and over sixty Negroes have received the degree of Ph. D. from leading American institutions.

4. The Emancipation of Democracy

Dramatically, the Negro is the central thread of American history. The whole story turns on him whether we think of the dark and flying slave ship in the sixteenth century, the expanding plantations of the seventeenth, the swelling commerce of the eighteenth, or the fight for freedom in the nineteenth. It was the black man that raised a vision of democracy in America such as neither Americans nor Europeans conceived in the eighteenth century and such as they have not even accepted in the twentieth century; and yet a conception which every clear-sighted man knows is true and inevitable.

Democracy in the United States as elsewhere in the world has been a slow development and not a sudden and complete realization. At first, the right to vote was limited by possession of property and then later, the color line was established to limit the franchise of the black worker. Nevertheless, from the beginning, Negroes have voted in the United States. In every colony, North and South, a free Negro with requisite qualifications had the legal right to vote at some time before 1787. Probably few actually voted, but we know that Negroes did vote in Delaware, Maryland, Virginia, North and South Carolina, and Louisiana; and in the North, many Negroes voted for the acceptance of the Federal Constitution.

The influence of Negroes on American democracy has been continuous. First, the appeal of their degraded position and lack of opportunity greatly influenced the earlier writers and thinkers, like Jefferson, Garrison, and John Brown. Then there was the active efforts of Negroes themselves toward insurrection. The slave trade itself was war.

It cost Negro Africa sixty million souls to land ten million slaves in America. The history of the West Indies, where American slavery was incubated, was a history of continuous insurrection, from 1522 on the sugar plantation of Diego Columbus, down to the great Haitian revolt. The history of the Maroons in Jamaica, from 1565 to 1795, reads like a saga. In the United States, there were revolts from colonial times down to the Civil War, but for the most part, they were small and unsuccessful because of the careful organization of the whites to prevent revolt and especially because of the fugitive slave.

Along the Great Black Way stretched swamps and rivers and the forests and crests of the Alleghanies. A widening, hurrying stream of fugitives swept to the havens of refuge, taking the restless, the criminal, and the unconquered— the natural leaders of the more timid mass. These men saved slavery and killed it. They saved it by leaving it to a false dream of peace and the eternal subjugation of the laboring class. They destroyed it by presenting themselves before the eyes of the North and the world as living specimens of the real meaning of slavery.

The fugitive slaves, by the help of whites and Negroes, organized and systematized their work under the Underground Railroad and in this way thousands of Negroes escaped to freedom in the North and in Canada. After emancipation, Negroes by the use of their political power, by appeal and agitation, kept up a continual fight for full inclusion in American democracy.

Negroes received the ballot after the Civil War for the part they took as soldiers and laborers, and more especially because only in this way could the North readmit the southern states immediately to full power and yet not fear the reestablishment of slavery, or an attack upon the fiscal and commercial policies of the North. The Negro voters helped to establish the public-school system in the South and tried to distribute land and strengthen labor laws. They lacked intelligent leadership, but they did start the mass of the slaves well on the road toward free labor and land ownership. When their vote was nullified in 1876, they retained their political power in the North, and their power as laborers and consumers in the South.

The political power thus indicated is not always effectively used. But, on the other hand, it has been able to protect the essential rights of Negroes so that even in the South there is increasing difficulty in making the disfranchisement of Negroes effective, and most southerners realize that the restoration of the Negroes to political rights in the South is simply a matter of time.

One-fifth of the Negro population now lives in the North. Negroes are members of the legislature in twelve states and members of city councils in a large number of cities. Three or more states today have had black judges on the bench. Twenty-two Negroes have sat in Congress and there is one member at present.[3] As democracy in industry increases, the power of the Negro as a worker and consumer is bound to increase. Negroes, therefore, must be reckoned with as a great force in the future development of democracy throughout the United States.

5. *The Black Soldier*

The world is coming to realize the futility and evil of war. But this does not deny that many of the soldiers who are compelled to fight are brave and conscientious and struggling for the highest ideals. This is the tragedy of war, and particularly the tragedy of the American Negro soldier.

In only one of the great American wars did he have any direct interest, and that was in the Civil War. He fought in the colonial and Revolutionary wars, and the War of 1812, in order to vindicate his right to be regarded as an American citizen.

It was a Negro, Crispus Attucks, who in a sense first began the actual fighting in the Revolutionary War, and our first national holiday commemorated the day of his death. Seven hundred Haitian soldiers saved the American Army at the Siege of Savannah in 1779, and the War of 1812 was based largely upon complaints about the impressment of American sailors who were of Negro descent. It was after the Battle of New Orleans that Andrew Jackson thanked the Negro regiment for helping him.

"I invited you to share in the perils and divide the glory of your white countrymen. . . . I have found in you that noble enthusiasm which impels to great deeds. . . ."

In these wars, the Negro fought to prove his right to be considered an American citizen. In the Civil War, he fought directly for freedom. His services were at first refused, but eventually both North and South sought his aid, and 200,000 soldiers and at least 300,000 servants and laborers aided the Union cause. Abraham Lincoln said that without the help of Negroes the war could not have been won. In the Spanish-American War, Negro regular troops took a part, and in the World War the Negroes, forming only one-tenth of the population, furnished 13 percent of the draftees. In this war, 367,710 Negroes were drafted and 150,000 eventually went to France.

6. *The Spirit of Religion*

The Negro has projected a peculiar spiritual quality into American life. It consists of a joyousness, a tropical love of living, and an intense sensitiveness to spiritual values. America early became a refuge for religion, and all sorts of men and sects came hither searching for truth and freedom in the wilderness. With them came the Negro, and his presence was a concrete test of the sincerity of those who professed religion in America. Great missionary movements arose. The first native bishop of the Catholic Church, Francisco Xavier de Luna Victoria, was a Negro and became bishop of Panama in the middle of the seventeenth century.

However, in the confines of the present United States, with the exception of Louisiana and Maryland, the Catholic Church did little proselyting among Negroes, being held back by the economic rivalry of its Irish members. In the twentieth century, the zeal and money of Katherine Drexel has started a new movement to spread the Catholic Church among Negroes.

The Protestant churches, and especially the Methodist and Baptist, have been the chief churches to receive the Negro; and in these churches the Negro has not been a passive convert but has taken an active part, assuming largely the responsibility for his own church organizations and led by the Negro priest, whose authority dates back to Africa.

We must think of the transplanting of the Negro as transplanting to the United States a certain spiritual entity, and an unbreakable set of world-old beliefs, manners, morals, superstitions, and religious observances. The religion of Africa is the universal animism or fetishism of primitive peoples, rising to polytheism and approaching monotheism chiefly, but not wholly, as a result of Christian and Islamic missions.

At first sight, it would seem that slavery completely destroyed every vestige of spontaneous social movement among the Negroes; the home had deteriorated; political authority and economic initiative was in the hands of the masters; property, as a social institution, did not exist on the plantation; and, indeed, it is usually assumed by historians and sociologists that every vestige of internal development disappeared, leaving the slaves no means of expression for their common life, thought, and striving. This is not strictly true; the vast power of the priest in the African state still survived; his realm alone— the province of religion and medicine— remained largely unaffected by the plantation system in many important particulars.

The Negro priest, therefore, early became an important figure on the plantation and found his function as the interpreter of the supernatural, the comforter of the sorrowing, and as the one who expressed, rudely, but picturesquely, the longing and disappointment and resentment of a stolen people. From such beginnings arose and spread with marvelous rapidity the Negro church, the first distinctively Negro American social institution. This church today has 42,585 organizations with 5,203,487 members, owning $205,782,628 worth of property and spending $43,000,000 a year.

This, then, is the gift of black folk to the New World. Thus in singular and fine sense the slave became master, the bond servant became free, and the meek not only inherited the earth, but made the heritage a thing of questing for eternal youth, of fruitful labor, of joy and music, of the

free spirit and of the ministering hand, of wide and poignant sympathy with men in their struggle to live and
love, which is, after all, the end of being.

7. *Texas*

As this pamphlet commemorates the one-hundredth anniversary of the establishment of the Republic of Texas in
1836, it cannot close without a word concerning the relation of the Negro to this great state.

The Negro has from the beginning occupied a central
place in Texas history. The organization and growth of
this section was due to the Negro. Here was a rich country
that of itself would have attracted settlers, but the settlers
came much earlier and in larger numbers because of cheap
slave labor that was made available in Texas through the
slave trade, and because of the rich land, especially adapted to cotton culture.

It began with Aury's slave market on Galveston Island
early in the nineteenth century, where slaves pirated from
the regular traders were gathered and smuggled into the
United States. By 1818 the traffic became large and prosperous, and a slave who would cost $1,000 in the United
States could be bought here for $140.

A natural expansion of vigorous pioneers into a new,
rich country became suddenly transformed into a determined attempt to extend the slave system. There were
dreams of a slave empire which would reach from the
Mississippi Valley to Central America. Even when Texas
began the fight for independence in 1836, three blacks
helped defend the Alamo.

The grants made by the Spanish government to American settlers, between 1821 and 1830, brought 20,000
whites and 5,000 Negroes, and by 1850, there were 154,-
000 whites and 58,000 Negroes. Cotton kept pace with
the slaves. Fifty-eight thousand slaves raised 58,000 bales
of cotton in 1850, and in 1860, 182,000 slaves raised
182,000 bales of cotton. The slave population was confined mainly to northeast, east, and central Texas along
the rich river bottoms. And here it still stays. It has not
gone into the West, but it is moving slowly but surely

from the farms to the great cities. This rush of the slave barons precipitated the Mexican War and resulted in the annexation of Texas to the United States.

With the vast territory of Texas, and with the large numbers of slaves which had been taken there during the Civil War, Texas seemed, and in a sense was, the impregnable outpost of the Confederacy. But her mission was changed because, after all, an increasing majority of the people of Texas were not slaveholders and were not interested in slavery as such. Before and after the Civil War, real farmers began to pour into Texas. They began to raise cotton. They began to establish industries and to build a modern state.

During Reconstruction, the Negro became a part of this new development and new organization. He played his part bravely and well. His leadership during Reconstruction was notable; J. T. Ruby, a colored man from Philadelphia, represented the white district from Galveston, and for fifteen years did an effective and courageous piece of work. After Reconstruction, Norris Wright Cuney became a leader of both whites and blacks. He was instrumental in perfecting the school system and gave the races equal accommodation. He ran for mayor of Galveston in 1875 and even his opponent attested to his honesty. For many years Cuney continued to be the incorruptible and intelligent leader of the Negroes of Texas.

There live today in Texas 4,284,000 whites, 855,000 Negroes, and nearly 684,000 Mexicans and Indians. They form a center for racial cooperation and understanding. They are in the midst of a vast and rich country. The bounty of nature in its land fertility, its oils and minerals, has endowed their people with a great gift which may be the basis of enduring prosperity. All that is necessary is justice and freedom and understanding between men.

Pamphlet, Texas Centennial Commission. Hall of Negro Life. Centennial Commission, 1936.

10

THE REVELATION OF
SAINT ORGNE THE DAMNED

Dr. Du Bois delivered the commencement address at Fisk University in 1938. Already distinguished as a poet and writer of fiction, he combined these talents with his usual keen insight into the basic problems of the Negro people. The result was a truly unusual and remarkable commencement address.

Saint Orgne stood facing the morning and asked: What is this life I see? Is the dark damnation of color real? or simply mine own imagining? Can it be true that souls wrapped in black velvet have a destiny different from those swathed in white satin or yellow silk, when all these coverings are fruit of the same worm, and threaded by the same hands? Or must I, ignoring all seeming difference, rise to some upper realm where there is no color nor race, sex, wealth nor age, but all men stand equal in the Sun?

Thus Orgne questioned Life on his Commencement morning, in the full springtide of his day. And this is the Revelation and the answer that came to Saint Orgne the Damned as he came to be called, as he stood on his Mount of Transfiguration, looking full at life as it is and not as it might be or haply as he would have it.

"In very truth, thou art damned, and may not escape by vain imagining nor fruitless repining. When a man faces evil, he does not call it good, nor evade it; he meets it breastforward, with no whimper of regret nor fear of foe."

"Blessed is he that reads and they that hear the words of this prophecy for the time is at hand. Grace be unto you and peace, from him which was and which is and is to come and from the seven spirits which are before his throne."

I, who also am your brother and companion in tribulation and in the kingdom and the patience, was in the isle that is called America. I was in the spirit and heard behind me a great Voice saying, "I am Alpha and Omega, the first and the last; and what thou seest write." I turned to the voice. I saw seven golden candlesticks with one in the midst of the candlesticks; and in his hands seven stars and out of his mouth went a sharp two-edged sword. And when I saw him I fell at his feet as dead and he laid his right hand upon me saying unto me "Fear not. Write thou the things which thou has seen; the mystery of the seven stars and the seven golden candlesticks."

So Orgne turned and climbed the Seven Heights of Hell to view the Seven Stars of Heaven. The seven heights are Birth and Family; School and Learning; the University and Wisdom; the great snow-capped peak of Work; the naked crag of Right and Wrong; the rolling hills of the Freedom of Art and Beauty; and at last the plateau that is the Democracy of Race; beyond this there are no vales of Gloom — for the star above is the sun itself and all shadows fall straight before it.

Orgne descended into the valleys of the Shadow, lit only by the waving light of single candles set in seven golden candlesticks, struggling through noisom refuse of body and mind. Long years he strove, uphill and down, around and through seven groups of seven years until in the end he came back to the beginning, world-weary, but staunch; and this is the revelation of his life and thought which I, his disciple, bring you from his own hands.

A golden candlestick stood beneath a silver star, atop a high mountain and in the cold gray dawn of a northern spring. There the first hint of apple blossoms and faint melody in the air; within the melody was the whisper of a Voice, which sighed and said: "Why should we breed black folk in this world and to what end? Wherefore should we found families and how? Is not the world for such as are born white and rich?"

Then Orgne, half grown, lying prone, reared himself suddenly to his feet and shivering looked upward to light. The sun rose slowly above the mountain and with its light spake. Hear ye the Wisdom of the families of black folk:

Gentlemen are bred and not born. They are trained in childhood and receive manners from those who surround them and not from their blood. Manners maketh Man, and are the essence of good breeding. They have to do with forms of salutation between civilized persons; with the care and cleanliness and grooming of the body. They avoid the stink of bodily excretions; they eat their food without offense to others; they know that dirt is matter displaced and they seek to replace it. The elementary rules of health become to them second nature and their inbred courtesy one to another makes life liveable and gracious even among crowds.

Now this breeding and infinite detail of training is not learned in college and may not be taught in school. It is the duty and task of the family group and once the infinite value of that training is missed it can seldom be replaced through any later agency. It is in vain that the university seeks to cope with ill-bred youngsters, foul-mouthed loafers and unwashed persons who have happened to pass the entrance examinations. Once in the earlier mission schools among American Negroes men tried to do this, knowing of the irreparable harm slavery had done the family group. They had some success right here in this institution; but the day when such effort is possible is gone. Unless a new type of Negro family takes the burden of this duty, we are destined to be, as we are too largely today, a bad-mannered, unclean crowd of ill-bred young men and women who are under the impression that they are educated.

For this task we have got to create a new family group; and a cultural group rather than a group merely biological. The biology and blood relationship of families is entirely subordinate and unimportant as compared with its cultural entity; with the presence of two persons who take upon themselves voluntarily the sacrificial priesthood of parents to children, limited in number and interval by intelligent and scientific birth control, who can and will train in the elements of being civilized human beings: how to eat, how to sleep, how to wash, how to stand, how to walk, how to laugh, how to be reverent and how to obey.

It is not entirely our fault that we have missed, forgotten or are even entirely unaware of the cultural place of the family. In European and American civilization we have tried to carry out the most idiotic paradox that ever civilized folk attempted. We have tried to make babies both sins and angels. We have regarded sex as a disgrace and as eternal life. We talk in one breath of the Virgin Mary and of the Mother of God. And at the critical age of life for both men and women, we compel them to strain the last sinew of moral strength to repress a natural and beautiful appetite, or to smear it with deception and crime. We base female eligibility for marriage on exotic personal beauty and childlike innocence, and yet pretend to desire brains, common sense and strength of body. If an age thus immolates its ugly virgins, it will crucify its beautiful fools, with the result of making marriage a martyrdom that few will enter with open eyes. The change from this has got to recognize the sin of virginity in a world that needs proper children; the right of the so-called unfathered child to be; the legal adoption into the cultural family of gifted and promising children and the placing of black sheep, no matter who their parents are, under necessary restraint and correction. Amen.

The Voice ceased. As Orgne walked slowly down the mountain, he brooded long over the word he had heard, wondering vaguely how far the revelation was within or without his own soul; and then turning the message over in his mind, he thought of his own home, of the three small rooms, of the careful, busy mother and grandmother, of the dead father; and he mused: if one's start in life depends on breeding and not on color or unchangeable and unfathomable compulsions before births, surely I may live, even though I am black and poor.

There came a long space of seven years. Orgne stood by the bank of the Golden River, with the second candle-stick in his hand. He could not see the stars above, for it was nine o'clock of a sun-washed morning; but he knew they were there. He was celebrating all alone his entry into High School. None of his people save only his dead grandfather had ever gotten so far; but with the wave of disappointment which comes with all accomplish-ment, he muttered, "And why should they, why should I, dawdle here with elements of things and mere tools of knowledge while both I and the world wait." The river flowed softly as he slept in the summer mildness. Daisies and buttercups waved above him. The grey fleecy clouds gathered and swiftly low thunder rolled; a bolt of heat lightning flashed across the sky. He slept on, yet heard the second star as it spoke:

Hear ye! This is the wisdom of the elementary school.

The difficulty and essential difficulty with Negro educa-tion lies in the elementary school; lies in the fact that the number of Negroes in the United States today who have learned thoroughly to read, write, and count is small; and that the proportion of those who cannot read, cannot express their thoughts and cannot understand the fundamentals of arithmetic, algebra and geometry is dis-couragingly large. The reason that we cannot do thorough college work and cannot keep high university standards is that the students in institutions like this are fundamen-tally weak in mastery of those essential tools to human learning. Not even the dumbest college professor can spoil the education of the man who as a child has learned to read, write, and cipher; so too Aristotle, Immanuel Kant and Mark Hopkins together are powerless before the illiterate who cannot reason.

The trouble lies primarily, of course, in the elementary schools of the South; in schools with short terms; with teachers inadequate both as to numbers and training; with quarters ill-suited physically and morally to the work in hand; with colored principals chosen not for executive ability but for their agility in avoiding race problems; and with white superintendents who try to see how large a statistical showing can be made without expenditure of funds, thought nor effort.

This is the fault of a nation which does not thoroughly believe in the education of Negroes, and of the South which still to a large extent does not believe in any training for black folk which is not of direct commercial profit to those who dominate the state.

But the fault does not end there. The fault lies with the Negroes themselves for not realizing this major problem in their education and for not being willing and eager and untiring in their effort to establish the elementary school on a fundamental basis. Necessary as are laws against lynching and race segregation, we should put more money, effort, and breath in perfecting the Negro elementary school than in anything else, and not pause nor think of pausing until every Negro child between five and fifteen is getting at least nine months a year, five hours a day, five days in the week, in a modern schoolroom, with the best-trained teachers, under principals selected for training and executive ability, and serving with their teachers during efficiency and good behavior; and with the school under the control of those whose children are educated there.

Until this is done and so far as it is not done the bulk of university endowment is being wasted and high schools strive partially in vain. Amen.

Again flew seven years. Orgne was far from home and school and land. He was speaking an unknown tongue and looking upon the walls and towers, colors and sounds of another world. It was high noon and autumn. He sat in a lofty cathedral, glorious in the fretted stone lacework of its proudly vaulted roof. Its flying buttresses looked down upon a grey and rippled lake; beyond lay fields of flowers, golden chrysanthemums and flaming dahlias and further the ancient university, where for a thousand years men had sought Truth. Around rose a symphony of sound, a miraculous blending of strings and brass, trumpet and drum which was the Seventh Symphony with its lovely interlacing of melody and soft solemn marches, breaking to little hymns and dances. He listened to its revelation gazing rapt at candlesticks and gilded star and whispered: "Why should I know and what, and what is the end of knowing? Is it not enough to feel?" The angels in the choir sang No—Hear ye! For Wisdom is the principal thing.

There can be no iota of doubt that the chief trouble with the world and the overwhelming difficulty with American Negroes is widespread ignorance; the fact that we are not thoroughly acquainted with human history; of what men and peoples have thought and done in the seven thousand years of our cultural life. We are especially unacquainted with modern science; with the facts of matter and its constitution; with the meaning of time and space; with chemical reaction and electrical phenomena; with the history of the machine and the tool; with the unfolding of life in the vegetable and animal kingdoms; with the history of human labor; the development of our knowledge of the mind; the practical use of the languages of the world; and the methods of logical reasoning, beginning and ending with mathematics.

This great body of knowledge has been growing and developing for thousands of years, and yet today its mastery is in the hands of so few men, that a comparative small death roll would mean the end of human culture. Without this knowledge there can be no planning in economy; no substantial guidance in character building; no intelligent development of art. It is for acquaintanceship with this knowledge and the broadening of its field that the college and university exist. This is the reason and the only reason for its building among American Negroes and the work that it is accomplishing today is so infinitely less than that which with any real effort it might accomplish that one has a right to shudder at the misuse of the word university. Amen.

Orgne stood at twilight in the swamp. In seven more years, all the romance and glamour of Europe had sunk to the winter of America. It was twilight, and the swamp glowed with the mystery of sunset—long shafts of level burning light—greens and yellows, purples and red; the whisper of leaves, the ghosts of dead and dying life. The sun died dismally, and the clouds gathered and a drizzling rain began to fall with slow determination. Orgne shrank within himself. He saw the toil of labor and revolted. He felt the pinch of poverty and wept. "What is this stuff I hear," he cried: "how can we marry and support a family without money? How can we control our schools without economic resource? How can we turn our churches from centers of superstition into intelligent building of character; and beyond this how shall we have time for real knowledge; and freedom of art; and effort toward worldwide democracy, until we have the opporunity to work decently and the resources to spend, which shall enable us to be civilized human beings?"

Suddenly across the swamp and across the world and up from the cotton fields of Georgia rolled a Negro folk song. Orgne saw in music Jehovah and his angels, the Wheel in a Wheel. He saw the Golden Candlestick and heard the revelation of the Star: Hear ye! This is the teaching of the World of Work.

The most distressing fact in the present world is poverty; not absolute poverty, because some folk are rich and many are well-to-do; not poverty as great as some lands and other historical ages have known; but poverty more poignant and discouraging because it comes after a dream of wealth; of riotous, wasteful and even vulgar accumulation of individual riches, which suddenly leaves the majority of mankind today without enough to eat; without proper shelter; without sufficient clothing.

Nowhere was the dream of wealth, for all who would work and save, more vivid than here in the United States. We Negroes sought to share that vision and heritage. Moreover, the poverty which the world now experiences, comes after a startling realization of our national endowment of rich natural resources and our power to produce. We have the material goods and forces at command, the machines and technique sufficient to feed, clothe the world, educate children and free the human soul for creative beauty and for the truth that will widen the bounds of all freedom.

That does not mean that we could have enough goods

and services for present extravagance, display and waste; but if there were neither idle rich nor idle poor; if sharing of wealth were based not on owning but only on effort, and if all who are able did their share of the world's work or starved, and limited their consumption to reasonable wants, we could abolish poverty.

Why have we not done this? It is because of greed in the production and distribution of goods and human labor. We discovered widely in the eighteenth century and the nineteenth the use of capital and it was a great and beneficent discovery; it was the rule of sacrificing present wealth for greater wealth to come. But instead of distributing this increase of wealth primarily among those who make it we left most workers as poor as possible in order further to increase the wealth of a few. We produced more wealth than the wealthy could consume and yet used this increased wealth to monopolize materials and machines; to buy and sell labor in return for monopoly ownership in the products of labor and for further wealth.

We thus not only today produce primarily for the profit of owners and not for use of the mass of people, but we have grown to think that this is the only way in which we can produce. We organize industry for private wealth and not for public weal, and we argue often honestly and conscientiously, that no human planning can change the essentials of this process. Yet the process itself has failed so many times and so abysmally, that we are bound to change or starve in the midst of plenty. We are encouraging war through fear of poverty that need not exist; we face the breakdown of production by persistent overproduction of the kinds of goods which we cannot afford to consume.

What can we do? There is only one thing for civilized human beings to do when facing such a problem, and that is to learn the facts, to reason out their connection and to plan the future; to know the truth; to arrange it logically and to contrive a better way. In some way, as all intelligent men acknowledge, we must in the end, produce for the satisfaction of human needs and distribute in accordance with human want. To content that this cannot be done is to face the Impossible Must. The blind cry of reaction, on the one hand, which says that we cannot have a planned economy and, therefore, must not try; and the cry of blood which says that only by force can selfishness be curbed, are equally wrong. It is not a question of deliberate guilt but of selfish stupidity. The economic world can only be reformed by Spartan restraint in the consumption of goods and the use of services; by the will to work not simply for individual profit but for group weal; not simply for one group but for all groups; and the freedom to dream and plan.

This reformation of the world is beginning with agony of soul and strain of muscle. It can and must go on, and we black folk of America are faced with the most difficult problem of realizing and knowing the part which we have got to play in this economic revolution for our own salvation and for the salvation of the world. This is not easy, for we are cut off from the main effort by the lesions of race, by the segregation of color, by the domination of caste. And yet nothing could be more fatal to our own ideals and the better ideals of the world than for us with unconscious ignorance or conscious perversity or momentary applause to join the forces of reaction; to talk as though the twentieth century presented the same oversimplified path of economic progress which seemed the rule in the nineteenth: work, thrift and wealth by individual effort no matter what the social cost.

The economic illiteracy prevalent among American Negroes is discouraging. In a day when every thinker sees the disorganization of our economic life and the need of radical change, we find the teachers of economics in colored colleges, the Negro businessmen, Negro preachers and writers to a very large extent talking the language of the early nineteenth century; seeking to make themselves believe that work for any kind of wages, saving at any sacrifice and wealth on any terms not excluding cheating, murder, and theft, are ways of the world still open and beckoning to us. Selah!

Orgne listened and sat staring at the sodden cotton field beyond the somber swamp. Always the swinging thunder of song surged above—Jordan rolled; the rocks and the mountains fled away, the Way was crowded; and Moses went down, away down among the cabins in the cotton patch to the crazy church and hysterical crowd of penitents all praying madly to escape debt. Orgne talked to the planter and said "let my people go," and worked with the tenants seven long years.

Seven years he toiled and in the end had a little nest of landholders owning one large unmortgaged farm in twenty shares; working their crops and buying their provisions in common and dividing them with equal justice. Poor, Orgne came to them and poor he finally went away leaving them poor too but fed and sheltered. They called him Saint. He smiled and looked upward to the star; but the preacher looked down to the dirt and mortgaged it behind the backs of the trusting flock and ran away with the money.

Saint Orgne cursed and cried how shall we plan a new earth without honest men and what is this thing we call a church. So, angry, disillusioned and weary he came to a land where it was always afternoon, and he laid him prone on the earth and slept.

Seven years he slept and in seven years came a thousand miles and more to Ohio, to teach in college. At high noon he stood before the chapel and heard the singing of a hymn in the haze of early springtime. Around him stretched the wide, undulating valleys of the Miami, the Ohio, and the realm of the Mississippi. He looked up and suddenly hated the walls that shut out the stars; he hated the maudlin words of the hymn quite as much as he loved the lilt of the voices that raised it. He loved the flowers — the violets and morning glory, the blossoming fruit that filled the yards about. Then came the earthquake; then the earth trembled and swayed; far off in San Francisco a city fell and around the nation quivered. In the midst of the rushing, swaying crowd, again Orgne, after seven years, awoke and found the Golden Candlestick in his hands, and heard the low clear revelation of the Star:

Saint Orgne the Damned, behold the Vision of the Seven Black Churches of America — the Baptist, the four wings of Methodism, the Roman and Episcopal Catholics.

Their five millions of members in 40,000 groups, holding $200,000,000 in their hands, are the most strongly orga-

nized body among us; the first source of our group culture, the beginning of our education — what is this church
doing today toward its primary task of teaching men right
and wrong, and the duty of doing right?

The flat answer is nothing if not less than nothing. Like
other churches and other religions of other peoples and
ages, our church has veered off on every conceivable side
path, which interferes with and nullifies its chief duty of
character-building.

It has built up a body of dogma and fairy tale, fantastic
fables of sin and salvation, impossible creeds and impossible demands for ignorant unquestioning belief and
obedience. Ask any thorough churchman today and he
will tell you, not that the object of the church is to get
men to do right and make the majority of mankind happy,
but rather that the whole duty of man is to "believe in the
Lord Jesus Christ and be saved"; or to believe "that Cod
is God and Mohammed is his prophet"; or to believe in the
"one Holy and Catholic church," infallible and omniscient;
or to keep the tomb of one's grandfather intact and his
ideas undisputed.

Considering how desperately, great and good men have
inveighed against these continuing foibles of priesthood
for many thousand years, and how little in essence has been
accomplished, it may seem hopeless to return to the attack
today, but that is precisely what this generation has to do.
The function of the Negro church, instead of being that of
building edifices, paying old debts, holding revivals and
staging entertainments, has got to be brought back, or
shall we say forward, to the simple duty of teaching ethics.
For this purpose the Hebrew scriptures and the New
Testament canon will not suffice. We must stop telling children that the lying and deceitful Jacob was better than the
lazy Esau, or that the plan of salvation is anything but
the picture of the indecent anger and revenge of a bully.

We can do this, not so much by the attacking of outworn
superstition and conventional belief as by hearty research
into real ethical questions. When is it right to lie? Do low
wages mean stealing? Does the prosperity of a country
depend upon the number of its millionaires? Should the

state kill a murderer? How much money should you give to the poor? Should there be any poor? And as long as there are, what is crime and who are the criminals?

So Saint Orgne preached the word of life from Jeremiah, Shakespeare and Jesus, Confucius, Buddha and John Brown; and organized a church with a cooperative store in the Sunday-school room; with physician, dentist, nurse and lawyer to help, serve and defend the congregation; with library, nursery school, and a regular succession of paid and trained lecturers and discussion; they had radio and moving pictures and out beyond the city a farm with house and lake. They had a credit union, group insurance, and building and loan association. The members paid for this not by contributions but by ten dollars a month each of regular dues and those who would join this church must do more than profess to love God.

Seven years he served and married a woman not for her hair and color but for her education, good manners, common sense and health. Together they made a home and begot two strong intelligent children. Looking one day into their eyes Orgne became suddenly frightened for their future. He prayed "Oh life let them be free!"

So soon, so soon, Orgne sighed, the world rolls around its sevens of years. It was midsummer and he was sailing upon the sea. He was bound for Africa on a mission of world brotherhood. Behind and waiting were wife and children, home and work. Ahead was the darker world of men of yellow, brown, and black. Dinner was done and the deck empty save for himself; all were within the magnificent saloon massed with tall vases of roses and lilies, priceless with tapestry and gilding, listening to the great organ which the master played. The *largo* whispered, smiled and swelled upward to tears. Then the storm swept down. Then the ocean, lashed to fury by the wind, bellowed and burned; the vast ship tossed like a tortured soul, groaned and twisted in its agony. But Orgne smiled. He knew that behind the storm and above the cloud the evening stars were singing, and he listened to the rhythm of their words: Hear Ye! This is the Freedom of Art which is the Beauty of Life.

Life is more than meat, even though life without food dies. Living is not for earning, earning is for living. The man that spends his life earning a living, has never lived. The education that trains men simply for earning a living is not education.

What then is Life—What is it for—What is its great End? Manifestly in the light of all knowledge, and according to the testimony of all men who have lived, Life is the fullest, most complete enjoyment of the possibilities of human existence. It is the development and broadening of the feelings and emotions, through sound and color, line and form. It is technical mastery of the media that these paths and emotions need for expression of their full meaning. It is the free enjoyment of every normal appetite. It is giving rein to the creative impulse, in thought and imagination. Here roots the rise of the Joy of Living, of music, painting, drawing, sculpture and building; hence come literature with romance, poetry, and essay; hence rise Love, Friendship, emulation, and ambition, and the ever widening realms of thought in increasing circles of apprehended and interpreted Truth.

It is the contradiction and paradox of this day that those who seek to choke and conventionalize art, restrict and censor thought and repress imagination are demanding for their shriveled selves, freedom in precisely those lines of human activity where control and regimentation are necessary; and necessary because upon this foundation is to be built the widest conceivable freedom in a realm infinitely larger and more meaningul than the realm of economic production and distribution of wealth. The less freedom we leave for business exploitation the greater freedom we shall have for expression in art.

We have got to think of the time when poverty approaches abolition; when men no longer fear starvation and unemployment; when health is so guarded that we may normally expect to live our seventy years and more, without excess of pain and suffering. In such a world living begins; in such a world we will have freedom of thought and expression, and just as much freedom of action as maintenance of the necessary economic basis of life permits; that is, given three or six hours of work under rule and duress, we ought to be sure of at least eighteen hours of recreation, joy, and creation with a minimum of compulsion for anybody.

Freedom is the path of art, and living in the fuller and broader sense of the term is the expression of art. Yet those who speak of freedom talk usually as fools talk. So far as the laws of gravitation are concerned there can be no freedom; so far as the physical constitution of the universe is concerned, we must produce and consume goods in accordance with that which is inexorable, unmoved by sentiment or dream. But this realm of the physical need be only the smaller part of life and above it is planning, emotion and dream; in the exercising of creative power; in building, painting and literature there is a chance for the free exercise of the human spirit, broad enough and lofty enough to satisfy every ambition of the free human soul. Limited though it be by birth and death, by time and space, by health and mysterious native gift, nevertheless its realm is so magnificent that those who fear that freedom may end with the abolition of poverty or that disease is needed to insure room on the earth or that war and murder are the only handmaids of courage are all talking utter nonsense.

The freedom to create within the limits of natural law; the freedom to love without limit; the freedom to dream of the utter marriage of beauty and art; all this men may have if they are sufficiently well-bred to make human contact bearable; if they have learned to read and write and reason; if they have character enough to distinguish between right and wrong and strength enough to do right; if they can earn a decent living and know the world in which they live.

The vastest and finest truth of all, is that while wealth diminishes by sharing and consuming and calls for control; Art, which is experience of life, increases and grows, the more widely it is shared. Here lie the rock foundations of democracy. Selah.

So now again pass seven years. It is midnight of an autumn day; and Saint Orgne, risen beatified on the dark frustration of his soul, to the quiet peace of pain, stands in an old forest amid falling leaves, with the starry heavens above him. He knows where, months before, the heavy fragrance of purple wisteria had hallowed this air and dipped great festoons of blooms down into a scented world. But tonight these are gone. All is death. There is no sound; and yet somehow somewhere beneath lies some Tone too deep for sound — a silent chord of infinite harmony. Saint Orgne lifts his hands and waves back to the skies the seven golden candlesticks and the seven silver stars, and speaks, saying, "It is enough!" But the Voice replies:

"I see a new Heaven and a new Earth." "How can that be," wails Saint Orgne. "What is new about War and Murder? What is new in deified and organized race hate? What is new in breadlines and starvation, crime and disease? Is not our dream of Democracy gone?"

The stars shine silently on, but in his own heart Saint Orgne's answer comes — Hear ye! This is the Truth of Democracy and Race.

The world compels us today as never before to examine and reexamine the problem of democracy. In theory we know it by heart: all men are equal and shoud have equal voice in their own government. This dictum has been vigorously attacked. All men are not equal. Ignorance cannot speak logically or clearly even when given voice. If sloth, dullness and mediocrity hold power, civilization is diluted and lowered, and government approaches anarchy. The mob cannot rule itself and will not choose the wise and able and give them the power to rule.

This attack began in 1787 during the French Revolution and it rose to crescendo sixty years later in 1867 when our fathers were enfranchised. The original dictum of human equality and the right of the governed to a voice in their government has never been universally accepted and only seldom has it been attempted. In the world today, universal suffrage is coerced by force as was true here in the South during Reconstruction; or by intimidation as was true in the South after 1876; or by economic pressure, either through threat of poverty or bribery of increased income, as has been true in the United States for years. Today finally we have entered the period of propaganda, when people to be sure may vote but cannot think freely nor clearly because of falsehood forced on their eyes and ears; or equally by the deliberate suppression of the whole truth. It is thus that there has arisen in our day, on an astonishing scale, the fascism of despair; the acquiescence of great masses of men in irresponsible tyranny, not because they want it, but because they see no other escape from greater disaster.

Let us then examine anew the basic thesis of democracy. It does not really mean to say that all men are equal; but it does assert that every individual who is a part of the state must have his experience and his necessities regarded by that state if the state survive; that the best and only ultimate authority on an individual's hurt and desire is that individual himself no matter how inarticulate his inner soul may be; that life, as any man has lived it, is part of that great national reservoir of knowledge without use of which no government can do justice.

But this is not the main end of democracy. It is not only that the complaints of all should be heard, or the hurts of the humblest healed; it is for the vastly larger object of loosing the possibilities of mankind for the development of a higher and broader and more varied human culture. Democracy then forms not merely a reservoir of complaint but of ability, hidden otherwise in poverty and ignorance. It is the astonishing result of an age of enlightenment, when the ruling classes of the world are the children of peasants, slaves and gutter snipes, that the still dominant thought is that education and ability are not today matters of chance, but mainly of individual desert and effort. As a matter of fact the chances of real ability today getting opportunity for development are not one-tenth as great as the chance of their owners dying in childbirth, being stunted by poverty or ending in prison or on the gallows. Democracy means the opening of opportunity to the disinherited to contribute to civilization and the happiness of men.

Given a chance for the majority of mankind to be educated, healthy and free to act, it may well turn out that human equality is not so wild a dream as many seem to hope.

The intelligent democratic control of a state by its citizens does not of itself and by any mechanical formula mean good government. It must be supplemented by the thrift and unselfishness of its citizens. The citizen of a democracy who thinks of democratic government chiefly as a means of his own advancement, meets and ought to meet disappointment. Only insofar as he conceives of democracy as the only way to advance the interests of the mass of people, even when those interests conflict with his, is he playing the heroic role of a patriot. And whenever he excludes from that mass the interests of the poor and the foolish; the Jew and Negro; the Asiatic and the South Sea Islander; he kills the effort at democracy.

Democracy does not and cannot mean freedom. On the contrary it means coercion. It means submission of the individual will to the general will and it is justified in this compulsion only if the will is general and not the will of special privilege.

Far from this broad conception of democracy, we have increasingly allowed the idea to be confined to the opportunity of electing certain persons to power without regard as to whether they can or will exercise power or for what. Even this choice of the voter, in current democracies, is confined mostly to comparatively minor matters of administration; but in the great realm of making a living, the fundamental interest of all; in the matter of determining what goods shall be produced, what services shall be rendered, and how goods and services shall be shared by all, there has been deep and bitter determination, that here democracy shall never enter; that here the Tyrant or the King by the grace of God shall always and forever rule.

It is widely in vain that the basic argument for democratic control has here been brought to bear; that these goods and services are the product of the labor of the mass of men and not solely of the rich and talented; and that therefore all men must have some decisive voice in the conduct of industry and the division of wealth. To be sure this calls for more intelligence, technical knowledge of intricate facts and forces, and greater will to work and sacrifice than most men today have; which is only saying that the mass of men must more and more largely acquire this knowledge, skill and character; and that meantime its wide absence is no valid excuse for surrendering the control of industry to the anarchy of greed and the tyranny of chance.

This faces us directly with our problem in America. Our best brains are taught and want to be taught in large northern universities where dominant economic patterns and European culture, not only prevail, but prevail almost to the exclusion of anything else.

Naturally these men are then grabbed up with rolling eyes and eager mien by the best southern Negro schools. Now if these Negro universities have any real meaning it is that in them other points of view should be evolved. They may or may not be radically different. They may bring something entirely new or be an adaptation of surrounding civilization; but certainly they should logically bring a newness of view and a reexamination of the old, of the European, and of the white, which would be stimulating and which would be real education.

But right here we have not simply little or no advance, but we have attitudes which make advance impossible. On the matter of race, for instance, we are ultramodern. There are certainly no biological races in the sense of people with large groups of unvarying inherited gifts and instincts thus set apart by nature as eternally separate. We have seen the whole world reluctantly but surely approaching this truth. We have therefore hastened to conclude there is no sense in studying racial subjects or inculcating racial ideals or writing racial textbooks or projecting vocational guidance from the point of view of race. And yet standing in stark contradiction of all this are the surrounding facts of race: the Jim Crow seats in the streetcars every day, the Jim Crow coaches on the railroads, the separate sections of the city where the races dwell; the discrimination in occupations and opportunities and in law; and beyond that the widespread division of the world by custom into white, yellow and black, ruler and eternally ruled.

We American Negroes form and long will form a perfectly definite group, not entirely segregated and isolated from our surroundings, but differentiated to such a degree that we have very largely a life and thought of our own. And it is this fact that we as scientists, and teachers and persons engaged in living, earning a living, have got to take into account and make our major problem. In the face of that, we have these young intellectual exquisites who smile if they do not laugh outright at our writhings. Their practical program is so far as our race or group is concerned: do nothing, think nothing, become absorbed in the nation.

To which the flat answer is: this is impossible. We have got to do something about race. We have got to think and think clearly about our present situation. Absorption into the nation, save as a long, slow intellectual process, is unthinkable and while it may eventually come, its trend and result depends very largely upon what kind of a group is being absorbed; whether such racial integration has to do with poverty-stricken and half-starved criminals; or whether with intelligent self-guided, independently acting men, who know what they want and propose at any civilized cost to get it. No, separated and isolated as we are so largely, we form in America an integral group, call it by any name you will, and this fact in itself has its meaning, its worth and its values.

In no line is this clearer than in the democratization of industry. We are still a poor people, a mass of laborers, with few rich folk and little exploitation of labor. We can be among the first to help restore the idea of high culture and limited income and dispel the fable that riotous wealth alone is civilization. Acting together, voluntarily or by outer compulsion, we can be the units through which universal democracy may be accomplished.

We black folk have striven to be Americans. And like all other Americans, we have longed to become rich Americans. Wealth comes easiest today through the exploitation of labor by paying low wages; and if we have not widely exploited our own and other labor the praise belongs not to us, but to those whites whose monopoly of wealth and ruthless methods have outrun our tardy and feeble efforts. This is the place to pause and look about, as well backward as forward. The leaders of the labor movement in America as in Europe, deceived us just as they deceived themselves. They left us out. They paid no attention to us, whether we were drudging in

colonies or slaving in cotton fields or pleading in vain
at the door of union-labor factories. The object of white
labor was not the uplift of all labor; it was to join capital in sharing the loot from exploited colored labor. So
we too, only half-emancipated, hurled ourselves forward,
too willing if it had but been possible, to climb up to a
bourgeois heaven on the prone bodies of our fellows.
But white folk occupied and crowded these stairs. And
white labor loved the white exploiter of black folk far
more than it loved its fellow black proletarian.

Such is the plight of democracy today. Where in this
picture does the American Negro come? With few exceptions, we are all today "white folks' niggers." No, do not
wince. I mean nothing insulting or derogatory, but this
is a concrete designation which indicates that very, very
many colored folk: Japanese, Chinese, Indians, Negroes;
and, of course, the vast majority of white folk; have been
so enthused, oppressed, and suppressed by current white
civilization that they think and judge everything by its
terms. They have no norms that are not set in the nineteenth and twentieth centuries. They can conceive of no future world which is not dominated by present white nations and thoroughly shot through with their ideals, their
method of government, their economic organization, their
literature and their art; or in other words their throttling
of democracy, their exploitation of labor, their industrial
imperialism and their color hate. To broach before such
persons any suggestion of radical change; any idea of
intrusion, physical or spiritual, on the part of alien races
is to bring down upon one's devoted head the most tremendous astonishment and contempt.

What to do? We went to school. But our industrial schools
taught no industrial history, no labor movement, no social
reform — only technique, just when the technique of skilled
trades was changing to mass industry. Our colleges taught
the reactionary economics of northern schools. We landed in bitter and justifiable complaint and sought a way
out by complaining. Our mistake lay not in the injustice
of our cause, but in our naive assumption that a system of
industrial monopoly that was making money out of our

exploitation, was going voluntarily to help us escape its talons.

On the other hand when we turn to join the forces of progress and reform we find again no easy or obvious path. As the disinherited both of labor and capital; as those discriminated against by employer and employee, we are forced to a most careful and thoroughgoing program of minority planning. We may call this self-segregation if we will, but the compulsion is from without and inevitable. We may call it racial chauvinism but we may make it the path to democracy through group culture. This path includes sympathy and cooperation with the labor movement; with the efforts of those who produce wealth, to assert their right to control it. It has been no easy path. What with organized, intelligent and powerful opposition and ignorant and venal and dogmatic leadership, the white labor movement has staggered drunkenly for two hundred years or more and yet it has given the world a vision of real democracy, of universal education and of a living wage. It is the most promising movement of modern days and we who are primarily laborers must eventually join it.

In addition to this, no matter how great our political disfranchisement and social exclusion, we have in our hands a voting power which is enormous, and that is the control we can exercise over the production and distribution of goods through our expenditure as consumers. The might and efficiency of this method of economic reform is continually minimized by the obvious fact that it does not involve radical change and that without other and more thoroughgoing changes it can bring no immediate millenium. But notwithstanding, for a minority group it is the most powerful weapon at hand and to refuse to use an instrument of power because it is not all-powerful is silly.

A people who buy each year at least a half-billion dollars worth of goods and services are not helpless. If they starve it is their own fault. If they do not achieve a respected place in the surrounding industrial organization, it is because they are stupid.

Here then is the plight and the steps toward remedy. Yet we are not awake. We have let obvious opportunities slip by during these awful days of depression when we have lost much of the land we used to own; when our savings have been dissipated; when our business enterprises have failed and when, if not a majority, a strikingly large minority of us are existing on public charity. We have not asked for the advantage of public housing as we should. We have not taken advantage of the possibilities of the TVA. We have not pushed energetically into plans of resettlement and the establishment of model villages. We have almost refused the subsistence homestead. We have not begun to think of socialized medicine and consumers' cooperation. We have no comprehensive plans concerning our unemployment, our economic dependence, the profit economy and the changing technique of industry. The day of our reckoning is at hand. "Awake, Awake/ put on thy strength, O Zion."

The martyrdom of man may be increased and prolonged through primitive, biological racial propaganda, but on the other hand through cooperation, education and understanding the cultural race unit may be the pipeline through which human civilization may extend to wider and wider areas to the fertilization of mankind.

It is to this use of our racial unity and loyalty that the United States impels us. We cannot escape it. Only through racial effort today can we achieve economic stability, cultural growth and human understanding. The way to democracy lies through race loyalty if only that is its real and consciously comprehended end. Selah and Amen.

This then is the revelation of Saint Orgne the Damned, as given me by his hand; and the philosophy of life out of which he strove to climb, despite the curse, to broader and more abundant life. Bearing this revelation, men and women of the Class of 1938, there return to you today, three pilgrims, and the ghosts of three others, whose memories await us. Fifty years ago we stood where you stand and received the Light of the Seven Stars. We return, not all-wise, but wise; for we have seen ten presidents rule in

America and five kings reign in England; we have seen the fall of three great empires; a whole world at war to commit twenty-six million murders; the rise of dark Japan and fall of darker Ethiopia. We have seen our own race in America nearly double in number from less than seven to more than twelve million souls.

We return home today worn and travel-stained, yet with the Light which Alma Mater laid upon our hands; it does not burn so high nor flash so fiercely — yet it has lighted thousands of other candles, and it is still aflame. We hand it on to you, that fifty years hence you give it again to others — and so on forever.

W. E. Burghardt Du Bois, *The Revelation of Saint Orgne the Damned.* Commencement 1938, Fisk University, n.p., n.d.

11

PROSPECT OF A WORLD
WITHOUT RACIAL CONFLICT

In the midst of the Second World War, Dr. Du Bois was frequently invited to speak on the prospect of a postwar world without racial conflict. His address on the subject was published in the American Journal of Sociology *of March 1944.*

It is with great regret that I do not see after this war, or within any reasonable time, the possibility of a world without race conflict; and this is true despite the fact that race conflict is playing a fatal role in the modern world. The supertragedy of this war is the treatment of the Jews in Germany. There has been nothing comparable to this in modern history. Yet its technique and its reasoning have been based upon a race philosophy similar to that which has dominated both Great Britain and the United States in relation to colored people.

This philosophy postulates a fundamental difference among the greater groups of people in the world, which makes it necessary that the superior peoples hold the inferior in check and rule them in accordance with the best interest of these superiors. Of course, many of the usual characteristics were missing in this outbreak of race hate in Germany. There was in reality little of physical difference between German and Jew. No one has been able to accuse the Jews of inferiority; rather it was the superiority of the Jews in certain respects which was the real cause of conflict. Nevertheless, the ideological basis of this attack was that of fundamental biological difference showing itself in spiritual and cultural incompatibility. Another difference distinguishes this race war. Usually the cure for race persecution and subordination has been thought to be segregation, but in this case the chance to segregate the Jews, at least partially, in Palestine, has practically been vetoed by the British government.

In other parts of the world the results of race conflict are clear. The representative of Prime Minister Churchill presiding over the British war cabinet has been the prime minister of the Union of South Africa. Yet South Africa has without doubt the worst race problem of the modern world. The natives have been systematically deprived of their land, reduced to the status of a laboring class with the lowest of wages, disfranchised, living and working under caste conditions with only a modicum of education, and exposed to systematic public and private insult. There is a large population of mixed-bloods, and the poverty, disease, and crime throughout the Union of South Africa are appalling. Here in a land which furnishes gold and diamonds and copper, the insignia of the luxury and technique of modern civilization, this race hate has flourished and is flourishing. Smuts himself, as political leader of the Union of South Africa, has carried out much of the legislation upon which this race conflict is based; and, although from time to time he has expressed liberal ideas, he has not tried or succeeded in basically ameliorating the fundamental race war in that part of the world.

The situation in India is another case of racial conflict. The mass of people there are in the bondage of poverty, disfranchisement, and social caste. Despite eminent and widely known leadership, there has not come on the part of the British any effective attempt fundamentally to change the attitude of the governing country toward the subject peoples. The basic reason for this, openly or by inference, is the physical difference of race which makes it, according to British thought, impossible that these peoples should within any reasonable space of time become autonomous or self-governing. There have been promises, to be sure, from time to time, and promises are pending; but no one can doubt that if these people were white and of English descent, a way out of the present impasse would have long since been found.

There is no doubt but that India is a congery of ignorant, poverty-stricken, antagonistic groups who are destined to go through all the hell of internal strife before they
emancipate themselves. But it is just as true that Europe of
the sixteenth century was no more ready for freedom and
autonomy than India. But Europe was not faced and
coerced by a powerful overlord who did not believe Europeans were men and was determined to treat them as serfs
to minister to his own comfort and luxury.

In India we have the first thoroughgoing case of modern
colonial imperialism. With the capitalism built on the
African slave trade and on the sugar, tobacco, and cotton
crops of America, investment in India grew and spread for
three hundred years, until there exists the greatest modern
case of the exploitation of one people by another. This
exploitation has been modified in various ways: some
education has been furnished the Indians, a great system
of railroads has been installed, and industrialism has been
begun. But nothing has been done to loosen to any appre-
ciable degree the stranglehold of the British Empire on the
destinies of four hundred million human beings. The prestige and profit of the control of India have made it impossible for the British to conceive of India as an autonomous
land.

The greatest and most dangerous race problem today is
the problem of relations between Asia and Europe: the
question as to how far "East is East and West is West" and
of how long they are going to retain the relation of master
and serf. There is in reality no difference between the
reaction to this European idea on the parts of Japan and
China. It is a question simply of the method of eliminating
it. The idea of Japan was to invoke war and force—to
drive Europe out of Asia and substitute the domination of
a weak Asia by a strong Japan. The answer of China was
cooperation and gradual understanding between Great
Britain, France, America, and China.

Chinese leaders are under no illusions whatever as to the
past attitude of Europe toward Chinese. The impudence,
browbeating, robbery, rape, and insult is one long trail of
blood and tears, from the Opium War to the kowtowing
before the emperor in Berlin. Even in this present war and

alliance, there has occurred little to reassure China: certain courtesies from the British and belated and meager justice on the part of the United States, after the Soong sister had swept in on us with her retinue, jade, and jewels. There has not only been silence concerning Hong Kong, Burma, and Singapore, but there is the continued assumption that the subjugation of Japan is in the interest of Europe and America and not of Asia. American military leaders have insisted that we must have in the Pacific after this war American bases for armed force. But why? If Asia is going to develop as a self-governing, autonomous part of the world, equal to other parts, why is policing by foreigners necessary? Why cannot Asia police itself? Only because of the deep-seated belief among Europeans and Americans that yellow people are the biological inferiors to the whites and not fit for self-government.

Not only does Western Europe believe that most of the rest of the world is biologically different, but it believes that in this difference lies congenital inferiority; that the black and brown and yellow people are not simply untrained in certain ways of doing and methods of civilization; that they are naturally inferior and inefficient; that they are a danger to civilization, as civilization is understood in Europe. This belief is so fundamental that it enters into the very reforms that we have in mind for the postwar world.

In the United States, the race problem is peculiarly important just now. We see today a combination of northern investors and southern Bourbons desiring not simply to overthrow the New Deal but to plunge the United States into a fatal reaction. The power of the southerners arises from the suppression of the Negro and poor-white vote, which gives the rotten borough of Mississippi four times the political power of Massachusetts and enables the South through the rule of seniority to pack the committees of Congress and to dominate it. Nothing can be done about this situation until we face fairly the question of color discrimination in the South; until the social, political, and economic equality of civilized men is recognized, despite race, color, and poverty.

In the Caribbean area, in Central and South America, there has been for four hundred years wide intermixture of

European, African, and Red Indian races. The result in one respect is widely different from that of Europe and North America; the social equality of Negroes, Indians, and mulattoes who were civilized was recognized without question. But the full results of this cultural liberalism were largely nullified by the economic control which Western Europe and North America held over these lands. The exploitation of cheap colored labor through poverty and low prices for materials was connived at as usual in the civilized world and the spoils shared with local white politicians. Economic and social prestige favored the whites and hindered the colored. A legend that the alleged backwardness of the South Americans was due to race mixture was so far stressed in the world that South America feared it and catered to it; it became the habit to send only white Brazilians, Bolivians, and Mexicans abroad to represent their countries; to encourage white immigration at all costs, even to loss of autonomy; to draw color lines in the management of industry dominated by Europe and in society where foreigners were entertained. In short, to pretend that South America hated and distrusted dark blood as much as the rest of the world, often even when the leaders of this policy were known themselves to be of Negro and Indian descent.

Thus the race problem of South and Central America, and especially of the islands of the Caribbean, became closely allied with European and North American practice. Only in the past few decades are there signs of an insurgent native culture, striking across the color line toward economic freedom, political self-rule, and more complete social equality between races.

There still is a residual sense of racial difference among parts of Europe; a certain contemptuous attitude toward Italy has been manifest for a long time, and the Balkans have been a byword for inefficiency and muddle. The pretensions of the Greeks to represent ancient Greek culture and of the Rumanians to be Roman have been laughed at by Western Europe. The remainder of the Balkans and Russia have been looked upon as Asiatic barbarism, aping civilization. As quasi-Asiatic, they have come in for the racial contempt poured upon the yellow peoples. This attitude greeted the Russian Revolution and staged almost a race war to uphold tottering capitalism, built on racial contempt. But in Eastern Europe today are a mass of awakening men. They know and see what Russia has done for her debased masses in a single generation, cutting across race lines not only between Jew and Gentile but between White Russians, Ukrainians, Tartars, Turks, Kurds, and Kalmuks.

As Sidney and Beatrice Webb declared: "All sections of the community—apart from those legally deprived of citizenship on grounds unconnected with either race or nationality—enjoy, throughout the USSR, according to law, equal rights and duties, equal privileges and equal opportunities. Nor is this merely a formal equality under the law and the federal constitution. Nowhere in the world do habit and custom and public opinion approach nearer to a like equality in fact. Over the whole area between the Arctic Ocean and the Black Sea and the Central Asian mountains, containing vastly differing races and nationalities, men and women, irrespective of conformation of skull or pigmentation of skin, even including the occasional African Negro admitted from the United States, may associate freely with whom they please; travel in the same public vehicles and frequent the same restaurants and hotels; sit next to each other in the same colleges and places of amusement; marry wherever there is mutual liking; engage on equal terms in any craft or profession for which they are qualified; join the same churches or other societies; pay the same taxes and be elected or appointed to any office or position without exception."[1] This, Eastern Europe knows, while Western Europe is still determined to build its culture on race discrimination and expects Russia to help her. But how far can Russia be depended upon to defend, in world war, British and American investments in Asia and Africa?

The attitude of America and Britain toward de Gaulle is puzzling until we remember that, since Gobineau, racial assumptions have entered into the relations between France and the Nordic world. During the First World War the United States was incensed at the social-equality attitudes of the "Frogs," while Britain as well as Germany resented

the open dependence of France on her black colonial soldiers. One present great liberal statesman, Smuts, led a
crusade against arming blacks in any future European
war. Yet de Gaulle not only uses Senegalese soldiers but
recognizes the Negro governor of a strategic French colonial province; while Burman, writing of the history of
the Free French, exclaims: "I am witnessing a miracle,
the rebirth of France in the jungles of Africa!" Racial caste
and profitable investment after the war indicate a halt
in our support of de Gaulle. France since the eighteenth
century has insisted on recognizing the social equality
of civilized men despite race. She has for this reason
been regarded as traitor to the white colonial front, in
government and in society, despite her investors who
have supported British methods. Hitler is not the only
modern statesman who has sneered at "mongrel" France.

These are some, but by no means all, of the race problems which face the world; yet they are not being discussed
except indirectly. The Atlantic Charter as well as the agree-
ments in Moscow and Teheran have been practically silent
on the subject of race. It is assumed that certain fundamental matters and more immediate issues must be met and
settled before this difficult question of race can be faced.
Let us now ask ourselves if this is true. What *are* the fundamental questions before the world at war?

If we measure the important matters by current discussion, we may range them somewhat as follows: (1) defense against aggression; (2) full employment after the
war; (3) eventual fair distribution of both raw materials
and manufactured goods; (4) abolition of poverty; and
(5) health.

To anyone giving thought to these problems, it must be
clear that each of them, with all of its own peculiar difficulties, tends to break asunder along the lesions of race
difference and race hate. Among the primary factors entering into the discussion is the folklore and superstition
which lurk in the minds of modern men and make them
thoroughly believe, in accord with inherited prejudice and
unconscious cerebration, that the peoples of the world are
divided into fundamentally different groups with differences
that are eternal and cannot be forgotten and cannot be

removed. This philosophy says that the majority of the people of the world are impossible.

Therefore, when we discuss any of the listed problems, we usually see the solution within the frame of race and race difference. When we think of defense against aggression, we are thinking particularly of Europe, and the aggregation which we have in mind is not simply another Hitler but a vaster Japan, if not all Asia and the South Sea Islands. The "yellow peril" as envisaged by the German Emperor William II has by no means passed from the subconscious reactions of Western Europe. That is the meaning of the world police and "our way of life."

When we think of the problem of unemployment, we mean especially unemployment in the developed countries of Western Europe and America. We do not have in mind any fundamental change so far as the labor of the darker world is concerned. We do not think of full employment and a living wage for the East Indian, the Chinese coolie, and the Negro of South Africa or even the Negro of our own South. We want the white laborer in England and in America to receive a living wage and economic security without periodic unemployment. In such case we can depend on the political power of white labor to maintain the present industrial organization. But we have little or no thought of colored labor, because it is disfranchised and kept in serfdom by the power of our present governments.

This means, of course, that the industrial organization of these countries must be standardized; they must not clog their own avenues of trade by tariff restrictions and cartels. But these plans have very seldom gone far enough to envisage any change in the relations of Europe and America to the raw material of Africa and Asia or to accepting any idea of so raising the prices of this raw material and the wages of the laborers who produce it that this mass of labor will begin to approach the level of white labor. In fact, any such prospect the white laborers with votes in their hands would in vast majorities oppose.

In both the United States and the Union of South Africa it has been the organized white laborers who have systematically, by vote and mob, opposed the training of the black worker and the provision of decent wages for him. In this respect, they have ranged themselves with exploiting investors and disseminators of race hatred like Hitler. When recently in the United States the President's Fair Employment Practices Commission sought to secure some steps of elementary justice for black railway workers, the railway unions refused even to attend the hearings. Only the Communists and some of the CIO unions have ignored the color line— a significant fact.

Our attitude toward poverty represents the constant lesion of race thinking. We have with difficulty reached a place in the modern white world where we can contemplate the abolition of poverty; where we can think of an industrial organization with no part of its essential cooperators deprived of income which will give them sufficient food and shelter, along with necessary education and some of the comforts of life. But this conception is confined almost entirely to the white race. Not only do we refuse to think of similar possibilities for the colored races but we are convinced that, even though it were possible, it would be a bad thing for the world. We must keep the Negroes, West Indians, and Indonesians poor. Otherwise they will get ambitious: they will seek strength and organization; they will demand to be treated as men, despite the fact that we know they are not men; and they will ask social equality for civilized human beings the world over.

There is a similar attitude with regard to health: we want white people to be well and strong, to "multiply and replenish the earth"; but we are interested in the health of colored people only insofar as it may threaten the health and wealth of whites. Thus in colonies where white men reside as masters, they segregate themselves in the most healthful parts of the country, provided with modern conveniences, and let the natives fester and die in the swamps and lowlands. It is for this reason that Englishmen and South Africans have seized the high land of Kenya and driven the most splendid of races of East Africa into the worst parts of the lowland, to the parts which are infested by the tsetse fly, where their cattle die, and they are forced laborers on white farms.

Perhaps in no area of modern civilized endeavor is the matter of race revealed more startlingly than in the question of education. We have doubts as to the policy of so educating the colored races that they will be able to take part in modern civilization. We are willing to educate them so that they can help in our industrial development, and we want them to become good workmen so long as they are unorganized. But when it comes to a question of real acquaintanceship with what the more advanced part of the world has done and is doing, we try to keep the backward races as ignorant as possible. We limit their schools, their travel, and their knowledge of modern tongues.

There are, of course, notable exceptions: the Negro colleges of the southern United States, the Indian universities, and some advance even in university training in South Africa and in East and West Africa. But this advance is hindered by the fact that popular education is so backward that the number of persons who can qualify for higher training is very small, especially the number who can enter the professions necessary to protect the economic status of the natives and to guide the natives in avoidance of disease. In all these matters race interferes with education.

Beyond this we have only to mention religion. There is no denying that certain missionaries have done fine work in ameliorating the lot of backward people, but at the same time there is not a ghost of a doubt that today the organized Christian church is unfavorable toward race equality. It is split into racial sections and is not disposed to disturb to any great degree the attitude of civilization toward the Chinese, the Indians, and the Negroes. The recent pronouncement of the Federation of Churches of Christ was a fine and forward-looking document, but it has aroused no attention, much less enthusiasm, among the mass of Christians, and will not. The Catholic Church never champions the political or economic rights of subject peoples.

This insistent clinging to the older patterns of race thought has had extraordinary influence upon modern life. In the first place, it has for years held back the progress of the social sciences. The social sciences from the beginning were deliberately used as instruments to prove the inferiority of the majority of the people of the world, who were being used as slaves for the comfort and culture of the masters. The social sciences long looked upon this as one of their major duties. History declared that the Negro had no history. Biology exaggerated the physical differences among men. Economics even today cannot talk straight on colonial imperialism. Psychology has not yet recovered from the shame of its "intelligence" tests and its record of "conclusions" during the First World War.

Granted, therefore, that this is the basic attitude of the majority of civilized people, despite exceptions and individual differences, what must we expect after this war? In the first place, the British Empire is going to continue, if Mr. Churchill has his way, without "liquidation"; and there is slight chance that the English Labour Party or any other democratic elements in England are going to be able to get past the suspensory veto of the House of Lords and the overwhelming social power of the British aristocracy. In America the control of wealth over our democracy is going to be reinforced by the action of the oligarchic South. A war-weary nation is going to ignore reform and going to work to make money. If, of course, the greedy industrial machine breaks down in 1950 as it did in 1929, there will be trouble; but the Negroes will be its chief victims and sufferers. Belgium has held its Congo empire with rare profit during the war, and the homeland will recoup its losses in Europe by more systematic rape of Africa. So Holland will batten down again upon the South Seas, unless the Japanese interlude forces some slight change of heart. South America will become an even more closely integrated part of British and American industry, and the West Indies will work cheaply or starve, while tourists throw them pennies.

The only large cause for disquiet on the part of Western Europe and North America is the case of Russia. There they are reassured as to the attitude of Stalin toward the working people of the Western world. Evidently he has decided that the Western European and American workers with votes in their hands are capable of deciding their own destiny; and, if they are not, it is their own

fault. But what is going to be the attitude of Russia toward colonial peoples? How far and where and when is
Russia going to protect and restore British and American
investments and control in Asia and Africa? Certainly
her attitude toward the Chinese has shown in the past
and still shows that she has the greatest sympathy with
coolie labor and no love for Chiang Kai-shek. Will she
have a similar attitude toward the other peoples of Asia,
of Africa, and of the South Seas? If so, smooth restoration of colonial imperialism is not going to be easy.

What now can be done by intelligent men who are aware
of the continuing danger of present racial attitudes in the
world? We may appeal to two groups of men: first, to those
leaders of white culture who are willing to take action, and
second, to the leaders of races which are victims of present
conditions. White leaders and thinkers have a duty to perform in making known the conclusions of science on the
subject of biological race. It takes science long to percolate
to the mass unless definite effort is made. Public health is
still handicapped by superstitions long disproved by science;
and race fiction is still taught in schools, in newspapers,
and in novels. This careless ignorance of the facts of race
is precisely the refuge where antisocial economic reaction
flourishes.

We must then, first, have wide dissemination of truth.
But this is not all: we need deliberate and organized action
on the front where race fiction is being used to prolong economic inequality and injustice in the world. Here is a
chance for a modern missionary movement, not in the interest of religious dogma, but to dissipate the economic illiteracy which clouds modern thought. Organized industry has
today made the teaching of the elementary principles of
economic thought almost impossible in our schools and
rare in our colleges; by outlawing "communistic" propaganda, it has effectually in press and on platform almost
stopped efforts at clear thinking on economic reform. Protest and revelation fall on deaf ears, because the public
does not know the basic facts. We need a concerted and
determined effort to make common knowledge of the facts
of the distribution of property and income today among
individuals; accurate details of the sources of income and

conditions of production and distribution of goods and use
of human services, in order that we may know who profits
by investment in Asia and Africa as well as in America and
Europe, and why and how they profit.

Next we need organized effort to release the colored laborer from the domination of the investor. This can best be
accomplished by the organization of the labor of the world
as consumers, replacing the producer attitude by knowledge
of consumer needs. Here the victims of race prejudice can
play their great role. They need no longer be confined to
two paths: appeal to a white world ruled by investors in
colored degradation, or war and revolt. There is a third
path: the extrication of the poverty-striken, ignorant laborer
and consumer from his bondage by his own efforts as a
worker and consumer, united to increase the price of his
toil and reduce the cost of the necessities of life. This is
being done here and there, but the news of it is suppressed,
the difficulties of united action deliberately increased, and law
and government united in colonial areas to prevent organization, manipulate prices, and stifle thought by force. Here
colored leaders must act; but, before they act, they must
know. Today, naturally, they are for the most part as economically illiterate as their masters. Thus Indian money-
lenders are the willing instruments of European economic
oppression in India; and many American and West Indian
Negroes regard as economic progress the chance to share in
the exploitation of their race by whites:

A union of economic liberals across the race line, with
the object of driving exploiting investors from their hideout
behind race discrimination, by freeing thought and action
in colonial areas is the only realistic path to permanent
peace today.

A great step toward this would be an international mandates commission with native representation, with power to
investigate and report, and with jurisdiction over all areas
where the natives have no effective voice in government.

American Journal of Sociology, vol. XLIX, March 1944,
pp. 450-56.

12

JACOB AND ESAU

On June 5, 1944, Dr. Du Bois delivered the Commence-
ment Address at Talladega College, a Negro institution at
Talladega, Alabama. Once again he demonstrated that he
presented no ordinary address to college graduates. In-
stead of glittering generalities and optimistic forecasts, he
traced for the students the history of exploitation of colonial
people, the enslavement of the African people, and the
oppression of the majority by the powerful, wealthy minor-
ity. "We have got to stop making income," he declared,
"by unholy methods; . . . to stop lying . . . that a civiliza-
tion based upon the enslavement of the majority of men for
the income of the smart minority is the highest aim of
man."

I remember very vividly the Sunday-school room where
I spent the Sabbaths of my early years. It had been newly
built after a disastrous fire; the room was large and full
of sunlight; nice new chairs were grouped around where the
classes met. My class was in the center, so that I could
look out upon the elms of Main Street and see the passers-
by. But I was interested usually in the lessons and in my
fellow students and the frail rather nervous teacher, who
tried to make the Bible and its ethics clear to us. We were
a trial to her, full of mischief, restless and even noisy; but
perhaps more especially when we asked questions. And on
the story of Jacob and Esau we did ask questions. My
judgment then and my judgment now is very unfavorable
to Jacob. I thought that he was a cad and a liar and I did

not see how possibly he could be made the hero of a Sunday-school lesson.

Many days have passed since then and the world has gone through astonishing changes. But basically, my judgment of Jacob has not greatly changed and I have often promised myself the pleasure of talking about him publicly, and especially to young people. This is the first time that I have had the opportunity.

My subject then is "Jacob and Esau," and I want to examine these two men and the ideas which they represent; and the way in which those ideas have come to our day. Of course, our whole interpretation of this age-old story of Jewish mythology has greatly changed. We look upon these Old Testament stories today not as untrue and yet not as literally true. They are simple, they have their truths, and yet they are not by any means the expression of eternal verity. Here were brought forward for the education of Jewish children and for the interpretation of Jewish life to the world, two men: one small, lithe and quick-witted; the other tall, clumsy and impetuous; a hungry, hard-bitten man.

Historically, we know how these two types came to be set forth by the Bards of Israel. When the Jews marched north after escaping from slavery in Egypt, they penetrated and passed through the land of Edom; the land that lay between the Dead Sea and Egypt. It was an old center of hunters and nomads, and the Israelites, while they admired the strength and organization of the Edomites, looked down upon them as lesser men; as men who did not have the Great Plan. Now the Great Plan of the Israelites was the building of a strong, concentered state under its own God, Jehovah, devoted to agriculture and household manufacture and trade. It raised its own food by careful planning. It did not wander and depend upon chance wild beasts. It depended upon organization, strict ethics, absolute devotion to the nation through strongly integrated planned life. It looked upon all its neighbors, not simply with suspicion, but with the exclusiveness of a chosen people, who were going to be the leaders of earth.

This called for sacrifice, for obedience, for continued planning. The man whom we call Esau was from the land of Edom, or intermarried with it, for the legend has it that he was twin of Jacob the Jew but the chief fact is that, no matter what his blood relations were, his cultural allegiance lay among the Edomites. He was trained in the free out-of-doors; he chased and faced the wild beasts; he knew vast and imperative appetite after long self-denial, and even pain and suffering; he gloried in food, he traveled afar; he gathered wives and concubines and he represented continuous primitive strife.

The legacy of Esau has come down the ages to us. It has not been dominant, but it has always and continually expressed and re-expressed itself; the joy of human appetites, the quick resentment that leads to fighting, the belief in force, which is war.

As I look back upon my own conception of Esau, he is not nearly as clear and definite a personality as Jacob. There is something rather shadowy about him; and yet he is curiously human and easily conceived. One understands his contemptuous surrender of his birthright; he was hungry after long days of hunting; he wanted rest and food, the stew of meat and vegetables which Jacob had in his possession, and determined to keep unless Esau bargained. "And Esau said, Behold, I am at the point to die: and what profit shall this birthright be to me? And Jacob said, Swear to me this day; and he swore unto him: and he sold his birthright unto Jacob."

On the other hand, the legacy of Jacob which has come down through the years, not simply as a Jewish idea, but more especially as typical of modern Europe, is more complicated and expresses itself something like this: life must be planned for the Other Self, for that personification of the group, the nation, the empire, which has eternal life as contrasted with the ephemeral life of individuals. For this we must plan, and for this there must be timeless and unceasing work. Out of this, the Jews as chosen children of Jehovah would triumph over themselves, over all Edom and in time over the world.

Now it happens that so far as actual history is concerned, this dream and plan failed. The poor little Jewish nation was dispersed to the ends of the earth by the overwhelming power of the great nations that arose East, North, and

South and eventually became united in the vast empire of Rome. This was the diaspora, the dispersion of the Jews. But the idea of the Plan with a personality of its own took hold of Europe with relentless grasp and this was the real legacy of Jacob, and of other men of other peoples, whom Jacob represents.

There came the attempt to weld the world into a great unity, first under the Roman Empire, then under the Catholic Church. When this attempt failed, and the empire fell apart, there arose the individual states of Europe and of some other parts of the world; and these states adapted the idea of individual effort to make each of them dominant. The state was *all,* the individual subordinate, but right here came the poison of the Jacobean idea. How could the state get this power? Who was to wield the power within the state? So long as power was achieved, what difference did it make how it was gotten? Here then was war — but not Esau's war of passion, hunger and revenge, but Jacob's war of cold acquisition and power.

Granting to Jacob, as we must, the great idea of the family, the clan, and the state as dominant and superior in its claims, nevertheless, there is the bitter danger in trying to seek these ends without reference to the great standards of right and wrong. When men begin to lie and steal, in order to make the nation to which they belong great, then comes not only disaster, but rational contradiction which in many respects is worse than disaster, because it ruins the leadership of the divine machine, the human reason, by which we chart and guide our actions.

It was thus in the middle age and increasingly in the seventeenth and eighteenth and more especially in the nineteenth century, there arose the astonishing contradiction: that is, the action of men like Jacob who were perfectly willing and eager to lie and steal so long as their action brought profit to themselves and power to their state. And soon identifying themselves and their class with the state they identified their own wealth and power as that of the state. They did not listen to any arguments of right or wrong; might was right; they came to despise and deplore the natural appetites of human beings and their very lives, so long as by their suppression, they themselves got rich and powerful. There arose a great, rich Italy; a fabulously wealthy Spain; a strong and cultured France and, eventually, a British Empire which came near to dominating the world. The Esaus of those centuries were curiously represented by various groups of people: by the slum-dwellers and the criminals who, giving up all hope of profiting by the organized state, sold their birthrights for miserable messes of pottage. But more than that, the great majority of mankind, the peoples who lived in Asia, Africa and America and the islands of the sea, became subordinate tools for the profit-making of the crafty planners of great things, who worked regardless of religion or ethics.

It is almost unbelievable to think what happened in those centuries, when it is put in cold narrative; from whole volumes of tales, let me select only a few examples. The peoples of whole islands and countries were murdered in cold blood for their gold and jewels. The mass of the laboring people of the world were put to work for wages which led them into starvation, ignorance and disease. The right of the majority of mankind to speak and to act; to play and to dance was denied, if it interfered with profit-making work for others, or was ridiculed if it could not be capitalized. Karl Marx writes of Scotland: "As an example of the method of obtaining wealth and power in nineteenth century; the story of the Duchess of Sutherland will suffice here. This Scottish noblewoman resolved, on entering upon the government of her clan of white Scottish people to turn the whole country, whose population had already been, by earlier processes, reduced to 15,000, into a sheep pasture. From 1814 to 1820 these 15,000 inhabitants were systematically hunted and rooted out. All their villages were destroyed and burnt, all their fields turned into pasture. Thus this lady appropriated 794,000 acres of land that had from time immemorial been the property of the people. She assigned to the expelled inhabitants about 6,000 acres on the seashore. The 6,000 acres had until this time lain waste, and brought in no income to their owners. The Duchess, in the nobility of her heart, actually went so far as to let these at an average rent of 50 cents per acre to the clansmen, who for centuries had

shed their blood for her family. The whole of the stolen
clan-land she divided into 29 great sheep farms, each
inhabited by a single imported English family. In the
year 1835 the 15,000 Scotsmen were already replaced by
131,000 sheep."[1]

"The discovery of gold and silver in America, the extir-
pation, enslavement and entombment in mines of the Indian population, the beginning of the conquest and looting
of the East Indies, the turning of Africa into a warren for
the commercial hunting of black-skins, signalized the rosy
dawn of power of those spiritual children of Jacob, who
owned the birthright of the masses by fraud and murder.
These idyllic proceedings are the chief momenta of primary accumulation of capital in private hands. On their
heels tread the commercial wars of the European nations,
with the globe for a theater. It begins with the revolt of
the Netherlands from Spain, assumes giant dimensions in
England's anti-jacobin war, and continues in the opium
wars against China. . . .

"Of the Christian colonial system, Howitt says: 'The
barbarities and desperate outrages of the so-called Christians, throughout every region of the world, and upon
people they have been able to subdue, are not to be par-
alleled by those of any other race, in any age of the
earth.' This history of the colonial administration of Holland — and Holland was the head capitalistic nation of the
seventeenth century— is one of the most extraordinary
relations of treachery, bribery, massacre, and meanness.'

"Nothing was more characteristic than the Dutch system
of stealing men, to get slaves for Java. The men-stealers
were trained for this purpose. The thief, the interpreter,
and the seller were the chief agents in this trade; the native
princes, the chief sellers. The young people stolen, were
thrown into the secret dungeons of Celebes, until they
were ready for sending to the slave ships. . . .

"The English East India Company, in the seventeenth
and eighteenth centuries, obtained, besides the political
rule in India, the exclusive monopoly of the tea trade,
as well as of the Chinese trade in general, and of the
transport of goods to and from Europe. But the coasting
trade of India was the monopoly of the higher employees

of the company. The monopolies of salt, opium, betel nuts and other commodities, were inexhaustible mines of wealth. The employees themselves fixed the price and plundered at will the unhappy Hindus. The Governor General took part in this private traffic. His favorites received contracts under conditions whereby they, cleverer than the alchemists, made gold out of nothing. Great English fortunes sprang up like mushrooms in a day; investment profits went on without the advance of a shilling. The trial of Warren Hastings swarms with such cases. Here is an instance: a contract for opium was given to a certain Sullivan at the moment of his departure on an official mission. Sullivan sold his contract to one Binn for $200,000; Binn sold it the same day for $300,000 and the ultimate purchaser who carried out the contract declared that after all he realized an enormous gain. According to one of the lists laid before Parliament, the East India Company and its employees from 1757 to 1766 got $30,000,000 from the Indians as gifts alone. . . .

"The treatment of the aborigines was, naturally, most frightful in plantation colonies destined for export trade only, such as the West Indies, and in rich and well-populated countries, such as Mexico and India, that were given over to plunder. But even in the colonies properly so called, the followers of Jacob outdid him. These sober Protestants, the Puritans of New England, in 1703, by decrees of their assembly set a premium of $200 on every Indian scalp and every captured redskin: in 1720 a premium of $500 on every scalp; in 1744, after Massachusetts Bay had proclaimed a certain tribe as rebels, the following prices prevailed: for a male scalp of 12 years upward, $500 (new currency); for a male prisoner, $525; for women and children prisoners, $250; for scalps of women and children, $250. Some decades later, the colonial system took its revenge on the descendants of the pious pilgrim fathers, who had grown seditious in the meantime. At English instigation and for English pay they were tomahawked by redskins. The British Parliament, proclaimed bloodhounds and scalping as 'means that God and Nature had given into its hands.'" [2]

"With the development of national industry during the

eighteenth century, the public opinion of Europe had lost the last remnant of shame and conscience. The nations bragged cynically of every infamy that served them as a means to accumulating private wealth. Read, e. g., the naive *Annals of Commerce* of Anderson. Here it is trumpeted forth as a triumph of English statecraft that at the Peace of Utrecht, England extorted from the Spaniards by the Asiento Treaty the privilege of being allowed to ply the slave trade, between Africa and Spanish America. England thereby acquired the right of supplying Spanish America until 1743 with 4,800 Negroes yearly. This threw, at the same time, an official cloak over British smuggling. Liverpool waxed fat on the slave trade. . . . Aikin (1795) quotes that spirit of bold adventure which has characterized the trade of Liverpool and rapidly carried it to its present state of prosperity; has occasioned vast employment for shipping and sailors, and greatly augmented the demand for the manufactures of the country; Liverpool employed in the slave trade, in 1730, 15 ships; in 1760, 74; in 1770, 96; and in 1792, 132." [3]

Henry George wrote of *Progress and Poverty* in the 1890s. He says: "At the beginning of this marvelous era it was natural to expect, and it was expected, that labor-saving inventions would lighten the toil and improve the condition of the laborer; that the enormous increase in the power of producing wealth would make real poverty a thing of the past. Could a man of the last century [the eighteenth]—a Franklin or a Priestley—have seen, in a vision of the future, the steamship taking the place of the sailing vessel; the railroad train, of the wagon; the reaping machine, of the scythe; the threshing machine, of the flail; could he have heard the throb of the engines that in obedience to human will, and for the satisfaction of the human desire, exert a power greater than that of all the men and all the beasts of burden of the earth combined; could he have seen the forest tree transformed into finished lumber—into doors, sashes, blinds, boxes or barrels, with hardly the touch of a human hand; the great workshops where boots and shoes are turned out by the case with less labor than the old-fashioned cobbler could have put on a sole; the factories where, under the eye of one girl, cotton becomes cloth faster than hundreds of stalwart weavers could have turned it out with their hand-looms; could he have seen steam hammers shaping mammoth shafts and mighty anchors, and delicate machinery making tiny watches; the diamond drill cutting through the heart of the rocks, and coal oil sparing the whale; could he have realized the enormous saving of labor resulting from improved facilities of exchange and communication—sheep killed in Australia eaten fresh in England, and the order given by the London banker in the afternoon executed in San Francisco in the morning of the same day; could he have conceived of the hundred thousand improvements which these only suggest, what would he have inferred as to the social condition of mankind?

"It would not have seemed like an inference; further than the vision went it would have seemed as though he saw; and his heart would have leaped and his nerves would have thrilled, as one who from a height beholds just ahead of the thirst-stricken caravan the living gleam of rustling woods and the glint of laughing waters. Plainly, in the sight of the imagination, he would have beheld these new forces elevating society from its very foundations, lifting the very poorest above the possibility of want, exempting the very lowest from anxiety for the material needs of life; he would have seen these slaves of the lamp of knowledge taking on themselves the traditional curse, these muscles of iron and sinews of steel making the poorest laborer's life a holiday, in which every high quality and noble impulse could have scope to grow." [4]

This was the promise of Jacob's life. This would establish the birthright which Esau despised. But, says George "Now, however, we are coming into collision with facts which there can be no mistaking. From all parts of the civilized world," he says speaking fifty years ago, "come complaints of industrial depression; of labor condemned to involuntary idleness; of capital massed and wasting; of pecuniary distress among businessmen; of want and suffering and anxiety among the working classes. All the full, deadening pain, all the keen, maddening anguish, that to great masses of men are involved in the words 'hard times,' afflict the world today."⁵ What would Henry George have said in 1933 after airplane and radio and mass production, turbine and electricity had come?

Science and art grew and expanded despite all this, but it was warped by the poverty of the artist and the continuous attempt to make science subservient to industry. The latter effort finally succeeded so widely that modern civilization became typified as industrial technique. Education became learning a trade. Men thought of civilization as primarily mechanical and the mechanical means by which they reduced wool and cotton to their purposes, also reduced and bent humankind to their will. Individual initiative remained but it was cramped and distorted and there spread the idea of patriotism to one's country as the highest virtue, by which it became established, that just as in the case of Jacob, a man not only could lie, steal, cheat and murder for his native land, but by doing so, he became a hero whether his cause was just or unjust.

One remembers that old scene between Esau who had thoughtlessly surrendered his birthright and the father who had blessed his lying son; "Jacob came unto his father, and said, My Father: and he said, Here am I; who art thou? And Jacob said unto his father, I am Esau thy firstborn; I have done according as thou badest me: arise, I pray thee, sit and eat of my venison, that thy soul may bless me." In vain did clumsy, careless Esau beg for a blessing—some little blessing. It was denied and Esau hated Jacob because of the blessing: and Esau said in his heart, "The days of mourning for my father are at hand; then I will slay my brother Jacob." So revolution entered—so revolt darkened a dark world.

The same motif was repeated in modern Europe and America in the nineteenth and twentieth centuries, when there grew the superstate called the Empire. The Plan had now regimented the organization of men covering vast territories, dominating immense force and immeasurable wealth and determined to reduce to subserviency as large a part as possible, not only of Europe's own internal world, but of the world at large. Colonial imperialism swept over the earth and initiated the First World War, in envious scramble for division of power and profit.

Hardly a moment of time passed after that war, a moment in the eyes of the eternal forces looking down upon us when again the world, using all of that planning and all of that technical superiority for which its civilization was noted; and all of the accumulated and accumulating wealth which was available, proceeded to commit suicide on so vast a scale that it is almost impossible for us to realize the meaning of the catastrophe. Of course, this sweeps us far beyond anything that the peasant lad Jacob, with his petty lying and thievery had in mind. Whatever was begun there of ethical wrong among the Jews was surpassed in every particular by the white world of Europe and America and carried to such length of universal cheating, lying and killing that no comparisons remain.

We come therefore to the vast impasse of today: to the great question, what was the initial right and wrong of the original Jacobs and Esaus and of their spiritual descendants the world over? We stand convinced today, at least those who remain sane, that lying and cheating and killing will build no world organization worth the building. We have got to stop making income by unholy methods; out of stealing the pittances of the poor and calling it insurance; out of seizing and monopolizing the natural resources of the world and then making the world's poor pay exhorbitant prices for aluminum, copper and oil, iron and coal. Not only have we got to stop these practices, but we have got to stop lying about them and seeking to convince human beings that a civilization based upon the enslavement of the majority of men for the income of the smart minority is the highest aim of man.

But as is so usual in these cases, these transgressions of Jacob do not mean that the attitude of Esau was flawless. The conscienceless greed of capital does not excuse the careless sloth of labor. Life cannot be all aimless wandering and indulgence if we are going to constrain human beings to take advantage of their brain and make successive generations stronger and wiser than the previous. There must be reverence for the *birthright* of inherited *culture* and that birthright cannot be sold for a dinner course, a dress suit or a winter in Florida. It must be valued and conserved.

The method of conservation is work, endless and tireless and planned work and this is the legacy which the Esaus of today who condemn the Jacobs of yesterday have got to substitute as their path of life, not vengeful revolution, but building and rebuilding. Curiously enough, it will not be difficult to do this, because the great majority of men, the poverty-stricken and diseased are the *real workers* of the world. They are the ones who have made and are making the *wealth* of this universe, and their future path is clear. It is to accumulate such knowledge and balance of judgment that they can reform the world, so that the workers of the world receive just share of the wealth which they make and that all human beings who are capable of work shall work. Not national glory and empire for the few, but food, shelter and happiness for the many. With the disappearance of systematic lying and killing, we may come into that birthright which so long we have called Freedom: that is, the right to act in a manner that seems to us beautiful; which makes life worth living and joy the only possible end of life. This is the experience which is Art and planning for this is the highest satisfaction of civilized needs. So that looking back upon the allegory and the history, tragedy and promise, we may change our subject and speak in closing of Esau and Jacob, realizing that neither was perfect, but that of the two, Esau had the elements which lead more naturally and directly to the salvation of man; while Jacob with all his crafty planning and cold sacrifice, held in his soul the things that are about to ruin mankind: exaggerated national patriotism, individual profit, the despising of men who are not the darlings of our particular God and the consequent lying and stealing and killing to monopolize power.

May we not hope that in the world after this catastrophe of blood, sweat and fire, we may have a new Esau and Jacob; a new allegory of men who enjoy life for life's sake; who have the Freedom of Art and wish for all men of all sorts the same freedom and enjoyment that they seek themselves and who work for all this and work hard.

Gentlemen and ladies of the class of 1944: in the days of the years of my pilgrimage, I have greeted many thou-

sands of young men and women at the commencement of
their careers as citizens of the select commonwealth of
culture. In no case have I welcomed them to such a world
of darkness and distractions as that into which I usher
you. I take joy only in the thought that if work to be
done is measure of man's opportunity you inherit a
mighty fortune. You have only to remember that the
birthright which is today in symbol draped over your
shoulders is a heritage which has been preserved all too
often by the lying, stealing and murdering of the Jacobs
of the world, and if these are the only means by which
this birthright can be preserved in the future, it is not
worth the price. I do not believe this, and I lay it upon
your hearts to prove that this not only need not be true,
but is eternally and forever false.

The Talladegan, Vol. LXII, November 1944, pp. 1-6.

13

THE NEGRO AND IMPERIALISM

On November 15, 1944, shortly after his return to the NAACP, Dr. Du Bois delivered a radio address over Station WEVD in New York City in which he told his radio audience that unless colonial peoples received a share of power proportionate to their numbers in the new world organization set up after the war, their rulers were inviting future wars among themselves and against subject peoples in revolt. He criticized the preliminary conference of the United Nations Organization at Dumbarton Oaks for failing to provide any direct representation for the billion people in colored colonial areas. Was this a sign that imperialism was still very much alive and did this indicate that colonial powers would seek to recoup their wartime losses by more vigorous exploitation of backward areas? The history of imperialism and racism, which Dr. Du Bois brilliantly but briefly outlined in his speech, indicated that the answer to this question would be in the affirmative.

He predicted, too, that the workers in the imperialist countries would be bribed by government aid at home into supporting a continuation of imperialism. "The working people of the civilized world will thus largely be induced to put their political power behind imperialism, and democracy in Europe will continue to impede and nullify democracy in Asia and Africa." Events were all too soon to bear out the truth of these words, although they were also to reveal that it was the United States imperialists who were to play the biggest role in impeding and nullifying democracy in Asia and Africa.

The government of the United Nations according to the proposals made at Dumbarton Oaks will consist of five great powers comprising perhaps five hundred million white and yellow people who will rule the world through a Security Council and have military power to enforce their decision. However, the three hundred and fifty million yellow people represented by China may not for historic reasons be recognized as racial equals and because of present economic disruption may be largely in the power of white nations. The proposal for a racial-equality declaration among nations, once made by Japan before the League of Nations and lately as persistent rumor has it, repeated at Dumbarton Oaks by China, does not appear in the published proposals.

An indeterminate number of free nations, mostly white folk and comprising about one thousand million people, will function in an assembly in which each nation is represented; the Assembly will have the right of petition, discussion, advice; and action insofar as the Security Council allows. Some of these nations, however, are so under the economic domination of great powers that they will hardly be able to take an independent stand. The Assembly will choose representatives of six nations who will be associated with the great powers in the Security Council; but their ability to influence those powers will depend largely upon the method of voting in the Security Council, which has not yet been decided.

There will be six hundred million colored and black folk inhabiting colonies owned by white nations, who will have no rights that white people are bound to respect.[1] Any revolt on their part can be put down by military force at the disposal of the Security Council. This mass of people will have no right of appeal to the Security Council or to the Assembly.

The Economic and Social Council of the Assembly may make recommendations and consider complaints; but they will apparently have no direct power of investigation; and on this Economic and Social Council no colony will have representation. It may be said that the interests of these colonial peoples will be represented in the world government by the master nations. In the same way it was said in 1787 in the United States that slaves would be represented by their masters.

There is no designated function for the enemy states which have been guilty of imperial aggression in this war. They will comprise perhaps one hundred fifty million people. Presumably they will eventually take their places among the friendly nations and possibly at some day among the great powers.

Evidently the weak point in this outline for a government of men is the fact that at least one-fourth of the inhabitants of the world have no part in it; no democratic power, not even a recognized right of petition. This puts all effort at reform and uplift on the shoulders of imperial countries and does this at a time when the countries, because of loss and disruption in this war, are least able to undertake philanthropic enterprise.

Classifying autonomous colonies like Canada and Australia as Free Nations in the meaning of the proposals, there remain therefore not less than six hundred million persons disfranchised in the General Assembly and represented only by the master nations. In addition there are on earth, a number of other nations, nominally independent, who by reason of accumulated debt owed creditor nations and current control of their labor and industry by absentee capital, will be in no position to act independently or speak freely, even if admitted to seats in the Assembly. Thus perhaps a thousand millions of human beings will have no direct voice, nor exercise any real degree of democratic control in the proposed United Nations.

There is no need here to discuss the advantages or disadvantages of modern imperialism, nor to attempt to assess the gain or loss to peoples arising from their subordination to the great nations. That the colonial system has involved in the past much that was horrible and inhuman will be admitted. That vast numbers of backward peoples have made notable cultural advance under the colonial regime is equally true. Despite this, if the world believes in democracy and is fighting a war of incredible cost to establish democracy as a way of life, it is both intolerable in ethics and dangerous in statecraft to allow, for instance, eight million Belgians to represent ten million Congolese in the new internation[al organization] without giving these black folk any voice even to complain.

It is equally unfair that seven and a half million Portuguese should dominate eleven million in their colonies; or that nine million Dutchmen should be the sole arbiters and spokesmen for sixty-seven million brown men of the South Seas. It cannot be reconciled with any philosophy of democracy that fifty million white folk of the British Empire should be able to make the destiny of four hundred and fifty million yellow, brown and black people a matter solely of their own internal decision. Or again, inside that same empire, it is astonishing to see among the leading "Free Nations," battling for democracy, the Union of South Africa, where two million white folk, not only in international affairs but openly in their established government, hold eight million black natives in a subordination unequalled elsewhere in the world.

This is not for a moment to deny the technique and elementary schools which Belgium has given black Congo; or the fact that the Netherlands has perhaps the most liberal colonial program of any modern empire; or that Great Britain gave the African freedom and education after the slave trade and slavery. But it is equally true that the advance of colonial peoples has been hesitant and slow, and retarded unnecessarily because of the denial of democratic method to the natives, and because their treatment and government have had, and still have, objects and methods incompatible with their best interests and highest progress. The substantial and permanent advance of a group cannot be allowed to depend on the philanthropy of a master, if the desires and initiative of its members are given no freedom, no democratic expression; and if, on the other hand, the will of the master is swayed by strong motives of selfish aggrandizement and gain. How often this selfish interest has prevailed in the past is too well known to require reminder. But today the temptation is stronger rather than less; with Holland reeling under murder, theft and destruction, can the world expect unselfish surrender by the present generation of the profit of rich colonies capable of helping restore her losses? Is it likely that Belgium after her crucifixion will be satisfied with less profit from the Congo and greater expenditure for education, health and social service? With Great Britain straining every nerve to satisfy the demands of her own laboring classes, is it likely that she will of her own initiative extend these reforms to India coupled with the autonomy necessary for Indian initiative and self-government?

No. The united effort of world opinion should now be brought earnestly to bear on the nations owning colonies to make them realize that great as the immediate sacrifice may be, it is the only way to peace. To set up now an internation[al organization] with near half mankind disfranchised and socially enslaved is to court disaster. In the past and the recent past we know how the lure of profit from rich, unlettered and helpless countries, has tempted great and civilized nations and plunged them into bloody rivalry. We know what part colonial aggression has played in this present world disaster. We know that capital investment can earn more in Africa, Asia and the South Seas, because there it suffers few of the restrictions of civilized life; that the foreign investor in these lands is himself the prime ruler and seat of power and without local democratic control, he has but to appease public opinion at home, which is not only ignorant of the local facts, but perhaps all too willing to remain ignorant as long as dividends continue.

If this situation is not frankly faced and steps toward remedy attempted, we shall seek in vain to find peace and security; we shall leave the door wide open for renewed international rivalry to secure colonies and eventually and inevitably for colonial revolt.

Evidently there is indicated here the necessity of earnest effort to avoid the nondemocratic and race-inferiority philosophy here involved. There should be consultation among colonial peoples and their friends as to just what measures ought to be taken. This consultation should look toward asking for the following successive steps:

One, representation of the colonial peoples alongside

the master peoples in the Assembly. Whether such representatives should at first have a right to vote or only the right to complain and petition should be determined by the Assembly.

Two, the organization of a Mandate Commission under the Economic and Social Council with distinct power to investigate complaints and conditions in colonies and make public their findings.

Three, a clear statement of the intentions of each imperial power gradually but definitely to take all measures designed eventually to grant the peoples of the colonies political and economic equality with the peoples of the master nations and eventually either to incorporate them into the polity of the master nations or to allow them to become independent free peoples.

We are in this war even more than in the last war facing the problem of democracy: how far are we going to have a world [in which] the people who are ruled are going to have effective voice in their government. We have stated and reiterated that this democratic method of government is going to be applied just as widely as possible. But of course in this program we recognize that beyond the logic of democracy looms the inevitable logic of facts; and the fact is that most of the people of the world have not been ruled in the past by democratic methods; and that the progress toward democracy has been disappointingly slow.

A century ago the explanation of this was clear. You had in the world a minority of people who were capable of civilization; who by their inherent gifts and by long and difficult trial and experience were the natural rulers of the world. They composed most of the white people of the world, although even among those people there was a certain proportion of the lower classes who were incapable because of deficiency in natural gifts to take effective part in democracy.

On the other hand, the majority of the people of the world, composing mainly the colored and black races were naturally so inferior that it was not to be hoped that in any reasonable time, if ever, they would be capable of self-government. This was supposed to be proven by their history, and current scientific investigation seemed to back up historical judgment.

Since the beginning of the twentieth century there has come great change in these judgments. In the first place we have practically given up the idea that there is any considerable portion of the civilized peoples who cannot by education and by the training of experience be made into effective voters and administrators in democratic governments. Further than this we are not nearly so sure today as we used to be of the inherent inferiority of the majority of the people of the earth who happen to be colored. We know, of course, that skin color itself has no particular significance and the other physical characteristics, whatever their significance, are not certain indications of inferiority. [In] the testimony of history we, of course, emphasize the accomplishments of certain people and decry or omit the work of other people. It is always astonishing for Americans to contrast the history of the Revolutionary War as set down in English and American textbooks. In addition to that the testimony of biology and anthropology and of various social sciences convinces us more and more that absolute and essential difference between races as self-perpetuating groups are difficult to fix if not nonexistent. That consequently we have no way of being certain that education and experience will not do for the backward races of man what it has already begun to do for the depressed classes in civilized states.

But these facts do not affect our actions today, because government and economic organization has already built a tremendous structure upon the nineteenth-century conception of race inferiority. This is what the imperialism of our day means. In order, therefore, to judge our present attitude and proposed action toward colonies we must note the growth of the colonial idea.

Roman imperialism did not involve national inferiority. It was simply a matter of political control and centralized taxation with a large degree of autonomy left to the individual states which submitted to Rome. The taxation, to be sure, was often oppressive and amounted to considerable subjection but the Roman Empire was not by any means the counterpart of modern empires. When during the Middle Ages Rome fell to pieces, the world established itself on the basis of separate states who were brought into correspondence with each other through trade and conference. A Marco Polo interpreted an independent Asia to an unknown Europe, and Othello, real or fictitious, was a respected stranger from Africa who offered aid to a European ruler. There arose in Asia and in the Sudan independent kingdoms equal in many respects and certainly distinguished from each other by no evident superiority or inferiority. It was the discovery of America and the sudden demand of labor supplied by the African slave trade that changed this; that based the new European capitalism upon extreme subjection of labor to an organized plantation system; and that rationalized slavery by a new doctrine of inevitable and unchangeable inferiority especially so far as the blacks were concerned.

Negro slavery in America was the passing phase of a great world labor problem but on it was built a new imperialism. Great Britain, from an empire supported by slavery, came to be an empire ruling a wide stretch of countries where cheap labor, more or less compulsory, exported valuable raw material in large quantity to manufacturing centers in the United Kingdom. Other countries followed suit, especially Holland and France. Spain sought to reorganize her empire of conquest and extortion but became in the long run subject to the British organization of industry. Finally Germany and Italy, seeing the tremendous advantage which imperial capital gave to Great Britain, Holland and France, tried to enter into effective competition.

The temptation in this situation was that colonial proprietorship gave the leading countries of the world certain tremendous advantages. The colonial contribution to imperial government was in itself small and often an actual loss; but to the individual investors in these countries, cheap labor and cheap raw material were the basis of tremendous and increasing wealth which made the luxury and power of the late nineteenth and early twentieth centuries remarkable. To enter into rivalry with these countries it was necessary for Germany, Italy and Japan to seek the control of colonies and in that way to gain a vast number of men, wide stretches of land and abundance of raw material.

The First World War was a war of rivalry between imperial powers, with the exploitation of Asia and Africa as the prize to be won. Germany felt that her share in Africa was too small to be commensurate with her manufacturing, commercial and technical possibilities. Japan felt that European imperialism was monopolizing the exploitation of Asia in which she was by situation and race the natural leader.

In the organization of the League of Nations, advantage was taken of the situation of the German colonies to attempt a solution to the whole colonial problem. The German colonies were distributed among France, Great Britain and Japan under the control of a Mandates Commission. The Mandates Commission was supposed to see that the people of these colonies were fairly treated; and that something was done for their social uplift and their economic betterment. The statute that governed the Mandates Commission was, however, deliberately limited in such a way that the Commission really had very little power. It could not of its own initiative inquire into or investigate facts in the various colonies; the colonial peoples themselves had no vested right of appeal to the Commission and as a matter of fact the mandated colony soon became indistinguishable from the other colonies of the countries holding the mandates. It had been hoped that the opposite would happen and that the authority of the Mandates Commission would eventually extend, not only to the former German colonies, but to all colonies of all nations. This never took place and the only organ of the League of Nations that helped the colonial situation was the International Labor Office which succeeded in setting up certain minimum standards of labor usage.

Meantime, between the two world wars there was at first an intensified effort, particularly in the British Empire and to some extent in France, to increase colonial exploitation in order to repay cost of war. This led to bitter complaints especially in British West Africa and finally to a colonial movement there which secured for five of the colonies the right of elected representation in the Governor's Councils; but these councils continued to have a majority of appointed officials representing the home government and also representing large investment interests in England. Elsewhere on the continent, in Kenya and in the Union of South Africa the deprivation of colonial people of their lands continued; while in Asia the new Japanese imperial expansion gained headway and purpose. Among the Dutch colonies some effort was made to increase the participation of colonial peoples in government and to systematize education. In the Belgian Congo elementary education under the Catholic Church was broadened in extent and recognition of local government throughout tribal organizations; but no secondary or high education and no participation in the colonial government was encouraged.

The Second World War, therefore, found the colonial question really unsettled and was precipitated by the determination of Italy to enter upon an imperial career in Africa. On the part of Germany there was a distinct and increasing pressure for the return of her colonies and for even larger colonial expansion. Thus the problem of colonies has been certainly a main cause of two world wars and unless it is frankly faced and its settlement begun, it may easily cause a third.

The colonial organization today is primarily economic. It is a method of carrying on industry and commerce and of distributing wealth. As such it not only confines colonial peoples to a low standard of living and encourages by reason of its high profit to investors a determined and interested belief in the inferiority of certain races but it also affects the situation of the working classes and minorities in civilized countries.

When, for instance, during and after this war the working people of Great Britain, the Netherlands, France and Belgium in particular are going to demand certain costly social improvements from the government: the prevention of unemployment, a rising standard of living, health insurance, increased education of children; the large cost of these improvements must be met by increased public taxation falling with greater weight than ever theretofore upon the rich. This means that the temptations to recoup and balance the financial burden of increased taxation by investment in colonies, where social services are at their lowest and standards of living below the requirements of civilization, are going definitely to increase; and the disposition of parties on the left, liberal parties and philanthropy to press for colonial improvement will be silenced by the bribe of vastly increased help of government to better their condition. The working people of the civilized world will thus largely be induced to put their political power behind imperialism, and democracy in Europe will continue to impede and nullify democracy in Asia and Africa.

In this way the modern world after this war may easily be lulled to sleep and to forget that the exclusion of something between one-fourth and one-half of the whole population of the world from participation in democratic government and socialized wealth is a direct threat to the spread of democracy and a certain promise of future war; and of war not simply as justifiable revolt on the part of colonial peoples who are increasing in intelligence and efficiency, but also of recurring wars of envy and greed because of the present inequitable distribution of colonial gain among civilized nations.

Moreover, the continuation of vested interest in the theory of racial inferiority and the oppression of minorities of any sort will be encouraged by failure to face the problem of the future of colonies.

Manuscript copy of speech in papers of the National Association for the Advancement of Colored People, Manuscripts Division, Library of Congress. Published with permission of the National Association for the Advancement of Colored People.

14

THE PAN-AFRICAN MOVEMENT

The Sixth Pan-African Congress was held October 15-21, 1945, in the Chorlton Town Hall at Manchester, England, headquarters of the recently formed Pan-African Federation. Chiefly responsible for this Congress was the secretary of the Federation, George Padmore, who was also elected a joint political secretary with Kwame Nkrumah to prepare the Congress and with Jomo Kenyatta as assistant secretary. Elected to preside over the first, as over most of the other sessions, Dr. Du Bois was hailed as "Father" of Pan-Africanism by Padmore, and unanimously elected International President of the Pan-African Congress. In this capacity, he delivered an address tracing the history and significance of the Pan-African Movement.

The idea of one Africa uniting the thought and ideals of all native peoples of the Dark Continent belongs to the twentieth century and stems naturally from the West Indies and the United States. Here various groups of Africans, quite separate in origin, became so united in experience and so exposed to the impact of a new culture that they began to think of Africa as one idea and one land. Thus, late in the eighteenth century when a separate Negro church was formed in Philadelphia, it called itself "African"; and there were various "African" societies in many parts of the United States.

It was not, however, until 1900 that a black West Indian barrister, H. Sylvester-Williams of Trinidad, practicing in London, called together a "Pan-African" Conference. This meeting attracted attention, put the word "Pan-African" in the dictionaries for the first time, and had some thirty delegates, mainly from England and the West Indies, with a few colored Americans. The Conference was welcomed by the Lord Bishop of London, and a promise was obtained from Queen Victoria, through Joseph Chamberlain, not to "overlook the interests and welfare of the native races."

This meeting had no deep roots in Africa itself, and the movement and the idea died for a generation. Then came the First World War, and at its close there was determined agitation among American Negroes for the rights of Negroes throughout the world, particularly in Africa. Meetings were held, a petition was sent to President Wilson, and finally, by indirection, I secured passage on the Creel press boat, the *Orizaba*, and landed in France in December 1918.

I went with the idea of calling a "Pan-African Congress" and trying to impress upon the members of the Peace Congress sitting at Versailles the importance of Africa in the future world. I was without credentials or influence, but the idea took on.

I tried to get a conference with President Wilson, but only got as far as Colonel House, who was sympathetic but noncommittal. The *Chicago Tribune* said, January 19, 1919, in a dispatch from Paris dated December 30, 1918:

"An Ethiopian Utopia, to be fashioned out of the German colonies, is the latest dream of leaders of the Negro race who are here at the invitation of the United States Government as part of the extensive entourage of the American peace delegation. Robert R. Moton, successor of the late Booker Washington as head of Tuskegee Institute, and Dr. William E. B. DuBois, Editor of the *Crisis*, are promoting a Pan-African Conference to be held here during the winter while the Peace Conference is on full blast. It is to embrace Negro leaders from America, Abyssinia, Liberia, Haiti, and the French and British colonies and other parts of the black world. Its object is to get out of the Peace Conference an effort to modernize the dark continent, and in the world reconstruction to provide international machinery looking toward the civilization of the African natives.

"The Negro leaders are not agreed upon any definite plan, but Dr. DuBois has mapped out a scheme which he has presented in the form of a memorandum to President Wilson. It is quite Utopian, and it has less than a Chinaman's chance of getting anywhere in the Peace Conference, but it is nevertheless interesting. As self-determination' is one of the words to conjure with in Paris nowadays, the Negro leaders are seeking to have it applied, if possible, in a measure to their race in Africa.

"Dr. DuBois sets forth that while the principle of self-determination cannot be applied to uncivilized peoples, yet the educated blacks should have some voice in the disposition of the German colonies. He maintains that in settling what is to be done with the German colonies, the Peace Conference might consider the wishes of the intelligent Negroes in the colonies themselves, the Negroes of the United States and of South America and the West Indies, the Negro Governments of Abyssinia, Liberia and Haiti, the educated Negroes in French West Africa and Equatorial Africa, and in British Uganda, Nigeria, Basutoland, Swaziland, Sierra Leone, Gold Coast, Gambia and Bechuanaland and in the Union of Africa.

"Dr. DuBois' dream is that the Peace Conference could form an internationalized Africa, to have as its basis the former German colonies, with their 1,000,000 square miles and 12,500,000 population.

"'To this,' his plan reads, 'could be added by negotiation the 800,000 square miles and 9,000,000 inhabitants of Portuguese Africa. It is not impossible that Belgium could be persuaded to add to such a State the 900,000 square miles and 9,000,000 natives of the Congo, making an international Africa with over 2,500,000 square miles of land and over 20,000,000 people.

"'This Africa for the Africans could be under the guidance of international organization. The governing international commission should represent not simply Governments, but modern culture, science, commerce, social reform, and religious philanthropy. It must represent not simply the white world, but the civilized Negro world.

" With these two principles the practical policies to be followed out in the government of the new States should involve a thorough and complete system of modern education, built upon the present government, religion, and customary law of the churches. Within ten years, 20,000,000 black children ought to be in school. Within a generation, young Africa should know the essential outlines of modern culture. From the beginning the actual general government should use both colored and white officials.

"'We can, if we will, inaugurate on the dark continent a last great crusade for humanity. With Africa redeemed, Asia would be safe and Europe indeed triumphant.'"

Members of the American delegation and associated experts assured me that no congress on this matter could be held in Paris because France was still under martial law; but the ace that I had up my sleeve was Blaise Diagne, the black deputy from Senegal and Commissaire-Général in charge of recruiting native African troops. I went to Diagne and sold him the idea of a Pan-African Congress. He consulted Clemenceau, and the matter was held up two wet, discouraging months. But finally we got permission to hold the Congress in Paris. "Don't advertise it," said Clemenceau, "but go ahead." Walter Lippmann wrote me in his crabbed hand, February 20, 1919: "I am very much interested in your organization of the Pan-African Conference, and glad that Clemenceau has made it possible. Will you send me whatever reports you may have on the work?"

The *Dispatch,* Pittsburgh, Pennsylvania, February 16, 1919, said: "Officials here are puzzled by the news from Paris that plans are going forward there for a Pan-African Conference to be held February 19. Acting Secretary Polk said today the State Department had been officially advised by the French Government that no such Conference would be held. It was announced recently that no passports would be issued for American delegates desiring to attend the meeting." But at the very time that Polk was assuring American Negroes that no Congress would be held, the Congress actually assembled in Paris.

First Pan-African Congress

This Congress represented Africa partially. Of the fifty-seven delegates from fifteen countries, nine were African countries with twelve delegates. The other delegates came from the United States, which sent sixteen, and the West Indies, with twenty-one. Most of these delegates did not come to France for this meeting, but happened to be residing there, mainly for reasons connected with the war. America and all the colonial powers refused to issue special visas.

The Congress influenced the Peace Conference. The New York *Evening Globe,* February 22, 1919, described it as "the first assembly of the kind in history, and has for its object the drafting of an appeal to the Peace Conference to give the Negro race of Africa a chance to develop unhindered by other races. Seated at long green tables in the council room today were Negroes in the trim uniform of American Army officers, other American colored men in frock coats or business suits, polished French Negroes who hold public office, Senegalese who sit in the French Chamber of Deputies. . . ."

The Congress specifically asked that the German colonies be turned over to an international organization instead of being handled by the various colonial powers. Out of this idea came the Mandates Commission. The resolutions of the Congress said in part:

"*a.* That the Allied and Associated Powers establish a code of law for the international protection of the natives of Africa, similar to the proposed international code for labor.

"*b.* That the League of Nations establish a permanent Bureau charged with the special duty of overseeing the application of these laws to the political, social, and economic welfare of the natives.

"*c.* The Negroes of the world demand that hereafter the natives of Africa and the peoples of African descent be governed according to the following principles:

"1. *The land* and its natural resources shall be held in trust for the natives and at all times they shall have effective ownership of as much land as they can profitably develop.

"2. *Capital*: The investment of capital and granting of concessions shall be so regulated as to prevent the exploitation of the natives and the exhaustion of the natural wealth of the country. Concessions shall always be limited in time and subject to State control. The growing social needs of the natives must be regarded and the profits taxed for social and material benefit of the natives.

"3. *Labor*: Slavery and corporal punishment shall be abolished and forced labor except in punishment for crime; and the general conditions of labor shall be prescribed and regulated by the State.

"4. *Education*: It shall be the right of every native child to learn to read and write his own language, and the language of the trustee nation, at public expense, and to be given technical instruction in some branch of industry. The State shall also educate as large a number of natives as possible in higher technical instruction in some branch of industry. The State shall also educate as large a number of natives as possible in higher technical and cultural training and maintain a corps of native teachers. . . .

"5. *The State*: The natives of Africa must have the right to participate in the Government as far as their development permits in conformity with the principle that the Government exists for the natives, and not the natives for the Government. They shall at once be allowed to participate in local and tribal government according to ancient usage, and this participation shall gradually extend, as education and experience proceeds, to the higher offices of State, to the end that, in time, Africa be ruled by consent of the Africans. . . . Whenever it is proven that African natives are not receiving just treatment at the hands of any State or that any State deliberately excludes its civilized citizens or subjects of Negro descent from its body politic and cultural, it shall be the duty of the League of Nations to bring the matter to the civilized world."

The New York *Herald*, Paris, February 24, 1919, said: "There is nothing unreasonable in the program, drafted at the Pan-African Congress which was held in Paris last week. It calls upon the Allied and Associated Powers to draw up an international code of law for the protection of the nations of Africa, and to create, as a section of the League of Nations, a permanent bureau to ensure obser-vance of such laws and thus further the racial, political, and economic interests of the natives."

Second Pan-African Congress

The idea of Pan-Africa having been thus established, we attempted to build a real organization. We went to work first to assemble a more authentic Pan-African Con-gress and movement. We corresponded with Negroes in all parts of Africa and in other parts of the world, and finally arranged for a Congress to meet in London, Brus-sels, and Paris, in August and September, 1921. Of the hundred and thirteen delegates to this Congress, forty-one were from Africa, thirty-five from the United States, twenty-four represented Negroes living in Europe, and seven were from the West Indies. Thus the African element showed growth. They came for the most part but not in all cases, as individuals, and more seldom as the representatives of organizations or of groups.

The Pan-African movement thus began to represent a growth and development; but it immediately ran into diffi-culties. First of all, there was the natural reaction of war and the determination on the part of certain elements in England, Belgium, and elsewhere to recoup their war losses by intensified exploitation of colonies. They were suspicious of native movements of any sort. Then, too, there came simultaneously another movement, stemming from the West Indies, which accounted for our small West Indian representation. This was in its way a people's movement rather than a movement of the intellectuals. It was led by Marcus Garvey, and it represented a poorly conceived but intensely earnest determination to unite the Negroes of the world, more especially in commercial enter-prise. It used all the nationalist and racial paraphernalia of popular agitation, and its strength lay in its backing by the masses of West Indians and by increasing numbers of American Negroes. Its weakness lay in its demagogic leadership, its intemperate propaganda, and the natural fear which it threw into the colonial powers.

The London meetings of the Congress were held in Central Hall, opposite Westminster Abbey, August 28 and 29, 1921. They were preceded by conference with the International Department of the English Labour Party, where the question of the relation of white and colored labor was discussed. Beatrice Webb, Leonard Wolf, Mr. Gillies, Norman Leys, and others were present.

Paul Otlet, once called "Father of the League of Nations," wrote me in April 1921: "I am very happy to learn your decision. We can put at your disposal the Palais Mondial for your Pan-African Conference, August 31 and September 1 and 2." Otlet and La Fontaine, the Belgian leaders of internationalism, welcomed the meeting warmly to Belgium, but strong opposition arose. The movement was immediately confounded by the press and others as a part of, if not the real, "Garvey Movement."

The Brussels *Neptune* wrote June 14: "Announcement has been made . . . of a Pan-African Congress organized at the instigation of the National Association for the Advancement of Colored People of New York. It is interesting to note that this association is directed by personages who it is said in the United States have received remuneration from Moscow (Bolsheviki). The association has already organized its propaganda in the lower Congo, and we must not be astonished if some day it causes grave difficulties in the Negro village of Kinshasa, composed of all the ne'er-do-wells of the various tribes of the Colony, aside from some hundreds of laborers."

Nevertheless, meetings of interest and enthusiasm were held. *The Crisis* reported: "The Congress itself was held in the marvelous Palais Mondial, the World Palace situated in the Cinquantenaire Park. We could not have asked for a better setting. But there was a difference. In the first place, there were many more white than colored people — there are not many of us in Brussels — and it was not long before we realized that their interest was deeper, more immediately significant, than that of the white people we had found elsewhere. Many of Belgium's economic and material interests center in Africa, in the Belgian Congo. Any interference with the natives might result in an interference with the sources from which so many Belgian capitalists drew their prosperity."

Resolutions which were passed without dissent at the meeting in London contained a statement concerning Belgium, criticizing her colonial regime although giving her credit for plans of reform for the future. This aroused bitter opposition in Brussels, and an attempt was made to substitute an innocuous statement concerning goodwill and investigation which Diagne declared adopted in the face of a clear majority in opposition.

At the Paris meeting, the original London resolutions, with some minor corrections, were adopted. They were, in part:

"To the World: The absolute equality of races, physical, political, and social, is the founding stone of world and human advancement. No one denies great differences of gift, capacity, and attainment among individuals of all races, but the voice of Science, Religion, and practical Politics is one in denying the God-appointed existence of superraces, or of races naturally and inevitably and eternally inferior.

"That in the vast range of time, one group should in its industrial technique, or social organization, or spiritual vision, lag a few hundred years behind another, or forge fitfully ahead, or come to differ decidedly in thought, deed, and ideal, is proof of the essential richness and variety of human nature, rather than proof of the coexistence of demigods and apes in human form. The doctrine of racial equality does not interfere with individual liberty: rather it fulfils it. And of all the various criteria of which masses of men have in the past been prejudged and classified, that of the color of the skin and texture of the hair is surely the most adventitious and idiotic. . . .

"The beginning of wisdom in interracial contact is the establishment of political institutions among suppressed peoples. The habit of democracy must be made to encircle the earth. Despite the attempts to prove that its practice is the secret and divine gift of the few, no habit is more natural or more widely spread among primitive people, or more easily capable of development among masses. Local self-government with a minimum of help and oversight can be established tomorrow in Asia, in Africa, America, and the Isles of the sea. It will in many instances need general control and guidance, but it will fail only when that guidance seeks ignorantly and consciously its own selfish ends and not the people's liberty and good.

"Surely in the twentieth century of the Prince of Peace, in the millennium of Mohammed, and in the mightiest Age of Human Wisdom, there can be found in the civilized world enough of altruism, yearning, and benevolence to develop native institutions whose aim is not profit and power of the few. . . .

"What, then, do those demand who see these evils of the color line and racial discrimination, and who believe in the divine right of suppressed and backward people to learn and aspire and be free? The Negro race, through their thinking intelligentsia, demand:

"1. *The recognition* of civilized men as civilized, despite their race or color.

"2. *Local self-government* for backward groups, deliberately rising as experience and knowledge grow to complete self-government under the limitation of a self-governed world.

"3. *Education* in self-knowledge, in scientific truth, and in industrial technique, undivorced from the art of beauty.

"4. *Freedom* in their own religion and social customs and with the right to be different and nonconformist.

"5. *Cooperation* with the rest of the world in government, industry, and art on the bases of Justice, Freedom, and Peace.

"6. *The return* to Negroes of their land and its natural fruits, and defense against the unrestrained greed of invested capital.

"7. *The establishment* under the League of Nations of an international institution for study of the Negro problems.

"8. *The establishment* of an international section of the Labor Bureau of the League of Nations, charged with the protection of native labor. . . .

"In some such words and thoughts as these we seek to

express our will and ideal, and the end of our untiring effort. To our aid, we call all men of the earth who love justice and mercy. Out of the depths we have cried unto the deaf and dumb masters of the world. Out of the depths we cry to our own sleeping souls. The answer is written in the stars."

The whole press of Europe took notice of these meetings, and more especially of the ideas behind the meeting. Gradually they began to distinguish between the Pan-African Movement and the Garvey agitation. They praised and criticized. Sir Harry Johnston wrote: "This is the *weakness* of all the otherwise grand efforts of the Colored People in the United States to pass on their own elevation and education and political significance to the Colored Peoples of Africa: they know so *little about real* Africa."

Even *Punch* took a good-natured jibe (September 7, 1921): "'A PAN AFRICAN MANIFESTO,' 'NO ETERNALLY INFERIOR RACES' (headlines in *The Times*). No, but in the opinion of our colored brothers some infernally superior ones!"

The Second Pan-African Congress had sent me with a committee to interview the officials of the League of Nations in Geneva. I talked with Rappard, who headed the Mandates Commission; I saw the first meeting of the Assembly; and especially I had an interesting interview with Albert Thomas, head of the I. L. O. Working with Monsieur Bellegarde of Haiti, a member of the Assembly, we brought the status of Africa to the attention of the League. The League published our petition as an official document, saying in part:

"The Second Pan-African Congress wished to suggest that the spirit of the world moves toward self-government as the ultimate aim of all men and nations, and that consequently the mandated areas, being peopled as they are so largely by black folk, have a right to ask that a man of Negro descent, properly fitted in character and training, be appointed a member of the Mandates Commission so soon as a vacancy occurs.

"The Second Pan-African Congress desires most earnestly and emphatically to ask the good offices and careful attention of the League of Nations to the condition of civilized persons of Negro descent throughout the world. Consciously and subconsciously, there is in the world today a widespread and growing feeling that it is permissible to treat civilized men as uncivilized if they are colored and more especially of Negro descent. The result of this attitude and many consequent laws, customs, and conventions is that a bitter feeling of resentment, personal insult, and despair is widespread in the world among those very persons whose rise is the hope of the Negro race.

"We are fully aware that the League of Nations has little, if any, direct power to adjust these matters, but it has the vast moral power of public world opinion, and as a body conceived to promote Peace and Justice among men. For this reason we ask and urge that the League of Nation take a firm stand on the absolute equality of races, and that it suggest to the colonial powers connected with the League of Nations to form an International Institute for the study of the Negro problem, and for the evolution and protection of the Negro race."

Later, Bellegarde revealed to the world the disgrace of the bombing of the African Bondelschwartz, and in retaliation was recalled by the American forces then in Haiti.[1]

We sought to have these meetings result in a permanent organization. A secretariat was set up in Paris and functioned for a couple of years, but it was not successful. Just as the Garvey movement made its thesis industrial cooperation, so the new young secretary of the Pan-African movement, a colored Paris public-school teacher, wanted to combine investment and profit with the idea of Pan-Africa. He wanted American Negro capital for this end. We had other ideas.

Third Pan-African Congress

This crucial difference of aim and method between our Paris office and the American Negro interested in the movement nearly ruined the organization. The Third Pan-African Congress was called for 1923, but the Paris secretary postponed it. We persevered and finally, without proper notice or preparation, met in London and Lisbon late in the year. The London session was small and was addressed by Harold Laski and Lord Olivier and attended by H. G. Wells. Ramsay MacDonald was kept from attending only by the' pending election, but wrote: "Anything I can do to advance the cause of your people on your recommendation, I shall always do gladly."

The meeting of the Congress in Lisbon was more successful. Eleven countries were represented there, and especially Portuguese Africa. The Liga Africana was in charge. "The great association of Portuguese Negroes with headquarters at Lisbon which is called the Liga Africana is an actual federation of all the indigenous associations scattered throughout the five provinces of Portuguese Africa and representing several million individuals . . . . This Liga Africana which functions at Lisbon in the very heart of Portugal, so to speak, has a commission from all the other native organizations and knows how to express to the Government in no ambiguous terms but in a highly dignified manner all that should be said to avoid injustice or to bring about the repeal of harsh laws. That is why the Liga Africana of Lisbon is the director of the Portuguese African movement; but not only in the good sense of the word, but without making any appeal to violence and without leaving constitutional limits."

Two former colonial ministers spoke, and the following demands were made for Africans:

1. *A voice* in their own government.

2. *The right* of access to the land and its resources.

3. *Trial by juries of their peers* under established forms of law.

4. *Free elementary education* for all; broad training in modern industrial technique; and higher training of selected talent.

5. *The development* of Africa for the benefit of Africans, and not merely for the profit of Europeans.

6. *The abolition* of the slave trade and of the liquor traffic.

7. *World disarmament* and the abolition of war; but

failing this, and as long as white folk bear arms against black folk, the right of blacks to bear arms in their own defense.

8. *The organization* of commerce and industry so as to make the main objects of capital and labor the welfare of the many rather than the enriching of the few. . . .

"In fine, we ask in all the world that black folk be treated as men. We can see no other road to Peace and Progress. What more paradoxical figure today fronts the world than the official head of a great South African state striving blindly to build Peace and Good Will in Europe by standing on the necks and hearts of millions of black Africans?"

From that Lisbon meeting I went to Africa for the first time, to see the land whose history and development I had so long been studying. I held from President Coolidge of the United States status as Special Minister Plenipotentiary and Envoy Extraordinary to represent him at the second inaugural of President King of Liberia.

So far, the Pan-African idea was still American rather than African, but it was growing, and it expressed a real demand for examination of the African situation and a plan of treatment from the native African point of view. With the object of moving the center of this agitation nearer other African centers of population, I planned a Fourth Pan-African Congress in the West Indies in 1925. My idea was to charter a ship and sail down the Caribbean, stopping for meetings in Jamaica, Haiti, Cuba, and the French islands. But here I reckoned without my steamship lines. At first the French Line replied that they could "easily manage the trip," but eventually no accommodation could be found on any line except at the prohibitive price of fifty thousand dollars. I suspect that colonial powers spiked this plan.

Fourth Pan-African Congress

Two years later, in 1927, a Fourth Pan-African Congress was held in New York. Thirteen countries were represented, but direct African participation lagged. There were two hundred and eight delegates from twenty-two American states and ten foreign countries. Africa was sparsely represented by representatives from the Gold Coast, Sierra Leone, Liberia, and Nigeria. Chief Amoah III of the Gold Coast spoke; Herskovits, then of Columbia [University], Mensching of Germany, and John Vandercook were on the program.

The resolution stressed six points. Negroes everywhere need:

1. *A voice* in their own government.

2. *Native rights* to the land and its natural resources.

3. *Modern education* of all children.

4. *The development* of Africa for the Africans and not merely for the profit of Europeans.

5. *The reorganization* of commerce and industry so as to make the main object of capital and labor the welfare of the many rather than the enriching of the few.

6. *The treatment* of civilized men as civilized despite difference of birth, race, or color.

The Pan-African Movement had been losing ground since 1921. In 1929, to remedy this, we made desperate efforts to hold the fifth Pan-African Congress on the continent of Africa itself, and selected Tunis because of its accessibility. Elaborate preparations were begun. It looked as though at last the movement was going to be geographically African. But two insuperable difficulties intervened: first, the French Government very politely but firmly informed us that the Congress could take place at Marseilles or any French city, but not in Africa; and finally, there came the Great Depression.

Fifth Pan-African Congress

The Pan-African idea died, apparently, until fifteen years afterwards, in the midst of the Second World War, when it leaped to life again in an astonishing manner. At the Trades Union Conference in London in the winter of 1945 there were black labor representatives from Africa and the West Indies. Among these, aided by colored persons resident in England, there came a spontaneous call for the assembling of another Pan-African Congress in 1945, when the International Trades Union had their meeting in Paris.

After consultation and correspondence, a Pan-African Federation was organized.

"On August eleventh and twelfth there was convened at Manchester, the headquarters of the Pan-African Federation, a Delegate Conference representing all of the organizations which have been invited to participate in the forthcoming Congress. At that ad hoc meeting, a review of the preparatory work was made. From the reports it revealed that the position was as follows:

"A number of replies had been received from Labor, Trade Union, Cooperative, and other progressive organizations in the West Indies, West Africa, South and East Africa, in acknowledgment of the formal invitation to attend the Conference. Most of these bodies not only approved and endorsed the agenda, making minor modifications and suggestions here and there, but pledged themselves to send delegates. In cases where either the time is too short or the difficulties of transport at the present time too great to be overcome at such short notice, the organizations will give mandates to the natives of the territories concerned who are traveling to Paris to attend the World Trades Union Conference. Where territories will not be sending delegates to the Trades Union Conference, organizations will mandate individuals already in Great Britain to represent them.

"In this way we are assured of the widest representation, either through people traveling directly from the colonial areas to Britain, or individuals from those territories who are already in the British Isles. Apart from these overseas delegates, more than fourteen organizations of Africans and peoples of African descent in Great Britain and Ireland will participate in the Conference."

There is no organization in the British colonial empire which has not been invited. The philosophy back of this meeting has been expressed by the West African Students Union of London in a letter to me:

"The idea of a Congress of African nations and all peoples of African descent throughout the world is both useful and timely. Perhaps it is even long overdue. But we observe that four of such Pan-African Congresses had been held in the past, all within recent memory, and that

he one at present under discussion will be the fifth. It is
unfortunate that all these important conferences should
have been held outside Africa, but in European capitals.
This point is significant, and should deserve our careful
attention. . . .

"Our Executive Committee are certainly not in favor of
his or any future Pan-African Congress being held anywhere in Europe. We do rather suggest the Republic of
Liberia as perhaps an ideal choice. All considerations
seem to make that country the most favorable place for
our Fifth Pan-African Congress. And, especially, at a time
like this when Liberia is planning to celebrate the centenary
of the founding of the Republic two years hence, the holding
of our Congress there seems most desirable. We have good
reason to believe that the Government of Liberia would
welcome this idea, and would give us the encouragement
and diplomatic assistance that might be necessary to ensure success."

The convening committee agrees that: "After reviewing
the situation, we do feel, like you, that our Conference
should be merely a preliminary one to a greater, more
representative Congress to be held some time next year,
especially as a new Government has come into being in
Britain since we started planning the forthcoming Conference." But they decided to call a congress this year in
Manchester; since "it is now officially announced that the
World Trades Union Conference will begin on September
twenty-fifth and close on October ninth, we are planning to
convene the Pan-African Congress on October fifteenth. It
should last a week. This will enable the colonial delegates
to get from France to England between the ninth and fifteenth of October. It will also enable us to hold some informal meetings and finish off our plans."

Difficulties of transportation and passport restrictions
may make attendance at this Congress limited. At the
same time there is real hope here that out of Africa itself,
and especially out of its laboring masses, has come a
distinct idea of unity in ideal and cooperation in action
which will lead to a real Pan-African movement.

Singularly enough, there is another "Pan-African" movement. I thought of it as I sat recently in San Francisco

and heard Jan Smuts plead for an article on "human rights" in the preamble of the Charter of the United Nations. It was an astonishing paradox. The Pan-African movement which he represents is a union of the white rulers of Kenya, Rhodesia, and Union of South Africa, to rule the African continent in the interest of its white investors and exploiters. This plan has been incubating since 1921, but has been discouraged by the British Colonial Office. Smuts is now pushing it again, and the white legislatures in Africa have asked for it. The San Francisco trusteeship left a door open for this sort of thing. Against this upsurges the movement of black union delegates working in cooperation with the labor delegates of Russia, Great Britain, and the United States in order to build a new world which includes black Africa. We may yet live to see Pan-Africa as a real movement.

George Padmore, editor, *Colonial and Coloured Unity: A Programme of Action. History of the Pan-African Congress.* London, n.d., pp. 13-26

15

HUMAN RIGHTS
FOR ALL MINORITIES

On November 7, 1945, Dr. Du Bois addressed a meeting of the East and West Association. He presented a brilliant and scholarly indictment of imperialism as it affected minority groups throughout the world which had one thing in common — the "various ways their rights have been denied." He also outlined a program for eradicating the evils he described so effectively.

You who have followed the discussion in this Peoples Congress have heard of problems of minorities as affecting Catholics, Moslems and Jews; peoples in the Pacific and peoples of Africa; the Indians and other folk in South America have been mentioned, and the minorities in Europe, especially in the Balkans; and minorities in India. There might have been further discussion of Negroes and Indians in the United States, and various minorities in China.

This covers a large number of people. Indeed so large that it is fair to say that minorities together form a majority, and the majority is a minority with power to enforce its will. But as one looks at this list of peoples, it is not at first clear that there is any interminority unity; there seems no logical or functional unity among these minorities. In certain sections and at certain times, one of these minorities might have majority power; and between them there often is friction, such as between Moslems and Jews; Africans and Indians, in the Caribbean; and native groups in China and India.

What have these groups in common save that repeatedly
and in various ways their rights have been denied? We
have seen in our own day a presidential campaign in this
land turn on the fact that one candidate was a Catholic;[1]
we have seen the Jews of Germany murdered and crucified
as seldom human beings have suffered in history; we see
a great and ancient land torn asunder with blood because
of suspicion between Hindu and Moslem; and the wail of
tortured Africa mocks Christianity today as it has for five
hundred years; in America, Negro slavery has not been
abolished; the American Indians, the peoples of the Balkans,
the inhabitants of the South Seas, the Japanese and Chinese,
all form today parts of a vast human congery of groups
subject again and again to inhuman treatment.

Beyond these facts can we see some common denomi-
nator? I believe we can. It is poverty — with the resultant
ignorance and disease of the mass of mankind and the
desperate fear of the few that they too may fall into this
disaster. This has led to the prolongation of the ancient
belief that there never has been, is not, and never will be
enough of goods and services to satisfy the needs of more
than a small minority of men; that the selection of the rich
must be an act of God or the deserved reward of human
effort; that any attempt to distribute wealth more widely
is not only sacrilege but a flying into the face of unchangeable scientific fact; that the defense of religion and civilization unfortunately but inevitably involves the continued and
persistent existence of poverty, ignorance and disease,
which may be alleviated but never eradicated.

Out of this basic myth has arisen, and persists in our
day, the denial to faiths, nations, groups and races of any
rights or privileges which infringe or threaten the status
of the privileged. Whenever a wave of sentiment, or surge
of conviction, or even scientific hypothesis starts to challenge
this basic and widespread belief of mankind, immediately
violence, hate and intolerance break forth, and we increase
denial to men of basic human rights.

Especially is this so when, as in the Reformation and the
Renaissance, a new vision of the possibilities and power of
mankind bursts forth. This was not only met by fear,
intolerance and disbelief, but by an astonishing new theory

of human effort based on the discovery of a new world, a vast migration of labor and a revolution in industrial processes more fundamental than any the world had ever seen. Not only a new prosperity, a new attack on poverty was evident, but it was accompanied by a new attack on humanity. The freeing of human energy and ingenuity in the fifteenth, sixteenth, seventeenth and eighteenth centuries was accompanied by a new degradation of labor through African slavery. The first impulsive recoil of religion and humanity from this horror of the slave trade to America was, in the face of the new wealth in crops, manufacture and commerce, quickly *rationalized* into a new defense of poverty. The rich were envisaged as the white nations of of earth, armed with a new and miraculous technique; the congenital poor were the peoples of the tropics born to be slaves and fulfill their destiny and the glory of God by working for the comfort and luxury of the whites. *But* the methods of exploitation of human toil could *not* be confined by barriers of race.

New patterns of cruelty and contempt for human beings were based on a doctrine of the inferiority of most men, which was announced as a scientific law and spread by the education of youth and the teachings of religion. This new economics regarded *all* labor — black, brown, yellow and white — as a *commodity.* It trafficked in the bodies of men in the slums of London as well as on the plantations of Virginia. Thus men built a new culture pattern in the nineteenth century, which was used even after chattel slavery of Negroes disappeared, to suppress any group different in body, thought and wish from the dominant group. It then came to be a weapon to exterminate rival groups — the German Jews, for example, were accused of taking economic opportunity from German youth. And, finally, the Church came repeatedly to be the center of propaganda against groups of different faith which did not represent the dominant majority.

These excuses, we are beginning to see clearly, come after the fact. They rationalize something that the world, or the dominant majority which calls itself the world, wants to believe to justify its acts. It is clear to those who think that what is needed in all these cases is understanding and sharing of knowledge and experience, and it is precisely this which comprehends the fundamental meaning of democracy.

Democracy is not merely a distribution of power among a vast number of individuals. It is not merely majority rule based on the fact that the majority has the physical force to prevail. It is something far more fundamental than this. It rests upon the fact that, when we have proven knowledge, interpreted through the experience of a large number of individuals, it is possible through this pooled knowledge and experience to come to decisions much more fundamental and much more far-reaching than can be had in any other way. This is so clear and logical that it needs no proof, but rests on certain fundamental assumptions. The people participating effectively in this pool of democracy must be alive and well, they must know the world which they are interpreting, and they must know themselves.

It is here that frustration of democracy comes, particularly in the case of minorities. Manifestly, there can be no hope of effective functioning of democracy among people who have not enough to eat or to live decently, among people who are sick and ignorant. Nor can we assume that poverty, ignorance and disease are always the fault of those who suffer from them. If a minority does suffer because of these disadvantages, we know immediately where the remedy lies and what we are compelled to do if we want decency and justice in the world.

We know that colonies, as centers of this frustration of democracy, are the starting point of injustice and cruelty toward all groups of people who form minority groups and who at the same time, in a sense, are the majority of the peoples of the world. And they are part of this majority even though unjustly treated minorities do not actually occupy colonial status. Often they occupy quasi-colonial status, even though segregated in the slums of a large and prosperous nation which is leading civilization.

It is, then, this colonial status that forms an integral and fundamental part of modern civilization. We must not let words mislead us and think of the modern colony as the pioneer group of Grecian days or of European exploration, when people of one country went out in search of adventure or to earn a living in another country through trade. This kind of colony in modern days changed. Either it became an independent state with its own economic organization, or it became a part of the economic organization of the mother country. In this later case in our era it was that part of our economy which illustrated and carried out logically the conception of labor as a commodity.

We know the growth of classical economics in England in the nineteenth century: its conception of the self-regulating world market, of labor and land as purchasable commodities, and of gold as the only real money. But we do not remember nor try to learn that in back of the industrial revolution, out of the experiences of which classical economics arose, lay African slavery, and that it was through the purchase of slaves in open market, where there was no floor to the price of labor, that the conception of labor as a commodity, and not as the effort of human beings, arose and became an axiom in modern industry.

Without this African slave trade it is doubtful if European labor, or even the larger part of the labor of Asia or Africa which came under its sway, could have been reduced to the commodity status. But once labor, paid at the lowest conceivable price, became the basis of prosperity in America and England under the capitalist system, then a pattern was laid which gripped the world.

It led to land seizure and land monopoly in colonial regions and in civilized lands as a method of further reducing the price of labor and increasing the profits of investors.

Thus we must conceive of colonies in the nineteenth and twentieth centuries as not something far away from the centers of civilization; not as comprehending problems which are not our problems — the local problems of London, Paris and New York. They are not something which we can consider at our leisure but rather a part of our own present local economic organization. Moreover, while the center of the colonial system (and its form and pattern) is set in the localities which are called definitely colonies and are owned politically and industrially by imperial countries, we must remember also that in the organized and dominant states there are groups of people who occupy the quasi-colonial status: laborers who are settled in the slums of large cities; groups like Negroes in the United States who are segregated physically and discriminated against spiritually in law and custom; groups like the South American Indians who are the laboring peons, without rights or privileges, of large countries; and whole laboring classes in Asia and the South Seas who are legally part of imperial countries and, as a matter of fact, have their labor treated as a commodity at the lowest wage, and the land monopolized. All these people occupy what is really a colonial status and make the kernel and substance of the problem of minorities.

The connection of these colonial and quasi-colonial conditions within our economy is so strong and intricate that we seldom realize or study it. Remember that today we depend upon colonial and quasi-colonial workers for coffee, tea and cocoa; for sugar, rubber and the increasingly valuable vegetable oils; for minerals like gold, diamonds, copper and tin; for fibers like cotton, hemp and silk; for rice, spices, quinine and gum arabic. Indeed, for a mass of materials so inextricably part of our modern life that it would practically be impossible for us to get on without them. Yet all of these materials are raised by labor which does not receive in return enough income to keep it healthy, trained or effective, or even physically able to reproduce itself. In order to force this labor to work, it is systematically deprived of ownership of land and of a share in the free bounty of nature. It is kept in ignorance, first because intelligence would bring active or passive revolt against these conditions; and secondly because the cost of education would reduce the profits which are pouring into the coffers of the investors and into our mouths and on our backs.

This means that every civilized man is part and parcel of the colonial system and is depending for his welfare and convenience, not to mention his luxury, upon the degradation of the majority of men.

Not only this but policies of suppression and repression, common in colonies and in slums, easily transport themselves to treatment of other minorities, whose oppression is not due directly to economic causes. We have all seen how racial antipathy evolves policies of religious intolerance; how economic exploitation is transmuted into color prejudice; how any refusal to submit to dominant cultural patterns, current at the particular time, tends to bring into use the whole machinery of suppression, which is born of economic exploitation. This is the basic reason for coupling in this series of lectures, religious, geographic, racial and other problems, which find their essential unity in the oppression of the poor and ignorant in segregated parts of the world known as colonies and slums; and result in widespread denial of human rights

For this reason, a more detailed study of colonial injustice may be here inserted. An excellent example is the cocoa crop. It would repay us to glance briefly at this tale of the cocoa crop as illustrating the methods of modern colonial exploitation and its results, even under a liberal administration. The world consumption of cocoa has increased from 77,000 tons in 1895 to 700,000 tons at present. Formerly three-fourths of the cocoa was raised in South America. Now two-thirds is raised in West Africa.

This development of a new industry has an interesting history. A black laborer, Tetteh Quarsie, in 1879 brought cocoa beans from Spanish Africa and distributed them among his friends on the Gold Coast, British West Africa. In 1891, eighty pounds of cocoa were raised by West African farmers. By 1936 this crop on the Gold Coast alone had been increased to 250,000 tons. It was purely an indigenous enterprise of black peasant farmers. The deeply laid plans to transfer the raising of cocoa from Spanish Africa to plantations in British West Africa, developed by the Cadbury-instituted "boycott," went astray, and the black peasants took over the job. On their own little farms, averaging about two and one-half acres, they increased crops and made the cocoa and chocolate in wide demand throughout the civilized world. Their fathers in Ashanti and Benin had fought Britain for centuries to retain ownership of this land.

For cocoa and chocolate today, consumers pay annually at least five hundred million dollars. Out of each dollar of this, less than three cents goes to the cocoa farmer; this is another instance of the manufacture of poverty out of progress.

Since the cocoa in West Africa is not raised on plantations, as it is in the West Indies and South America, the problem of the traders and manufacturers is to make profit by beating down the sale price and by manipulation of the world market. For this reason, the price to cocoa farmers varied from $44 per ton during the depression, to $188 per ton during the time of scarcity in 1927, and about $60 a ton today.

Ostensibly for correcting this price fluctuation, but really for controlling the price, the British buyers on the Gold Coast have for many years tried to come into agreement so as to make one price and one bid for all the cocoa offered. There are thirteen main buyers: the British Unilevers, Cadbury and Fry, buying for themselves and the Lyons' Teahouses; and others.

Finally, in 1937, these firms came to a buying agreement. The cocoa farmers desperately resisted. They staged a boycott for eight months, reducing the sale of cocoa from 250,000 tons to 50,000 tons. The buyers resisted. They applied pressure on the colonial office in London, and without showing it the text of the "buying agreement," induced it to advise the natives that the proposal was for their benefit and to accept it. The colonial governor, also without sight of the agreement, immediately followed this directive from London and strongly "advised" acquiescence by the natives. The natives still refused. Mr. Cadbury then went to the Gold Coast and talked to the chiefs and farmers. They demanded to see a copy of the agreement. He "regretted" that he had not brought a copy with him. Finally the British Government capitulated and sent a royal commission to the Coast. This commission secured a copy of the agreement, but made public only a part. After careful investigation, they recommended that the buying agreement be terminated and that cooperative enterprise be instituted with representation of the African farmers.

Before this plan could be implemented, however, the war broke out and the government proposed to take charge of the cocoa crop, set prices, and sell it for the farmers.

They promised to bear any losses and to distribute any profit among the farmers. This was satisfactory to the farmers, although they protested at the low price per ton which the government set in order to guard itself against loss.

The African colonial governments are virtually ruled by investors in England. Investors not only dictate the choice of governors, but these governors have broad rights of legislation under the colonial office in London. They are "advised" by councils, on which business interests are directly represented. Recently local natives have been elected to such councils; but even so, most of the real power still rests in the hands of the governor.

Government conduct of industry in West Africa is, therefore, conducted by London investors. The whole economy of the colony is rigged by outside business interests. Instead of a tax on imports to encourage local effort, the Gold Coast, for instance, claps an export duty on cocoa of $3.75 a ton; and during the war it added a surtax of $4.58, making a total of $8.33 on a ton of cocoa, for which the cocoa farmer has at times during this war received as little as $37 a ton; and on the average not more than $52 from 1939 to 1943. At the same time, English exporters of goods to Africa need pay no import tax. As a result, the cost of imported goods skyrocketed during the war, so that cotton print which sold before the war for $2.50 rose to $18, khaki from $0.60 to $3.20, and sheet iron from $1 to $20. "The result of this situation is that today many of the farmers have been completely impoverished and paralyzed economically."

However, the whole picture changed in the minds of the Negro farmers when the Labour Party came to power and took over the colonial office. Perhaps they were overoptimistic, but they were certainly justified in some degree by the results of government operations during World War II. Instead of the anticipated losses, the government in five years of operation, netted the neat profit of $25,-000,000. Indeed, if they had previously built proper storage facilities on the Gold Coast, instead of compelling farmers to sell and rush the crop immediately to Europe, regardless of prices or conditions of the market; and if they had ever encouraged simple processing operations, which would have saved freight and increased local employment; if such policies had been followed, much cocoa could have been saved from spoiling, and some 150,000 tons need not have been burned. The net profit might have been doubled.

But the Labour Party, to the indignation of the black cocoa farmers, now proposed to put all West African produce, under control of a board sitting in England, with representation of the manufacturers of cocoa and other materials, and with no representation of the farmers! In addition, instead of returning the profits of the cocoa pool to the farmers, as promised, the government now proposed to use the profits "for their benefit," including the hiring of a number of English "experts" at high salaries to protect the cocoa trees from disease. The farmers protested bitterly. They wanted the profits turned over to them and their own sons retained as experts.

Finally, after long argument and delay, the details of a new government control of West African cocoa have been announced. Two organizations are to be set up: one on the Gold Coast and one in Nigeria. These bodies are to fix the prices paid cocoa farmers, determine arrangements for purchasing, issue licenses to buyers, and set up and maintain executive machinery for purchasing, shipping and selling all the cocoa purchased. On the Gold Coast this marketing board will consist of ten members: six of these are nominated by the governor; two are nominated by local councils where the farmers have some representation; three are nominated by the merchants —which means that the power is overwhelmingly in the hands of the investors. The Nigerian cocoa-marketing board consists of members appointed solely by the governor but assisted by an advisory committee on which there will be representatives of producers and the commercial interests. In other words, the whole industry is strongly weighted in favor of the merchants. Among the most powerful of these mercantile companies is the United Africa Company.

A member of parliament recently declared: "I can give the House two quotations in regard to the United Africa

Company. The foreign secretary said at Blackpool that he was not prepared to leave the whole of Africa to the tender mercies of the United Africa Company, and the . . . gentleman who was formerly Secretary of State for the colonies, once indicated in this House that he was really frightened at the extent of the power which these monopolistic companies had; that they had even more power than certain governments."

The results of these beliefs and practices has been unrest and revolt in colonies, strikes in imperial countries, and war and suspicion among the exploiting peoples.

This turmoil has reached today a tense and frightful foreboding of increasing horror, so that we have efforts, not toward democracy and freedom, but rather toward hysterical curtailing of thought or expression of those who strive for the welfare of mankind but do not agree with the dominant majority in this nation.

There is no question as to the path that ought to be followed and, in the long run, will be followed. This path is the path of economic reorganization and reform. It means the definite refusal any longer to follow the dictates of classical economics; the definite rejection of the myth of a self-regulating world market; the refusal longer to regard labor as a commodity, or land as a private monopoly. It means a definite rejection of the idea that any one commodity, like gold, must be the inevitable measure of exchange.

What then is the clear path of reform before us? It is not merely pity and philanthropy so much as the determination of men of goodwill who are cognizant of what social science has learned in the twentieth century, to insist on four truths:

1. Poverty is unnecessary.
2. Production of goods should be planned according to need and not for private profit.
3. Distribution of goods and services should be made according to reason and right and not by chance, birth or privilege.
4. Education and health should be free and compulsory.

I mean by this a denial of the old argument, which I learned in high school, that you could not have rational distribution of wealth because there was simply not enough of the things that human beings need, to go around.

Under that belief, the world tried to distribute its bounty to certain preferred peoples; to certain persons who were superior, or thought to be superior, or who called themselves superior. That myth has been definitely put on the shelf by science; and science today knows that there can be plenty in this world for the wants of its people; not enough, of course, for everybody to wear a mink coat, or to have two automobiles; not enough for everybody to have a town house and a country villa; but enough for everybody to have sufficient to eat and to wear, and comfortable, sanitary housing. If there is any lack of these things for anybody at any time, we know perfectly well that it is because some people have more than they need or some are not contributing to the world's work as they should. It is difficult today to get people to admit that before anybody has *cake*, all human beings should have *bread*. Nevertheless, that is the inevitable ideal to which we have got to come.

Secondly, production can be *planned*. Production must *not* depend upon the individual profit which any producer may get out of the production of anything that he makes or anything he does. Production must be carefully and scientifically planned, according to the rational needs of human beings. We are beginning to do this, but we are doing it with hesitation and with a feeling that the whole program of planned industry is merely an emergency. It is not. It is a perpetual imperative.

Third, the goods and services of the world should be distributed in accordance with a rational plan. It should not be a matter of birth, chance or of good luck. We have recently been regaled by the story of a bright young man who borrowed twenty-six thousand dollars, made five million dollars, and finally enriched himself circling the world. What we do not realize is that this sort of thing makes it the legal right of anybody to take advantage of chance and monopoly, and secure for himself the services and produce of vast numbers of workers while they starve. This should be not only illegal but *immoral*. The moral ideal of distribution of goods and services according to need and desert must eventually prevail if civilization endures.

Next, *health* should be compulsory; not something which has to be bought of private individuals or doled out by charity. Governments should establish regimes to which every individual has to submit in order to avoid, so far as possible, sickness and death.

Finally, education must not be a luxury for the few or propaganda for the privileged but a compulsory discipline for every human being, at public cost. Illiteracy must become a crime.

It is perfectly clear that if we have people who live decently with a healthy and agreeable amount of work; and who know the world, past and present, with the accumulated results of scientific research — we can then begin to have a real democracy.

One of the first results of such democracy will be greater areas of freedom and less compulsion. In basic natural law — the law of gravity, of atomic weights, of the movement of the stars and the rotation of seasons — there can be *no freedom*, no argument, only *law*. If a man will eat, he must work — that is law and this law cannot be transgressed because a man is white-skinned, or because his father worked, or because he bet on the winner of the Derby. The attempt to flout this social law is disaster. On color and form, here is the freedom which is the true and inevitable child of democracy.

This is what real freedom means. With the doing away of poverty, needless sickness, premature death and investment in human degradation, we can have such freedom of expression as will let nobody tell any man whether he must believe in communism or capitalism, Christianity or Mohammedanism, but only the right freely to choose and follow his own beliefs.

This is the democracy which is the solution, and the only solution, to the problems of minorities and to the question of human rights for all men.

16

BOUND BY THE COLOR LINE

In February 1946, the left-wing weekly New Masses *sponsored a meeting at which it honored two score black and white Americans "whose achievements in the arts, sciences and public life are major contributions toward greater racial understanding." Dr. Du Bois was one of those honored, and he delivered the key address of the evening, "Bound by the Color Line."*

Many friends of American Negroes would say that we tend to emphasize our problem of race above that of the more basic problems of labor, poverty and ignorance. But to this we would reply that our problems are so fundamentally human that they often underlie the broader but more abstract social problems. Nothing illustrates this better than the history of America where development of work, income and education have had the greatest field for expansion the world has ever known; and yet continually have been hindered from the progress they might have made by problems of race and color which have been, and still form, the central thread of our history.

Despite desperate efforts to rewrite and distort this history, a few of us must recall that in 1776, when three million white Americans proclaimed the equality of all men, they were at that very moment holding five hundred thousand black folk in slavery and classifying them not even as animals but as real estate. Their prosperity had been built on two centuries of this slavery and the independence which they demanded was mainly freedom to pursue this exploitation of men in raw material and in trade.

When in the War for Independence these slaves threatened to revolt to the English, the American army not only used five thousand of them to win the war but welcomed volunteers from that Haiti which for a half century afterward they refused to recognize as a nation. The emancipation which was implicit in this use of the slave was thereupon begun in the United States, but it was halted in 1820 when the Cotton Kingdom, based on slave labor, together with plans for vaster empires centered in the Caribbean and South America, became backbone and vision of the American economy.

For the next half century the meaning of America was not the winning of the West, nor the development of democracy, as history insists, but a bitter fight as to whether American labor was to be slave or free. It flamed into bloody Civil War: a war caused by Negro slavery and in singular paradox stopped, as Abraham Lincoln himself testified, when two hundred thousand black soldiers reinforced the North and brought emancipation of both white labor and black to a nation that had never wanted it.

Thereupon the nation was faced by the logical contradiction that unless they used slaves as voters they could not control the former slaveholders or hold the United States in permanent union. Black votes and black labor, as well as white, reconstructed the union and attempted to reconstruct democracy, but northern capital and southern land monopoly bound southern labor to the chariot wheels of new free enterprise, which became powerful enough to disfranchise labor. This disfranchised labor was immediately thrown into two antagonistic competing groups by a legal caste of black folk reminiscent of the Middle Ages established by consent of the nation in the center of the twentieth century.

How in such a case could real democracy develop in this land? Remember that tonight in nine states of the Union a meeting like this would be illegal; and that in at least eight other states it would not be advisable because of the danger of mob law. Remember that today you cannot in the United States either attack this basic caste or carry out social reform by legal methods because in your way there stands a bloc of 134 electoral votes based on color caste, which makes a third-party movement impossible and prevents any clear-cut voting on education, economic security or health. It takes 126,000 of your votes to send a representative to Congress but it needs only 44,000 to send such a representative from the South. In Bilbo's Mississippi, 150,000 votes have the same power in the Senate as 6,000,000 votes in New York. These figures are so fantastic that most people do not know them and cannot believe them when they are stated. Yet it remains true that New York's 6,024,597 votes in 1944 elected the same number of Senators that Mississippi elected with 152,712. President Truman, backed by a majority of the voters of the nation, can implement no program of reform as long as the South, with political power based on disfranchisement and caste, can outcount the majority in the presidential election and in Congress.

Thus we Negroes insist that there can be no attack upon social problems by free democratic methods because we have neither freedom nor democracy. We have bound our own hands by the color line entrenched in the rotten boroughs of the South. By the same token the significance of America in the world is not freedom, democracy, education and economic security but rather alliance with colonial imperialism and class dictatorship in order to enforce the denial of freedom to the colored peoples of the world. Whatever may be the sentiment in this room and in this state or even in this section, we cannot tonight for a moment forget that there are millions of Americans of wealth, education and power who believe that the necessity of keeping black men from ever becoming free citizens is more important than the triumph of democracy in the world. Under such circumstances you cannot blame us if we stress, sometimes perhaps unduly, the importance of the Negro problem, not simply for ourselves but for you.

New Masses, February 12, 1946, p. 8.

17

BEHOLD THE LAND

In May 1934, W. E. B. Du Bois, one of the founders of the NAACP and editor of its official organ The Crisis *since its first issue in 1910, resigned from the organization's board and from editorship of the journal. He had become increasingly disillusioned with the slow, gradual process of attacking discrimination through the courts, and was more and more convinced that the Negro should build his own economic and political power along the path of socialism. Du Bois returned to Atlanta University as chairman of the Department of Sociology. In 1944 he returned to the NAACP as Director of Special Research. He delivered the following speech in Columbia, South Carolina, October 20, 1946, at the closing session of the Southern Youth Legislature, sponsored by the Southern Negro Youth Congress, and attended by 861 black and white delegates. In slightly more than two thousand words, Dr. Du Bois illuminated the basic nature of the social, political and economic life of the South.*

The future of American Negroes is in the South. Here three hundred and twenty-seven years ago, they began to enter what is now the United States of America; here they have made their greatest contribution to American culture; and here they have suffered the damnation of slavery, the frustration of Reconstruction and the lynching of emancipation. I trust then that an organization like yours is going to regard the South as the battleground of a great crusade. Here is the magnificent climate; here is the fruitful earth under the beauty of the southern sun; and here, if anywhere on earth, is the need of the thinker, the worker, and the dreamer. This is the firing line not simply for the emancipation of the American Negro but for the emancipation of the African Negro and the Negroes of the West Indies; for the emancipation of the colored races; and for the emancipation of the white slaves of modern capitalistic monopoly.

Remember here, too, that you do not stand alone. It may seem like a failing fight when the newspapers ignore you; when every effort is made by white people in the South to count you out of citizenship and to act as though you did not exist as human beings, while all the time they are profiting by your labor; gleaning wealth from your sacrifices, and trying to build a nation and a civilization upon your degradation. You must remember that despite all this, you have allies and allies even in the white South. First and greatest of these possible allies are the white working classes about you. The poor whites whom you have been taught to despise and who in turn have learned to fear and hate you. This must not deter you from efforts to make them understand, because in the past in their ignorance and suffering they have been led foolishly to look upon you as the cause of most of their distress. You must remember that this attitude is hereditary from slavery and that it has been deliberately cultivated ever since emancipation.

Slowly but surely the working people of the South, white and black, must come to remember that their emancipation depends upon their mutual cooperation; upon their acquaintanceship with each other; upon their friendship; upon their social intermingling. Unless this happens each is going to be made the football to break the heads and hearts of the other.

White youth in the South is peculiarly frustrated. There is not a single great ideal which they can express or aspire to, that does not bring them into flat contradiction with the Negro problem. The more they try to escape it, the more they land into hypocrisy, lying and double-dealing; the more they become, what they least wish to become, the oppressors and despisers of human beings. Some of them in larger and larger numbers are bound to turn toward the truth and to recognize you as brothers and sisters, as fellow travelers toward the dawn.

There has always been in the South that intellectual elite who saw the Negro problem clearly. They have always lacked, and some still lack, the courage to stand up for what they know is right. Nevertheless, they can be depended on in the long run to follow their own clear thinking and their own decent choice. Finally, even the politicians must eventually recognize the trend in the world, in this country, and in the South. James Byrnes, that favorite son of this commonwealth and secretary of state of the United States, is today occupying an indefensible and impossible position; and if he survives in the memory of men, he must begin to help establish in his own South Carolina something of that democracy which he has been recently so loudly preaching to Russia. He is the end of a long series of men whose eternal damnation is the fact that they looked *truth* in the face and did not see it; John C. Calhoun, Wade Hampton, Ben Tillman[1] are men whose names must ever be besmirched by the fact that they fought against freedom and democracy in a land which was founded upon democracy and freedom.

Eventually this class of men must yield to the writing in the stars. That great hypocrite, Jan Smuts, who today is talking of humanity and standing beside Byrnes for a United Nations, is at the same time oppressing the black people of Africa to an extent which makes their two countries, South Africa and the American South, the most reactionary peoples on earth. Peoples whose exploitation of the poor and helpless reaches the last degree of shame. They must in the long run yield to the forward march of civilization or die.

If now you young people, instead of running away from the battle here in Carolina, Georgia, Alabama, Louisiana and Mississippi, instead of seeking freedom and opportunity in Chicago and New York—which do spell opportunity—nevertheless grit your teeth and make up your minds to fight it out right here if it takes every day of your lives and the lives of your children's children; if you do this, you must in meetings like this ask your-

selves what does the fight mean? How can it be carried
on? What are the best tools, arms, and methods? And
where does it lead?

I should be the last to insist that the uplift of mankind
never calls for force and death. There are times, as both
you and I know, when

> Tho' love repine and reason chafe,
> There came a voice without reply,
> "Tis man's perdition to be safe
> When for truth he ought to die."

At the same time and even more clearly in a day like
this, after the millions of mass murders that have been
done in the world since 1914, we ought to be the last
to believe that force is ever the final word. We cannot
escape the clear fact that what is going to win in this
world is reason if this ever becomes a reasonable world.
The careful reasoning of the human mind backed by the
facts of science is the one salvation of man. The world, if
it resumes its march toward civilization, cannot ignore
reason. This has been the tragedy of the South in the
past; it is still its awful and unforgivable sin that it has
set its face against reason and against the fact. It tried to
build slavery upon freedom; it tried to build tyranny upon
democracy; it tried to build mob violence on law and law
on lynching and in all that despicable endeavor, the state
of South Carolina has led the South for a century. It
began not the Civil War — not the War between the States —
but the War to Preserve Slavery; it began mob violence
and lynching and today it stands in the front rank of
those defying the Supreme Court on disfranchisement.

Nevertheless reason can and will prevail; but of course
it can only prevail with publicity — pitiless, blatant publicity. You have got to make the people of the United
States and of the world know what is going on in the
South. You have got to use every field of publicity to
force the truth into their ears, and before their eyes. You
have got to make it impossible for any human being to
live in the South and not realize the barbarities that prevail here. You may be condemned for flamboyant methods;
for calling a congress like this; for waving your grievances

under the noses and in the faces of men. That makes no difference; it is your duty to do it. It is your duty to do more of this sort of thing than you have done in the past. As a result of this you are going to be called upon for sacrifice. It is no easy thing for a young black man or a young black woman to live in the South today and to plan to continue to live here; to marry and raise children; to establish a home. They are in the midst of legal caste and customary insults; they are in continuous danger of mob violence; they are mistreated by the officers of the law and they have no hearing before the courts and the churches and public opinion commensurate with the attention which they ought to receive. But that sacrifice is only the beginning of battle, you must rebuild this South.

There are enormous opportunities here for a new nation, a new economy, a new culture in a South really new and not a mere renewal of an old South of slavery, monopoly and race hate. There is a chance for a new cooperative agriculture on renewed land owned by the state with capital furnished by the state, mechanized and coordinated with city life. There is chance for strong, virile trade unions without race discrimination, with high wage, closed shop and decent conditions of work, to beat back and hold in check the swarm of landlords, monopolists and profiteers who are today sucking the blood out of this land. There is chance for cooperative industry, built on the cheap power of TVA and its future extensions. There is opportunity to organize and mechanize domestic service with decent hours, and high wage and dignified training.

There is a vast field for consumers' cooperation, building business on public service and not on private profit as the mainspring of industry. There is chance for a broad, sunny, healthy homelife, shorn of the fear of mobs and liquor, and rescued from lying, stealing politicians, who build the devilry on race prejudice.

Here in this South is the gateway to the colored millions of the West Indies, Central and South America. Here is the straight path to Africa, the Indies, China and the South Seas. Here is the path to the greater, freer, truer world. It would be shame and cowardice to surrender this glorious land and its opportunities for civilization and humanity to the thugs and lynchers, the mobs and profiteers, the monopolists and gamblers who today choke its soul and steal its resources. The oil and sulphur; the coal and iron; the cotton and corn; the lumber and cattle belong to you the workers, black and white, and not to the thieves who hold them and use them to enslave you. They can be rescued and restored to the people if you have the guts to strive for the real right to vote, the right to real education, the right to happiness and health and the total abolition of the father of these scourges of mankind, *poverty*.

"Behold the beautiful land which the Lord thy God hath given thee." Behold the land, the rich and resourceful land, from which for a hundred years its best elements have been running away, its youth and hope, black and white, scurrying North because they are afraid of each other, and dare not face a future of equal, independent, upstanding human beings, in a real and not a sham democracy.

To rescue this land, in this way, calls for the *Great Sacrifice*; this is the thing that you are called upon to do because it is the right thing to do. Because you are embarked upon a great and holy crusade, the emancipation of mankind, black and white; the upbuilding of democracy; the breaking down, particularly here in the South, of forces of evil represented by race prejudice in South Carolina; by lynching in Georgia; by disfranchisement in Mississippi; by ignorance in Louisiana and by all these and monopoly of wealth in the whole South.

There could be no more splendid vocation beckoning to the youth of the twentieth century, after the flat failures of white civilization, after the flamboyant establishment of an industrial system which creates poverty and the children of poverty which are ignorance and disease and crime; after the crazy boasting of a white culture that finally ended in wars which ruined civilization in the world; in the midst of allied peoples who have yelled about democracy and never practiced it either in the British Empire or in the American Commonwealth or in South Carolina.

Here is the chance for young women and young men of devotion to lift again the banner of humanity and to walk toward a civilization which will be free and intelligent; which will be healthy and unafraid; and build in the world a culture led by black folk and joined by peoples of all colors and all races — without poverty, ignorance and disease!

Once, a great German poet cried: *"Selig der den Er in Sieges Glanze findet."*

"Happy man whom Death shall find in Victory's splendor."

But I know a happier one: he who fights in despair and in defeat still fights. Singing with Arna Bontemps [2] the quiet, determined philosophy of undefeatable men:

> I thought I saw an angel flying low,
> I thought I saw the flicker of a wing
> Above the mulberry trees; but not again,
> Bethesda sleeps. This ancient pool that healed
> A host of bearded Jews does not awake.
> This pool that once the angels troubled does not move.
> No angel stirs it now, no Saviour comes
> With healing in His hands to raise the sick
> And bid the lame man leap upon the ground.
>
> The golden days are gone. Why do we wait
> So long upon the marble steps, blood
> Falling from our open wounds? and why
> Do our black faces search the empty sky?
> Is there something we have forgotten? Some precious
>   thing
> We have lost, wandering in strange lands?
>
> There was a day, I remember now,
> I beat my breast and cried, "Wash me God,"
> Wash me with a wave of wind upon
> The barley; O quiet one, draw near, draw near!
> Walk upon the hills with lovely feet
> And in the waterfall stand and speak!

18

AN APPEAL TO THE WORLD

In 1946, Dr. Du Bois, with the aid of a group of black and white scholars, prepared "An Appeal to the World," protesting the treatment of Negroes in the United States and presented it to the Commission on Human Rights of the United Nations. At first the Commission refused to receive the appeal except for filing, but eventually it was received formally by an undersecretary. At a public meeting on October 23, 1947, at the United Nations, Lake Success, New York, Walter White, executive secretary of the NAACP, made the speech of presentation. He said, "Because freedom is indivisible and can be denied to no human being anywhere on the face of the earth without abridgment of the freedom of all other human beings . . . Because injustice against black men in America has repercussion upon the status and future of brown men in India, yellow men in China, and black men in Africa, we submit that the lasting cure of the causes of war cannot be found until discrimination based on race or skin color is wiped out in the United States and throughout the world."

Making the formal presentation of the document, entitled "A Statement in the Denial of Human Rights to Minorities in the Case of the Citizens of Negro Descent in the United States of America and an Appeal to the United Nations for Redress," Dr. Du Bois stated: "This protest . . . is a frank and earnest appeal to all the world for elemental Justice against the treatment which the United States has visited upon us for three centuries. . . . It is to induce the nations of the world to persuade this nation to be just to its own people, that we have prepared and now present to you this . . . documented statement of grievances, and we firmly believe that the situation pictured here is as much your concern as ours."

The petition, a 155-page document, had an introduction by Dr. Du Bois, and subsections prepared by attorneys Earl B. Dickerson, Milton R. Konvitz, William R. Ming, Jr., and Leslie S. Perry, and the Howard University historian, Rayford W. Logan. It all added up to an irrefutable indictment of the United States in its treatment of its black citizens.

In a letter published in the New York Times of November 10, 1946, Dr. Du Bois severely denounced the barbaric treatment of eight million Africans by the South African government and condemned South African imperialism. He closed with a warning to the United Nations, writing:

"I am calling attention to all this, not simply as a plea for Africa, but as a warning to the United Nations. Is it possible to build one world, free and democratic, on the foundation of a continually enslaved Africa? Of an Africa, whose labor at twenty cents a day is in direct competition with the free labor of the world?

"Finally, what shall fifteen million Negroes in the United States, many more than the population of the Argentine, and of Belgium and Holland combined, do to secure recognition of their rights as human beings at the hands of the peoples of the world? They are in majority disfranchised. Their disfranchisement in the South makes democracy unworkable in the nation and a third-party movement impossible. Their rights of travel, domicile, use of public facilities, and right to work are widely infringed. Five thousand of them in fifty years have been lynched by mobs without trial and no lyncher has been punished; because as the attorney general of the nation admits, the law gives him no adequate ground on which to prosecute.

"Is this the way to build a new world? Is even the atomic bomb of greater importance than the freedom and manhood of 200,000,000 black men?"

The "Introduction" to the "Appeal," written by Dr. Du Bois, follows.

There were in the United States of America, 1940, 12,-865,518 citizens and residents, something less than a tenth of the nation, who form largely a segregated caste, with restricted legal rights, and many illegal disabilities. They are descendants of the Africans brought to America during the sixteenth, seventeenth, eighteenth and nineteenth centuries and reduced to slave labor. This group has no complete biological unity, but varies in color from white to black, and comprises a great variety of physical characteristics, since many are the offspring of white European-Americans as well as of Africans and American Indians. There are a large number of white Americans who also descend from Negroes but who are not counted in the colored group nor subjected to caste restrictions because the preponderance of white blood conceals their descent.

The so-called American Negro group, therefore, while it is in no sense absolutely set off physically from its fellow American, has nevertheless a strong, hereditary cultural unity, born of slavery, of common suffering, prolonged proscription and curtailment of political and civil rights; and especially because of economic and social disabilities. Largely from this fact, have arisen their cultural gifts to America — their rhythm, music and folk song; their religious faith and customs; their contribution to American art and literature; their defense of their country in every war, on land, sea and in the air; and especially the hard, continuous toil upon which the prosperity and wealth of this continent has largely been built.

The group has long been internally divided by dilemma as to whether its striving upward should be aimed at strengthening its inner cultural and group bonds, both for intrinsic progress and for offensive power against caste; or whether it should seek escape wherever and however possible into the surrounding American culture. Decision in this matter has been largely determined by outer compulsion rather than inner plan; for prolonged policies of segregation and discrimination have involuntarily welded the mass almost into a nation within a nation with its own schools, churches, hospitals, newspapers and many business enterprises.

The result has been to make American Negroes to a

wide extent provincial, introvertive, self-conscious and narrowly race-loyal; but it has also inspired them to frantic
and often successful effort to achieve, to deserve, to show
the world their capacity to share modern civilization. As
a result there is almost no area of American civilization
in which the Negro has not made creditable showing in
the face of all his handicaps.

If, however, the effect of the color caste system on the
North American Negro has been both good and bad, its
effect on white America has been disastrous. It has repeatedly led the greatest modern attempt at democratic government to deny its political ideals, to falsify its philanthropic assertions and to make its religion to a great
extent hypocritical. A nation which boldly declared "That
all men are created equal," proceeded to build its economy
on chattel slavery; masters who declared race mixture impossible, sold their own children into slavery and left a
mulatto progeny which neither law nor science can today
disentangle; churches which excused slavery as calling the
heathen to God, refused to recognize the freedom of con-
verts or admit them to equal communion. Sectional strife
over the profits of slave labor and conscientious revolt
against making human beings real estate led to bloody
civil war, and to a partial emancipation of slaves which
nevertheless even to this day is not complete. Poverty,
ignorance, disease and crime have been forced on these
unfortunate victims of greed to an extent far beyond any
social necessity; and a great nation, which today ought
to be in the forefront of the march toward peace and democracy, finds itself continuously making common cause
with race hate, prejudiced exploitation and oppression of
the common man. Its high and noble words are turned
against it, because they are contradicted in every syllable
by the treatment of the American Negro for three hundred
and twenty-eight years.

Slavery in America is a strange and contradictory story.
It cannot be regarded as mainly either a theoretical problem of morals or a scientific problem of race. From either
of these points of view, the rise of slavery in America is
simply inexplicable. Looking at the facts frankly, slavery
evidently was a matter of economics, a question of income

and labor, rather than a problem of right and wrong, or of the physical differences in men. Once slavery began to be the source of vast income for men and nations, there followed frantic search for moral and racial justifications. Such excuses were found and men did not inquire too carefully into either their logic or truth.

The twenty Negroes brought to Virginia in 1619 were not the first who had landed on this continent. For a century small numbers of Negroes had been arriving as servants, as laborers, as free adventurers. The southwestern part of the present United States was first traversed by four explorers of whom one was an African Negro. Negroes accompanied early explorers like D'Ayllon and Menendez in the southeastern United States. But just as the earlier black visitors to the West Indies were servants and adventurers and then later began to appear as laborers on the sugar plantations, so in Virginia these imported black laborers in 1619 and after came to be wanted for the raising of tobacco which was the money crop.

In the minds of the early planters, there was no distinction as to labor whether it was white or black; in law there was at first no discrimination. But as imported white labor became scarcer and more protected by law, it became less profitable than Negro labor which flooded the markets because of European slave traders, internal strife in Africa; and because in America the Negroes were increasingly stripped of legal defense. For these reasons America became a land of black slavery, and there arose first, the fabulously rich sugar empire; then the cotton kingdom, and finally colonial imperialism.

Then came the inevitable fight between free labor and democracy on the one hand, and slave labor with its huge profits on the other. Black slaves were the spearhead of this fight. They were the first in America to stage the "sit-down" strike, to slow up and sabotage the work of the plantation. They revolted time after time and no matter what recorded history may say, the enacted laws against slave revolt are unanswerable testimony as to what these revolts meant all over America.

The slaves themselves especially imperiled the whole slave system by escape from slavery. It was the fugitive slave more than the slave revolt, which finally threatened investment and income; and the organization for helping fugitive slaves through free northern Negroes and their white friends, in the guise of an underground movement, was of tremendous influence.

Finally it was the Negro soldier as a co-fighter with the whites for independence from the British economic empire which began emancipation. The British bid for his help, and the colonials against their first impulse had to bid in return and virtually to promise the Negro soldier freedom after the Revolutionary War. It was for the protection of American Negro sailors as well as white that the War of 1812 was precipitated and, after independence from England was accomplished, freedom for the black laboring class, and enfranchisement for whites and blacks was in sight.

In the meantime, however, white labor had continued to regard the United States as a place of refuge; as a place for free land; for continuous employment and high wage; for freedom of thought and faith. It was here, however, that employers intervened; not because of any moral obliquity but because the Industrial Revolution, based upon the crops raised by slave labor in the Caribbean and in the southern United States, was made possible by world trade and a new and astonishing technique; and finally was made triumphant by a vast transportation of slave labor through the British slave trade in the eighteenth and early nineteenth centuries.

This new mass of slaves became competitors of white labor and drove white labor for refuge into the arms of employers, whose interests were founded on slave labor. The doctrine of race inferiority was used to convince white labor that they had the right to be free and to vote, while the Negroes must be slaves or depress the wage of whites; western free soil became additional lure and compensation, if it could be restricted to free labor.

On the other hand, the fight of the slaveholders against democracy increased with the spread of the wealth and power of the Cotton Kingdom. Through political power based on slaves they became the dominant political force in the United States; they were successful in expanding into

Mexico and tried to penetrate the Caribbean. Finally they demanded for slavery a part of the free soil of the West, and because of this last excessive, and in fact impossible effort, a Civil War to preserve and extend slavery ensued.

This fight for slave labor was echoed in the law. The free Negro was systematically discouraged, disfranchised and reduced to serfdom. He became by law the easy victim of the kidnapper and liable to treatment as a fugitive slave. The Church, influenced by wealth and respectability, was predominately on the side of the slave owner and effort was made to make the degradation of the Negro, as a race, final by Supreme Court decision.

But from the beginning, the outcome of the Civil War was inevitable, and this not mainly on account of the predominant wealth and power of the North; it was because of the clear fact that the southern slave economy was built on black labor. If at any time the slaves or any large part of them, as workers, ceased to support the South; and if even more decisively, as fighters, they joined the North, there was no way in the world for the South to win. Just as soon then as slaves became spies for the invading northern armies, laborers for their camps and fortifications, and finally produced 200,000 trained and efficient soldiers with arms in their hands, and with the possibility of a million more, the fate of the slave South was sealed.

Victory, however, brought dilemma; if victory meant full economic freedom for labor in the South, white and black; if it meant land and education, and eventually votes, then the slave empire was doomed, and the profits of northern industry built on the southern slave foundation would also be seriously curtailed. Northern industry had a stake in the Cotton Kingdom and in the cheap slave labor that supported it. It had expanded for war industries during the fighting, encouraged by government subsidy and eventually protected by a huge tariff rampart. When war profits declined there was still prospect of tremendous postwar profits on cotton and other products of southern agriculture. Therefore, what the North wanted was not freedom and higher wage for black labor, but its control under such forms of law as would keep it cheap; and also stop its open competition with northern labor. The moral protest of abolitionists must be appeased but profitable industry was determined to control wages and government.

The result was an attempt at Reconstruction in which black labor established schools, tried to divide up the land and put a new social legislation in force. On the other hand, the power of southern landowners soon joined with northern industry to disfranchise the Negro, keep him from access to free land or to capital, and to build up the present caste system for blacks founded on color discrimination, peonage, intimidation and mob violence.

It is this fact that underlies many of the contradictions in the social and political development of the United States since the Civil War. Despite our resources and our miraculous technique; despite a comparatively high wage paid many of our workers and their consequent high standard of living, we are nevertheless ruled by wealth, monopoly and big-business organization to an astounding degree. Our railway transportation is built upon monumental economic injustice both to passengers, shippers and to different sections of the land. The monopoly of land and national resources throughout the United States, both in cities and in farming districts, is a disgraceful aftermath to the vast land heritage with which this nation started.

In 1876 the democratic process of government was crippled throughout the whole nation. This came about not simply through the disfranchisement of Negroes but through the fact that the political power of the disfranchised Negroes and of a large number of equally disfranchised whites was preserved as the basis of political power, but the wielding of that power was left in the hands and under the control of the successors to the planter dynasty in the South.

Let us examine these facts more carefully. The United States has always professed to be a democracy. She has never wholly attained her ideal, but slowly she has approached it. The privilege of voting has in time been widened by abolishing limitations of birth, religion and lack of property. After the Civil War, which abolished slavery, the nation in gratitude to the black soldiers and laborers who helped win that war, sought to admit to the suffrage all persons without distinction of "race, color or previous condition of servitude." They were warned by the great leaders of abolition, like Sumner, Stevens and Douglass, that this could only be effective, if the freedmen were given schools, land and some minimum of capital. A Freedmen's Bureau to furnish these prerequisites to effective citizenship was planned and put into partial operation. But Congress and the nation, weary of the costs of war and eager to get back to profitable industry, refused the necessary funds. The effort died, but in order to restore friendly civil government in the South the enfranchised freedmen, seventy-five percent illiterate, without land or tools, were thrown into competitive industry with a ballot in their hands. By herculean effort, helped by philanthropy and their own hard work, Negroes built a school system, bought land and cooperated in starting a new economic order in the South. In a generation they had reduced their illiteracy by half and had become wage-earning laborers and sharecroppers. They still were handicapped by poverty, disease and crime, but nevertheless the rise of American Negroes from slavery in 1860 to freedom in 1880 has few parallels in modern history.

However, opposition to any democracy which included the Negro race on any terms was so strong in the former slaveholding South, and found so much sympathy in large parts of the rest of the nation, that despite notable improvement in the condition of the Negro by every standard of social measurement, the effort to deprive him of the right to vote succeeded. At first he was driven from the polls in the South by mobs and violence; and then he was openly cheated; finally by a "gentlemen's agreement" with the North, the Negro was disfranchised in the South by a series of laws, methods of administration, court decisions and general public policy, so that today three-fourths of the Negro population of the nation is deprived of the right to vote by open and declared policy.

Most persons seem to regard this as simply unfortunate for Negroes, as depriving a modern working class of the minimum rights for self-protection and opportunity for progress. This is true as has been shown in poor educational opportunities, discrimination in work, health and protection and in the courts. But the situation is far more serious than this: the disfranchisement of the American Negro makes the functioning of all democracy in the nation difficult; and as democracy fails to function in the leading democracy in the world, it fails in the world.

Let us face the facts: the representation of the people in the Congress of the United States is based on population; members of the House of Representatives are elected by groups of approximately 275,000 to 300,000 persons living in 435 Congressional Districts. Naturally difficulties of division within state boundaries, unequal growth of population, migration from year to year, and slow adjustment of these and other changes, make equal population of these districts only approximate; but unless by and large, and in the long run, essential equality is maintained, the whole basis of democratic representation is marred and as in the celebrated "rotten borough" cases in England in the nineteenth century, representation must be eventually equalized or democracy relapses into oligarchy or even fascism.

This is exactly what threatens the United States today because of the unjust disfranchisement of the Negro and the use of his numerical presence to increase the political power of his enemies and of the enemies of democracy. The nation has not the courage to eliminate from citizenship all persons of Negro descent and thus try to restore slavery. It therefore makes its democracy unworkable by paradox and contradiction.

Let us see what effect the disfranchisement of Negroes has upon democracy in the United States. In 1944, 531 electoral votes were cast for the president of the United States. Of these, 129 came from Alabama, Arkansas, Georgia, Louisiana, Oklahoma, North and South Carolina, Texas, Virginia, Florida and Mississippi. The number of these votes and the party for which they were cast, depended principally upon the disfranchisement of the Negro and were not subject to public opinion or democratic control. They represented nearly a fourth of the power of the electoral college and yet they represented only a tenth of the actual voters.

If we take the voting population according to the census of 1940, and the vote actually cast in 1946 for members of Congress, we have a fair picture of how democracy is working in the United States. The picture is not accurate because the census figures are six years earlier than the vote; but this fact reduces rather than exaggerates the discrepancies. The following are the figures concerning the election of 1946.

United States

Total Population, 21 and over, 1940	79,863,451	
Total Voters, 1946	34,410,009	43.0%
Non-Voters: (Disfranchised, Incompetent, Careless)	45,453,442	57.0%

South Atlantic States

Total Population, 21 and over, 1940	10,402,423	
Negroes, 21 and over, 1940	2,542,366	24.4%
Actual Voters, 1946		22.2%
Non-Voters: (Disfranchised, Incompetent, Careless)		77.8%

East South Central States

Total Population, 21 and over, 1940	6,100,838	
Negroes, 21 and over	1,532,291	25.0%
Actual Voters		16.5%
Non-Voters: (Disfranchised, Incompetent, Careless)		83.5%

West South Central States

Total Population, 21 and over, 1940	7,707,724	
Negroes, 21 and over	1,382,482	17.9%
Actual Voters		14.2%
Non-Voters: (Disfranchised, Incompetent, Careless)		85.8%

Whole South

Actual Voters	18.0%
Non-Voters	82.0%

The number of persons of voting age who do not vote

in the United States is large. This is due partly to indifference; women particularly are not yet used to exercising the right to vote in large numbers. In addition to this, there is a dangerously large number of American citizens who have lost faith in voting as a means of social reform. To these must be added the incompetent and those who for various reasons cannot reach the polls. This explains why only 43 percent of the population of voting age actually voted in 1946. Rivalry and economic competition between city and country districts has led to deliberate curtailment of the power of the city vote. Notwithstanding all this, in New England, the Middle Atlantic states and the Middle and Far West, about 100,-000 persons cast their votes in a congressional election. In the sparsely settled mountain states this falls to 90,000. But where the Negro lives, in the Border states, less than 50,000 elect a congressman; while in the Deep South, where the Negro forms a large proportion of the population, men are sent to Congress by 22,000 votes; and in South Carolina by 4,000.

When we compare with this the record of the South, we see something more than indifference, carelessness and incompetence and discouragement. We see here the result of deliberate efforts not only to disfranchise the Negro but to discourage large numbers of whites from voting. In the South as a whole, eighty-two percent of the persons of voting age did not vote, and in the West South Central states this percentage reached nearly eighty-six percent.

Two tables follow which show the respective votes in three pairs of states where the same number of members of Congress were elected but the difference in number of votes cast is enormous. In the second table the number of votes cast for a single congressman is contrasted for a series of states, showing 138,000 votes to elect a congressman from Illinois and 4,000 votes to elect a congressman in South Carolina.

Election of 1946
Vote for 8 Members of Congress

Louisiana	106,009
Iowa	593,076

Vote for 9 Members of Congress

| Alabama | 179,488 |
| Minnesota | 875,005 |

Vote for 10 Members of Congress

| Georgia | 161,578 |
| Wisconsin | 983,918 |

Negro Congressmen

| Powell, New York | 32,573 in total of 53,087 |
| Dawson, Illinois | 38,040 in total of 66,885 |

Southern White Congressmen

| Dorn, South Carolina | 3,527 in total of 3,530 |
| Rankin, Mississippi | 5,429 in total of 5,429 |

How Many Voters Does It Take to Elect
a Representative in Congress?

Illinois	137,877 voters	
Rhode Island	136,197 "	
New York	104,720 "	North and West
California	101,533 "	
Iowa	74,135 "	
Kentucky	64,811 "	
North Carolina	37,685 "	
Virginia	28,207 "	Upper South
Arkansas	21,619 "	
Tennessee	19,345 "	
Alabama	19,943 "	
Texas	16,542 "	
Georgia	16,158 "	
Louisiana	13,251 "	Lower South
Mississippi	7,148 "	
South Carolina	4,393 "	

In other words while this nation is trying to carry on the government of the United States by democratic methods, it is not succeeding because of the premium which we put on the disfranchisement of the voters of the South. Moreover, by the political power based on this disfranchised vote the rulers of this nation are chosen and policies of the country determined. The number of congressmen is determined by the population of a state. The larger the number of that population which is disfranchised means greater power for the few who cast the vote. As one national Republican committeeman from Illinois declared, "The Southern states can block any amendment to the United States Constitution and nullify the desires of double their total of Northern and Western states."

According to the political power which each actual voter exercised in 1946, the southern South rated as 6.6, the Border states as 2.3 and the rest of the country as about 1.

When the two main political parties in the United States become unacceptable to the mass of voters, it is practically impossible to replace either of them by a third-party movement because of the rotten borough system based on disfranchised voters.

Not only this but who is interested in this disfranchisement and who gains power by it? It must be remembered that the South has the largest percentage of ignorance, of poverty, of disease in the nation. At the same time, and partly on account of this, it is the place where the labor movement has made the least progress; there are fewer unions and the unions are less effectively organized than in the North. Besides this, the fiercest and most successful fight against democracy in industry is centering in the South, in just that region where medieval caste conditions based mainly on color, and partly on poverty and ignorance, are more prevalent and most successful. And just because labor is so completely deprived of political and industrial power, investors and monopolists are today being attracted there in greater number and with more intensive organization than anywhere else in the United States.

Southern climate has made labor cheaper in the past. Slavery influenced and still influences the conditions under which southern labor works. There is in the South a reservoir of labor, more laborers than jobs, and competing groups eager for the jobs. Industry encourages the culture patterns which make these groups hate and fear each other. Company towns with control over education and religion are common. Machines displace many workers and increase the demand for jobs at any wage. The United States government economists declare that the dominant

characteristics of the southern labor force are: (1) greater
potential labor growth in the nation; (2) relatively larger
number of nonwhite workers (which means cheaper workers); (3) predominance of rural workers (which means
predominance of ignorant labor); (4) greater working
year span (which means child labor and the labor of
old people); (5) relatively fewer women in industrial employment. Whole industries are moving South toward this
cheaper labor. The recent concentration of investment and
monopoly in the South is tremendous.

If concentrated wealth wished to control congressmen or
senators, it is far easier to influence voters in South Carolina, Mississippi or Georgia where it requires only from
four thousand to sixteen thousand votes to elect a congressman, than to try this in Illinois, New York or Minnesota, where one hundred to one hundred and fifty thousand votes must be persuaded. This spells danger: danger
to the American way of life, and danger not simply to the
Negro, but to white folk all over the nation, and to the
nations of the world.

The federal government has for these reasons continually
cast its influence with imperial aggression throughout the
world and withdrawn its sympathy from the colored peoples and from the small nations. It has become through
private investment a part of the imperialistic bloc which
is controlling the colonies of the world. When we tried to
join the Allies in the First World War, our efforts were
seriously interfered with by the assumed necessity of ex-
tending caste legislation into our armed forces. It was
often alleged that American troops in France showed more
animosity against Negro troops than against the Germans.
During the Second World War, there was, in the Orient, in
Great Britain, and on the battlefields of France and Italy,
the same interference with military efficiency by the necessity of segregating and wherever possible subordinating
the Negro personnel of the American army.

Now and then a strong political leader has been able
to force back the power of monopoly and waste, and make
some start toward preservation of natural resources and
their restoration to the mass of the people. But such effort
has never been able to last long. Threatened collapse and

disaster gave the late President Roosevelt a chance to develop a New Deal of socialist planning for more just distribution of income under scientific guidance. But reaction intervened, and it was a reaction based on a South aptly called our "Number One Economic Problem": a region of poor, ignorant and diseased people, black and white, with exaggerated political power in the hands of a few resting on disfranchisement of voters, control of wealth and income, not simply by the South but by the investing North.

This paradox and contradiction enters into our actions, thoughts and plans. After the First World War, we were alienated from the proposed League of Nations because of sympathy for imperialism and because of race antipathy to Japan, and because we objected to the compulsory protection of minorities in Europe, which might lead to similar demands upon the United States. We joined Great Britain in determined refusal to recognize equality of races and nations; our tendency was toward isolation until we saw a chance to make inflated profits from the want which came upon the world. This effort of America to make profit out of the disaster in Europe was one of the causes of the depression of the thirties.

As the Second World War loomed, the federal government, despite the feelings of the mass of people, followed the captains of industry into attitudes of sympathy toward both fascism in Italy and Nazism in Germany. When the utter unreasonableness of fascist demands forced the United States in self-defense to enter the war, then at last the real feelings of the people were loosed and we again found ourselves in the forefront of democratic progress.

But today the paradox again looms after the Second World War. We have recrudescence of race hate and caste restrictions in the United States and of these dangerous tendencies not simply for the United States itself but for all nations. When will nations learn that their enemies are quite as often within their own country as without? It is not Russia that threatens the United States so much as Mississippi; not Stalin and Molotov but Bilbo and Rankin; internal injustice done to one's brothers is far more dangerous than the aggression of strangers from abroad.

Finally it must be stressed that the discrimination of which we complain is not simply discrimination against poverty and ignorance which the world by long custom is used to see: the discrimination practiced in the United States is practiced against American Negroes in spite of wealth, training and character. One of the contributors of this statement happens to be a white man, but the other three and the editor himself are subject to "Jim Crow" laws, and to denial of the right to vote, of an equal chance to earn a living, of the right to enter many places of public entertainment supported by their taxes. In other words, our complaint is mainly against a discrimination based mainly on color of skin, and it is that that we denounce as not only indefensible but barbaric.

It may be quite properly asked at this point to whom a petition and statement such as this should be addressed? Many persons say that this represents a domestic question which is purely a matter of internal concern; and that therefore it should be addressed to the people and government of the United States and the various states.

It must not be thought that this procedure has not already been taken. From the very beginning of this nation, in the late eighteenth century, and even before, in the colonies, decade by decade and indeed year by year, the Negroes of the United States have appealed for redress of grievances, and have given facts and figures to support their own contention.[1]

It must also be admitted that this continuous hammering upon the gates of opportunity in the United States has had effect, and that because of this, and with the help of his white fellow citizens, the American Negro has emerged from slavery and attained emancipation from chattel slavery, considerable economic independence, social security and advance in culture.

But manifestly this is not enough; no large group of a nation can lag behind the average culture of that nation, as the American Negro still does, without suffering not only itself but becoming a menace to the nation.

In addition to this, in its international relations, the United States owes something to the world; to the United Nations of which it is a part, and to the ideals which it professes to advocate. Especially is this true since the United Nations has made its headquarters in New York. The United States is in honor bound not only to protect its own people and its own interests, but to guard and respect the various peoples of the world who are its guests and allies. Because of caste custom and legislation along the color line, the United States is today in danger of encroaching upon the rights and privileges of its fellow nations. Most people of the world are more or less colored in skin; their presence at the meetings of the United Nations as participants and as visitors renders them always liable to insult and to discrimination; because they may be mistaken for Americans of Negro descent.

Not very long ago the nephew of the ruler of a neighboring American state was killed by policemen in Florida, because he was mistaken for a Negro and thought to be demanding rights which a Negro in Florida is not legally permitted to demand. Again and more recently in Illinois, the personal physician of Mahatma Gandhi, one of the great men of the world and an ardent supporter of the United Nations, was with his friends refused food in a restaurant, again because they were mistaken for Negroes. In a third case, a great insurance society in the United States in its development of a residential area, which would serve for housing the employees of the United Nations, is insisting and reserving the right to discriminate against the persons received as residents for reasons of race and color.

All these are but passing incidents, but they show clearly that a discrimination practiced in the United States against her own citizens and to a large extent a contravention of her own laws, cannot be persisted in, without infringing upon the rights of the peoples of the world and especially upon the ideals and the work of the United Nations.

This question then, which is without doubt primarily an internal and national question, becomes inevitably an international question and will in the future become more and more international, as the nations draw together. In this great attempt to find common ground and to maintain peace, it is therefore fitting and proper that the thirteen million American citizens of Negro descent should appeal to the United Nations and ask that organization in the proper way to take cognizance of a situation which deprives this group of their rights as men and citizens, and by so doing makes the functioning of the United Nations more difficult, if not in many cases impossible.

The United Nations surely will not forget that the population of this group makes it in size one of the considerable nations of the world. We number as many as the inhabitants of the Argentine or Czechoslovakia, or the whole of Scandinavia including Sweden, Norway and Denmark. We are very nearly the size of Egypt, Rumania and Yugoslavia. We are larger than Canada, Saudi Arabia, Ethiopia, Hungary or the Netherlands. We have twice as many persons as Australia or Switzerland, and more than the whole Union of South Africa. We have more people than Portugal or Peru; twice as many as Greece and nearly as many as Turkey. We have more people by far than Belgium and half as many as Spain. In sheer numbers then we are a group which has a right to be heard; and while we rejoice that other smaller nations can stand and make their wants known in the United Nations, we maintain equally that our voice should not be suppressed or ignored.

We are not to be regarded as completely ignorant, poverty-stricken, criminal or diseased people. In education our illiteracy is less than most of the peoples of Asia and South America, and less than many of the peoples of Europe. We are property holders, our health is improving rapidly and our crime rate is less than our social history and present disadvantages would justify. The census of 1940 showed that of American Negroes twenty-five years or over, one-fifth have had seven to eight years of training in grade schools; 4 percent have finished a four-year high-school course and nearly 2 percent are college graduates.

It is for this reason that American Negroes are appealing to the United Nations, and for the purposes of this appeal they have naturally turned toward the National Association for the Advancement of Colored People. This Association is not the only organization of American

Negroes; there are other and worthy organizations. Some of these have already made similar appeal and others doubtless will in the future. But probably no organization has a better right to express the wishes of this vast group of people than the National Association for the Advancement of Colored People.

The National Association for the Advancement of Colored People, incorporated in 1910, is the oldest and largest organization among American Negroes designed to fight for their political, civil and social rights. It has grown from a small body of interested persons into an organization which had enrolled at the close of 1946, 452,289 members in 1,417 branches. At present it has over a half million members throughout the United States. The Board of Directors of this organization, composed of leading colored and white citizens of the United States, has ordered this statement to be made and presented to the Commission on Human Rights of the Economic and Social Council of the United States, and to the General Assembly of the United Nations.

An Appeal to the World: A Statement on the Denial of Human Rights to Minorities in the Case of Citizens of the United States of America and an appeal to the United Nations for redress . . . Under the Editorial Supervision of W. E. Burghardt Du Bois, New York, 1947, pp. 1-14.

19

WE MUST KNOW THE TRUTH

Dr. Du Bois held the position of Director of Special Research in the NAACP until 1948 when he was dismissed from his post. His increasing radicalism brought him into sharp conflict with more conservative leaders of the organization. On June 26, 1947, at the thirty-eighth annual convention of the NAACP in Washington, D. C., Du Bois delivered his final address before the organization he had helped found and in which he was so important an influence. The speech clearly reveals his interest in socialism and communism and the struggles of the colonial countries for liberation from imperialism.

I wish to lay down and defend, four propositions:
Poverty is unnecessary.
Colonies and quasi-colonial regions are the most poverty-stricken portions of the earth and most human beings live in them.
Socialism is an attack on poverty.
The United Nations is the greatest hope of abolishing colonialism and thus abolishing poverty in all the world.
Poverty is unnecessary. Most intelligent people today, even in civilized parts of the earth, believe that it is normal and necessary that most human beings should not have enough to eat and wear and insufficient shelter; and that because of this inevitable poverty most human beings must be ignorant, diseased and to a large extent criminal. The persons who believe this mythical witchcraft are ignorant of the plain teaching of science and industrial technique of science and industrial technique especially in the nineteenth and twentieth centuries.

Yet we know better or could know better if we would use the brains with which even the most stupid are endowed. To be specific, we know that the present floods in the Missouri and Mississippi Valleys are due simply to carelessness and greed: we could dam these waters, store them in reservoirs, and use them for cheap irrigation and power production for a cost not one-tenth as great as the toll of dead farmers, lost crops and property; and ruined, rich soil which is annually taken from corn and wheat fields and deposited in the Gulf of Mexico to obstruct shipping.

We know that annually many times as many persons die of tuberculosis, cancer and heart disease as need to if we would apply our present medical knowledge; and that the lost value of their work would pay to society much more than our present medical care costs us.

We know that the money which we refuse for schools and teachers does not amount to a tenth of what we are compelled to pay for police, jails, courts and insane asylums, to take wretched care of the crime of ignorant young people whom we neglect as children, leave in ignorance during youth and imprison and hang before they are thirty.

If we were really trying to relieve the wants of men, we would not have to destroy potatoes, burn corn, let food rot in warehouses or prevent men from buying wool where wool can be raised cheapest and best, in a land like this where most of our surface is empty unused space, and where wood, iron and coal are more plentiful than anywhere else on earth, it is simply a monument to our stupidity that we should have and continue to have a housing shortage.

In fine, while it was true a thousand years ago, that human toil and energy was unable to feed, clothe and shelter all mankind, this has not been the case since the beginning of the nineteenth century; and today, with what we know of natural forces; with the land and labor at our disposal, with the known technique of processing materials and transport of goods, there is no adequate reason why a single human being on earth should not have sufficient food, clothing and shelter for healthy life.

Colonies and quasi-colonial regions are the most pover-

*ty-stricken portions of the earth and most human beings
live in them.*

We have grown into the habit of regarding colonial
questions as comparatively unimportant and far removed
from our immediate domestic interests. We can easily correct this tragic error, if we remember that we have spent
thousands of million dollars and killed millions of human
beings, and maimed and crazed tens of millions more,
mainly because of jealousy and greed arising primarily
over the control of labor, land and materials of colonial
peoples.

The basic reason for this is the fact that most of the
goods and materials which we need for living in civilized
lands comes from the land and labor of colonial people.
Colonial peoples are not simply those who live and work
in lands called colonies, but all those who live under
colonial conditions. This comprehends nearly all Asia
and Africa, most of South America and vast areas in the
islands of the sea.

Most human beings live in such lands, and here poverty
reaches a level which men in Europe and North America
simply cannot conceive. Four hundred million people in
India live on an average income of $25 a year per family;
the millions of China average no more than $30 perhaps;
the peoples of Africa probably do not average $20 a
year, while South America and the Caribbean area hardly
average $50.

This spells poverty at its harshest and crudest; and I
repeat it is unnecessary, and largely deliberate on the
part of the master nations of the world.

How can this happen? There is still in the minds of
many men the explanation of laziness and congenital stupidity as the cause of the poverty of so-called backward
peoples. In fact such people work harder than the people
in cultured lands. They furnish an astounding proportion
of the necessary goods and materials of the world, although this is largely concealed by the price system,
through which we measure value by the market price.

These prices are set by those who manipulate markets
for their own advantage. Consider, on the basis of human

needs, and not at the price paid, what we get from colonies: sugar, rice, spices, rubber, fruit, coffee, tea, cocoa, vegetable, oils, cotton, wool, flax, quinine, diamonds, gold, copper, tin, hides.

Does it make these materials less basically valuable, because after the application to them of special techniques of manufacture, the manufacturers and financiers can put so high a price on the finished product that no colonial can buy it?

Of the dollar which you pay for a box of chocolates, the cocoa farmer in West Africa gets three cents: yet chocolate is cocoa boiled with sugar and sold with fancy forms and wrappings. We are part of colonial exploitation, whenever we buy a pound of coffee and pay the machine which grinds it three times as much as the man who raises it.

Socialism is an attack on poverty

We can by our knowledge, by the use of our democratic power, prevent the concentration of political and economic power in the hands of the monopolists who rule colonies and make them the cesspools that they are.

These exploiters live in civilized lands and get their power by consent of the people living there. Many of these people are poor workers, but are deprived of their rightful democratic control by social forces and groups whose power comes from colonial exploitation.

Every leading land on earth is moving toward some form of socialism, so as to restrict the power of wealth, introduce democratic methods in industry, and stop the persistence of poverty and its children, ignorance, disease and crime.

The United Nations is the greatest hope of abolishing colonialism and thus abolishing poverty in all the world. In this situation what now is the meaning of the organization of the United Nations? The United Nations was established to stop war, we wish to stop war because otherwise civilization will end. Wars are so destructive and costly today that social reform is impossible, if world wars are to continue.

But the main and basic object of the United Nations is, of course, as everybody recognizes only preliminary.

If and when we succeed in outlawing war then the question is what can the united wisdom and effort of the peoples of the world do to uplift civilization?

The most distinct affirmation of what the world desires in this respect is the statement in the charter of the United Nations which touches upon colonies and non-self-governing peoples.

It says: "Members of the United Nations which have or assume responsibilities for administration of territories whose peoples have not yet attained a full measure of self-government recognize the principle that the interests of inhabitants of these territories are paramount, and accept as a sacred trust the obligation to promote to the utmost, within the system of international peace and security established by the present charter, the well-being of the inhabitants of these territories, and, to this end:

"*a*. To insure, with due respect for the culture of the peoples concerned, their political, economic, social, and educational advancement, their just treatment, and their protection against abuses;

"*b*. To develop self-government, to take due account of the political aspirations of the peoples, and to assist them in the progressive development of their free political institutions," according to the particular circumstances of each territory and its peoples and their varying stages of advancement; bitter and protracted opposition from the reactionary element at San Francisco developed over the acceptance of this paragraph. Why was this?

Because the United Nations in its basic charter promised to devote time and energy to the uplift politically, socially and educationally of the most poverty-striken portion of mankind. Whatever the United Nations does to implement this promise can and will be a precedent for attack on problems of poverty in the individual nations.

It makes no difference how strong and stubborn a stand the various nations may take to prevent world knowledge of their internal conditions or criticisms and interference with these conditions, this kind of reform is bound to come and is illustrated by the formation of the Commission on Human Rights.

It is here that the National Association for the Advancement of Colored People is making effort to do something toward the spread of justice and democracy in the world. We have written a book which will, when printed, extend to two hundred pages on the denial of human rights in the United States to persons of Negro descent.

We have examined in that statement the curtailment of our rights in law, in social progress and in education; and we have asked the United Nations to move toward correction of these abuses in the interest of democracy and justice.

This statement under my editorship has been written by Earl B. Dickerson, Milton R. Konvitz, William R. Ming Jr., Leslie S. Perry and Rayford W. Logan. It has already been presented to the Commission on Human Rights and there so far suppressed. It is going to be presented again to this Commission and also to the Economic and Social Council and finally to the General Assembly of the United Nations.

We hope to have the whole world eventually able to read the grievances of American Negroes in printed and widely disseminated form.

This is a beginning of methods by which we can help this parliament of man and federation of the world. But in the long run and fundamentally we can only back this up by doing away with the economic illiteracy so prevalent among us.

We must understand industrial profit; we must know what wealth is and what it means; we must stand back of democracy in industry and better methods of production and a more just distribution of wealth.

We must not let ourselves be scared and intimidated by the fear of being called Communist,[1] by the smearing of Henry Wallace,[2] by lies printed about Russia for the last thirty years or by the word-spread attempt of a monopolized and privately owned press to keep the peoples of the world from knowing the truth about work and income.

In order to support the United Nations and its wider objects and duties we must know the truth and the truth will make us free.

The Worker, July 13, 1947.

20

THE FREEDOM TO LEARN

As the post-World War II witch-hunt against Communists and all Americans of progressive thought mounted in intensity, Dr. Du Bois spoke out frequently for a return to sanity. Especially did he warn against restrictions on free inquiry in the colleges and universities and the dismissal of teachers who dared to differ with the established viewpoints. Here is Du Bois's defense of the freedom to learn. It was delivered frequently in speeches during 1948 and published early in 1949.

This is a time when any man who sincerely questions the efficiency of industrial organization in the United States is liable to be called a revolutionist, a traitor, and a liar, and to be accused of having selfish and unfair designs upon the progress and well-being of the people of this nation.

If he is so accused, no matter by whom or under what circumstances, anonymously, by rumor or innuendo, he is going to find it difficult to make answer or to prove his sincerity. He will find newspapers and radio filled with false interpretation of facts to such an extent that it is practically impossible for him to explain his belief or defend his conclusions. If he attempts to defend his position he may lose his friends, his influence, and what is more important, he may lose his chance to earn a decent living. Such a situation is one of the greatest dangers, not only to the person himself but even more to his family, his nation, and the civilization in which he lives.

What can we do about it? It is the temptation of every

civilization to think of itself as supremely modern; as the last word of accomplishment; as having reached such perfection and efficiency that any change in object or method must be regarded with fear and suppressed by force. This is the all-too-natural conclusion of those who are comfortable and reasonably content under present conditions. But for those who suffer discomfort, the poor, the ignorant and sick, this restriction upon education is not only unfair for them but fatal for their children.

The present organization of industry in the United States fears for the future, lest the great advances which we have undoubtedly made in technique and production, in transportation and distribution should be disturbed and ruined by new untried and unproven plans and doctrines. Nevertheless, it seems to wise men that now all the more it is necessary to know, to open as widely as possible the opportunity for careful study of our situation and careful training of youth to seek truth, and to judge it.

If, for instance, the United States fears the doctrines of Karl Marx and Frederick Engels; if Americans do not believe in the work and thought of Lenin and Stalin; if they regard Communism as not only dangerous but malevolent, then what this nation needs most of all is the free and open curriculum of a school where people may study and read Marx, know what Communism is or proposes to be, and learn actual facts and accomplishments.

I should think that the greatest disservice that this nation or any people could do to the United States would be to stop the study of economic change; to prevent people from pursuing knowledge of Marx and Communism, and to try not to answer the great arguments for change. But instead, to let our children believe that none of the great minds of the eighteenth, nineteenth, and twentieth centuries have advocated programs of fundamental change in our economic organization.

It is all the more dangerous to stop the education of youth and the pursuit of knowledge in any direction because of the fact that practically always some persons, some classes, and some nations are enjoying great advantage in any currect situation. Naturally, today those persons who own the capital and control the production and distribution of wealth enjoy distinct advantage, as compared with those who own little money or property, who are employees and not employers, and who have small voice in the organization or conduct of industry.

Of course, it is possible that persons who have the advantage in any particular social organization will, nevertheless, do the right thing, as far as they see it, and that the results of their actions will inure to the common good. But it is even more probable that power and influence will mislead them and work for the disadvantage of the nation. The question whether this is true or not can only be determined by honest study, by the encouragement of inquiry and argument, and by wide knowledge of the facts. To prevent this is, in the long run, to prevent progress.

What we need today, then, to ward off the threatened collapse of the civilization in which we live, is not only opposition to war as a method of human progress, but also a determination to keep the civil rights which modern civilization has gained at so vast a cost, and the possession of which is the surest preventive of war: the right to think, the right to express one's thought, the right to act in accordance with one's conclusions. Especially we should insist upon the right to learn, upon the right to have our children learn, and upon keeping our schools, uncoerced by the dominant forces of the present world, free to exercise the right to join with the great Goethe in a worldwide cry for "light, more light."

Of all the civil rights for which the world has struggled and fought for five thousand years, the right to learn is undoubtedly the most fundamental. If a people has preserved this right, then no matter how far it goes astray, no matter how many mistakes it makes, in the long run, in the unfolding of generations, it is going to come back to the right. But if at any time, or for any long period, people are prevented from thinking, children are indoctrinated with dogma, and they are made to learn not what is necessarily true but what the dominant forces in their world want them to think is true, then there is no aberration from truth and progress of which such a people may not be guilty.

We have had example upon example of this sort of thing. We have seen great priesthoods in Egypt and Babylon monopolize learning and keep the mass of people in ignorance. We have seen the Inquisition seek to make people righteous by fear and death. We have seen in the last one hundred and fifty years attempts to keep even elementary learning away from children, away from women, and away from certain classes and races.

The freedom to learn, curtailed even as it is today, has been bought by bitter sacrifice. And whatever we may think of the curtailment of other civil rights, we should fight to the last ditch to keep open the right to learn, the right to have examined in our schools not only what we believe, but what we do not believe; not only what our leaders say, but what the leaders of other groups and nations, and the leaders of other centuries have said. We must insist upon this in order to give our children the fairness of a start which will equip them with such an array of facts and such an attitude toward truth that they can have a real chance to judge what the world is and what its greater minds have thought it might be.

It is astonishing in days of crisis or disaster how quickly we turn toward the schools and assume that through them we can make people believe anything. This, of course, is a great compliment to learning, but it is an unfortunate comment upon our belief in current patterns of culture. If the school is so great an instrument of progress, then we ought at least to have the breadth of conviction that would allow us to make it the freest of our institutions and oppose bitterly any attempt to curtail learning or discussion.

Freedom always entails danger. Complete freedom never exists. But of all the freedoms of which we think, the freedom to learn is in the long run the least dangerous and the one that should be curtailed last.

The Midwest Journal, Winter 1949, pp. 9-11.

21

THE NATURE OF
INTELLECTUAL FREEDOM

*For three days, March 25, 26, and 27, 1949, under
the auspices of the National Council of the Arts, Sciences
and Professions, close to five thousand scholars, artists,
writers and other intellectuals met in a Cultural and Scientific Conference for World Peace. Naturally, Dr. Du Bois
was one of the prominent speakers, and in the panel
of writers and artists, he presented a paper which defined
at once both the scope of the creative intellectual's realm
and the limitations upon his freedom.*

Writing and publishing — knowing, expressing and thinking; dreaming and contriving, through the world-old ways
of poetry and story, drama and essay; history and the
interpretation of human emotion; experience and action —
these things occupy the broadest realm of freedom which
the mind can grasp. No sane person ever pictured freedom
everywhere and at all times. Parts of human action always have been, and always will be, subject to inexorable
law. We cannot abolish gravitation because we do not
like it; and the law of atomic weights will ever defy Congress. Even where natural law and human effort unite
to wrest life from nature, the freedom of human action
must yield in greater or lesser degree not simply to proba-
bilities or tendencies which refuse to conform entirely to
desire, but to enacted law, which insists that if we would
conquer ignorance, men must be made to learn; if we
would conquer poverty, thieves cannot be let to steal.
Many who scream for freedom, and despair because

struggling humanity is so often coerced by *Thou Shalt Not* appear to forget that, compared with the realm of physical law and even of biological and psychological compulsions, the regions where the spirit of man may range, free of all distortion and restraint, are infinitely larger, deeper and broader than the narrow margins of compulsion. Beyond that, while in our ignorance and fear, and with our utter lack of faith in the capacities of the human soul, we stand compelled here and today to remain prisoners of our bellies to an extent which disgraces our science and history. We nevertheless know that we also stand this instant tiptoe on the threshold of infinite freedoms, freedoms which outstretch this day of slavery as the universe of suns outmeasures our little earthly system.

We have but to think of the upsurging emotions of men: of the dreams and fantasies of mind, of imagination and contrivance, playing with the infinite possibilities of ever-revealing truth. We have but to let our minds contemplate for a moment what the human soul may do, once it is free to think and write and say but a morsel of what our thought is capable. Even the chained and barred fields of work and food and disease today will yield to vaster freedoms when men are let to think and talk and explore more widely in regions already really free.

There is of course a grey borderland, where human effort and natural law combine to raise food, build shelter and train the young. Here inflexible law merges with wish and will, and freedom is an indeterminate variable. Here men may restrain action in order to protect and guide ignorance and inexperience toward using freedom aright. It is in this borderland that more often too many men seek artificially to restrain such freedom as emerges for selfish and shortsighted aims. They choose ignorance, for fear too many will know; give the masses too little, so that a few may have too much; prefer hate to love, lest power change hands and prestige wane. They forget that it is the wide reaches of more complete freedom that can ultimately best teach and guide our twilight ignorance amid the inescapable iron of law. The borderland where

freedom chokes today may easily, as freedom grows, fade
into its more complete realm.

Two barriers and two alone hem us in and hurl us
back today: one, the persistent relic of ancient barbarism —
war: organized murder, maiming, destruction and insanity.
The other, the world-old habit of refusing to think ourselves, or to listen to those who do think. Against this
ignorance and intolerance we protest forever. But we do
not merely protest; we make renewed demand for freedom
in that vast kingdom of the human spirit where freedom
has ever had the right to dwell: the expressing of thought
to unstuffed ears; the dreaming of dreams by untwisted
souls.

Daniel S. Gillmor, editor, *Speaking of Peace. Report of the
Cultural and Scientific Conference for World Peace, New
York, March 25-27, 1949, under the auspices of the Na-
tional Council of the Arts, Sciences and Professions,* New
York, 1949, pp. 78-79.

22

AMERICA'S PRESSING PROBLEMS

"The peace movement in the United States is old and respectable," Dr. Du Bois *wrote in his book,* In Battle for Peace: The Story of My 83rd Birthday. *"I began to study it early and tried to get in close touch with it."* In his famous *"Credo,"* which first appeared in 1904, Du Bois wrote: *"I believe in the Prince of Peace. I believe that War is Murder."* Hence it is not surprising that when in 1949 he was asked to be the sponsor of a peace meeting in New York to bring together representatives of the nations of the world, he immediately agreed.

The Cultural and Scientific Conference for World Peace in March 1949, in which Du Bois participated, took a firm stand in favor of peaceful relations between the United States and the Soviet Union, thereby bringing down upon its participants a barrage of attacks in the press. In this era of the "Cold War," to call for peaceful relations with the Soviet Union was to risk the charge of "treason." But Du Bois was not to be intimidated. In April, he attended a world peace movement meeting in Paris, and in August 1949, he was one of twenty-five prominent Americans who were invited to attend an all-Soviet peace conference in Moscow. But only Du Bois had the courage to accept the invitation. In an address to the one thousand persons present at the Moscow peace conference, he brought greetings from the peace movement in the United States and presented a historical analysis of the reasons for the reactionary role his country was playing in world politics.

I represent millions of citizens of the United States who are just as opposed to war as you are. But it is not easy for American citizens either to know the truth about the world or to express it. This is true despite the intelligence and wealth and energy of the United States. Perhaps I can best perform my duty to my country and to the cause of world peace by taking a short time to explain the historic reasons for the part which the United States is playing in the world today. I can do this the more appropriately because I represent the large group of fourteen million Americans, one tenth of the nation, who in a sense explain America's pressing problems.

The two great advantages of the United States have been vast natural resources and effective labor force. The first effective labor force were slaves, at first both white and black, but increasingly as time went on black Africans brought in by an intense effort made by the English especially in the eighteenth century which succeeded in landing fifteen million black laborers in all the Americas from 1500 to 1800, at a cost of a hundred million souls to Africa, disrupting its culture and ruining its economy. This labor gave the world tobacco, cotton, sugar and numbers of other crops and opened America to the world. There followed an increasing migration of millions of workers chiefly from Europe who became energetic laborers with initiative and skill encouraged by the large and immediate returns from their efforts. With free land, favorable climate and freedom of trade, the individual laborer could make a living and often become rich without the necessity of any wide social control for the common good. Plenty for most workers, without socialism, marked America from 1800 to 1900.

But this was possible not only because of vast resources but also because of the slavery of the blacks. So long as a depressed class of slaves with no political nor social rights supplied a rich mass of basic materials and a whole area of personal service, the share of white capital and white labor was abnormally large. Even when the expanding mass of white labor tried to build a democratic form of government, inspired by the thinkers of the late eighteenth century, they faced the uncomfortable fact of slavery in the land of liberty. Some wanted to abolish Negro slavery forthwith: but slaves represented too much invested property and income for this to be easy. So in 1787, the United States declared "All men are equal" in the face of the fact that at the time nearly one American in every five was a slave. This was not complete hypocrisy. Most persons believed that Negro slavery could not continue without a slave trade so they arranged to suppress this African trade in twenty years and thus gradually, they hoped, the slave labor would disappear.

This did not happen, because slave labor in the United States even with a curtailed slave trade began to raise so valuable a cotton crop that this crop, by use of newly invented machinery, became one of the most profitable investments of the modern world. The spindles for spinning cotton cloth in Europe increased from five million in 1800 to 150 million in 1900 and black labor furnished the raw material. This was the Cotton Kingdom and it represented vast capital and the income of millions of people. Slavery therefore in the United States by 1820 had so firm an economic foundation that emancipation became impossible without cataclysm.

This pressure for social upheaval naturally did not come from the organizers of industry, nor from property owners, nor even at first from the white workers, who had been taught that their high wages depended on the slavery of Negroes. The pressure came primarily from the Negroes; first by their sheer physical expansion from 750,000 in 1790 to 3,000,000 in 1840, of whom nearly 400,000 had gained their freedom by purchase, escape or philanthropy. They organized systematic escape from the territory where the slave system prevailed: they joined with white men in an abolition movement; and their kin in Haiti and other West Indies Islands shook the world with bloody revolt.

But the struggle of the black slave for freedom did not gain the sympathy of the majority of citizens of the United States. This was because a persistent propaganda campaign had been spread as slave labor began to increase in value, to prove by science and religion that black men were not real men; that they were a subspecies fit only for slavery. Consequently the fight for democracy and especially the struggle for a broader social control of wealth and of individual effort was hindered and turned aside by widespread contempt for the lowest class of labor and the consequent undue emphasis put on unhampered freedom of individual effort, even at the cost of social loss and degradation. Therefore at the time when socialism and broad social control for the common good should have spread in the United States, as it was spreading in Europe, there grew on the contrary exaltation of industrial anarchy, tightening of the slave system and belief in individual or group success even at the expense of national welfare.

The catastrophe was precipitated as the workers gradually discovered that slavery of their black fellows was not to their advantage if slave labor spread to the free soil of the West. The nation went to Civil War therefore not to abolish slavery, but to limit it to the cotton states. The South was determined to spread slavery in the North and if not there, into the Caribbean and South America. This would cut northern capital off from its most valuable market, and the North fought to preserve this market. But the North could not win without the cooperation of the slaves themselves, since the slaves were raising food for the southern armies. Gradually by a general strike the Negroes began to desert to the northern armies as laborers, servants and spies, until at last 300,000 of them became armed soldiers while a million more stood ready to fight.[1] Thus American Negroes gained their freedom.

Now came the problem as to what to do with them. They were ignorant, poverty-stricken, sick. The northerners wanted to let them drift. The freedmen desperately wanted land and education. A plan of socialistic control with schools and land distribution was worked out by philanthropists, but industry rejected it as too costly and as alien to American individualism. Then came a hitch: unless the slaves were given the right to vote, their numerical voting strength would go to their white former masters, who would vote to lower the tariff on which war industry flourished and to scale the war debt owned by northern banks. Suddenly industry gave the black freedmen the vote, expecting them to fail but meantime to break the power of the planters. The Negroes did not fail; they enfranchised their white fellow workers, established public schools for all, and began a modern socialistic legislation for hospitals, prisons and land distribution. Immediately the former slave owners made a deal with the northern industrial leaders for the disfranchisement of the freedmen. The South would support the tariff and the debt. The freedmen lost the right to vote but retained their schools, poorly supported as they were by their own meager wages and northern philanthropy.

The history of the United States in the last seventy-five years has been one of the great series of events in human history. With marvelous technique based on scientific knowledge with organized expert management, vast natural resources and worldwide commerce, this country has built the greatest industrial machine in history — still capable of wide expansion. This organization is socialistic in its planning and coordination and methods but it is not under democratic control, nor are its objects those of the welfare state.

Our industry is today controlled, as George Seldes tells us, by one thousand individuals and is conducted primarily for their profit and power.[2] This does not exclude a great deal which is for the progress of America and the world, but human progress is not its main object nor its sole result. The American philosophy brought over from pioneer days was that individual success was necessarily social uplift, and today large numbers of Americans firmly believe that the success of monopolized industry controlled by an oligarchy is the success of this nation. It is not; and the high standard of living in the United States and its productive capacity is not due to monopoly and private profit, but has come in spite of this and indicates how much higher standards of living might have been reached not only in America but throughout the world, if the bounty of the United States and its industrial planning had been administered for the progress of the masses instead of the power and luxury of the few.

The power of private corporate wealth in the United States has throttled democracy and this was made possible by the color caste which followed Reconstruction after the Civil War. When the Negro was disfranchised in the South, the white South was and is owned increasingly by the industrial North. Thus, caste which deprived the mass of Negroes of political and civil rights and compelled them to accept the lowest wage, lay underneath the vast industrial profit of the years 1890 to 1900 when the greatest combinations of capital took place.

The fight of Negroes for democracy in these years was the main movement of the kind in the United States. They began to gain the sympathy and cooperation of those liberal whites who succeeded the abolitionists and who now realized that physical emancipation of a working class must be followed by political and economic emancipation or means nothing. For more than a half century this battle of a group of black and white Americans for the abolition of color caste has gone on and made striking progress: the American Negro is beginning to vote, to be admitted to labor unions and to be granted many civil rights. But the mischief and long neglect of democracy has already spread throughout the nation. A large percentage of eligible voters do not go to the polls. Democracy has no part in industry, save through the violence or threatened violence of the strike. No great American industry admits that it could or should be controlled by those who do its work. But unless democratic methods enter industry, democracy fails to function in other paths of life. Our political life is admittedly under the control of organized wealth and while the socialized organization of all our work proceeds, its management remains under oligarchical control and its objects are what that oligarchy decide. They may be beneficial decisions, they may be detrimental, but in no case are they arrived at by democratic methods.

The claim of the United States that it represents democracy in contrast to fascism or communism is patently false. Fascism is oligarchy in control of a socialized state which is run for the benefit of the oligarchs and their friends. Communism is a socialized state conducted by a group of workers for the benefit of the mass of the people. There may be little difference in the nature of the controls exercised in the United States, fascist Germany and the Soviet republics. There is a world of difference in the objects of that control. In the United States today the object is to center and increase the power of those who control organized wealth and they seek to prove to Americans that no other system is so successful in human progress. But instead of leaving proof of this to the free investigation of science, the reports of a free press, and the discussion of the public platform, today in the United States, organized wealth owns the press and chief news-gathering organs and is exercising increased control over the schools and making public discussion and even free thinking difficult and often impossible.

The cure for this and the way to change the socially planned United States into a welfare state is for the American people to take over the control of the nation in industry as well as government. This is proceeding gradually. Many Americans are not aware of this, but it is true: we conduct the post office; we are in the express and banking business; we have built the great Tennessee Valley river-control system; we exercise control in varying degrees over railroads, radio, city planning, air and water traffic; in a thousand other ways, social control for general welfare is growing and must grow in our country. But knowledge of this, of its success and of its prevalence in other lands, does not reach the mass of people. They are today being carried away by almost hysterical propaganda that the freedoms which they have and such individual initiative as remains are being threatened and that a Third World War is the only remedy.

Not all America has succumbed to this indefensible belief. The Progressive Party . . . has challenged this program; the voters in 1948 declared wide agreement but were induced by fear to vote for a man who has not carried out his promises; the Council of Arts, Sciences and Professions assembled a vast protest against war last year and the religious sect of Quakers have just issued a fine balanced statement in the same line. There are millions of other Americans who agree with these leaders of the peace movement. I bring you their greeting.

W. E. B. Du Bois, *In Battle for Peace: The Story of My 83rd Birthday, With Comment by Shirley Graham,* New York, 1952, pp. 182-86.

23

I TAKE MY STAND

On April 29, 1951, a conference, held under the auspices of the National Cultural Commission of the Communist Party of Great Britain, met at Holborn Hall, London to discuss the American threat to British culture. Defying the McCarthyites, Dr. Du Bois sent a paper to the conference which denounced the Cold-War warriors and called for a return to sanity in the United States.

The world is astonished at recent developments in the United States. Our actions and attitudes are discussed with puzzled wonder on the streets of every city in the world. Reluctantly the world is coming to believe that we actually want war; that we must have war; that in no other way can we keep our workers employed and maintain huge profits save by spending seventy thousand million dollars a year for war preparation and adding to the vast debt of over two hundred thousand millions which we already owe chiefly for war in the past.

Our present war expenditure must be increased, yet we cannot tax the rich much more since the lawyers who make the tax laws can also break them and let the bulk of wealth go untaxed. We cannot raise the taxes on the poor much higher because rising prices leave less and less to tax. Citizens have borrowed two hundred thousand million dollars on homes, farms and furniture, and the poor and middle class have spent nearly all their savings. Yet we cannot stop; either we spend more and more on top of what we are spending or our whole industrial organization, with its billions of private profit monopoly, will face collapse.

On the other hand, the Soviet Union, whom we are determined to destroy, does not at present seem willing to fight. We have warned and dared it. We have publicly and privately insulted it. We have eagerly given currency to every charge which anyone at any time makes against the Soviet Union, its economy, its morals, its plans. We thought that at last in Korea we had them where they must fight, and we prepared jauntily for World War III almost with shouts of joy.

We were sure the Russians had started the Korean uprising, were furnishing arms and were ready to march to war. Henry Wallace actually saw them and ran backwards so fast that he tripped over his own resolutions, and stepped in the faces of his friends. Still the Soviets did not fight and began instead to call for world peace, for union against the atom bomb, for peace congresses. But the United States was not misled; not they. They stopped the peace appeal. They picked up and jailed advocates of peace. They barred from our shores foreign advocates of peace, persons of the highest reputation.

Highly placed public officials and military men began openly to declare that if the Russians would not attack us, we would attack them to keep them from attacking us. The Wild Man of Tokyo, who remembers shooting down World War I veterans in Washington,[1] and who is turning Korea into a stinking desert, has received the President of the United States in audience. Whatever they talk about, the result, if MacArthur has his way, was not peace now or ever; until we seize China, conquer Southeast Asia and drop atom bombs on Moscow. Meantime, wave after wave of our young men are being trained for murder, and Congress is on the verge of calling every youth in the land for this purpose.

This is what Europe sees us set for, in contradiction to everything we once professed—liberty, free speech, truth and justice. To this our masters will lead us unless you intervene: unless right here and now you, the people of the United States, say *No! Enough of this hysteria, this crazy foolishness!*

Our slow but steady descent into belief in complete and universal war and our determination to make all men agree with what some believe, rather than to let them exercise their free American heritage of choosing truth — this literal descent into hell in our day, and in this our own country, has been so gradual and complete that many honest Americans cannot believe what they actually hear and see; and sit bewildered, rubbing their eyes in order to get some vague conception of what can have happened to the land which once declared "these truths to be self-evident, that all men are created equal; that they are endowed by their Creator with certain unalienable rights; that among these, are life, liberty, and the pursuit of happiness."

No American born before 1900 could possibly conceive that the United States would become a land approaching universal military service; with its armed forces in every continent and on every sea; pledged to conquer and control masses of mankind, order the thought and belief of the nations of the world, and ready to spend for these objects more money than it ever spent for religion, education or social uplift altogether.

When men arise and say this and try to prove its truth, every effort is made by secret police, organized spies and hired informers, by deliberate subversion of the fundamental principles of our law, to imprison, slander and silence such persons, and deprive them of earning an honest livelihood.

Avoiding all hysteria and exaggeration, all natural indignation and instinctive defense of the right of free speech and hatred of thought control, it is clear to all Americans who still dare to think, that my description of this America is true, and if true, frightening to all men who once thought of this land as the Land of the Free.

My platform then, like the platform of every honest American who still dares believe in peace and freedom, takes its unalterable stand against war and slavery. There was a day when most men believed that progress depended on war; that by war, and mainly by war, had modern men gained freedom, religion and democracy.

We believed this because we were taught this is our literature and science, in church and school, on platform and in newspaper. It was always a lie, and as war has become universal and so horrible and destructive that everybody recognizes it as murder, crippling, insanity and stark death of human culture, we realize that there is scarce a victory formerly claimed by war which mankind might not have gained more cheaply and more decently and even more completely by methods of peace. If that was true in the past, it is so clear and indisputable today that no sane being denies it. And yet of all nations of earth today, the United States alone wants war, prepares for war, forces other nations to fight and asks you and me to impoverish ourselves, give up health and schools, sacrifice our sons and daughters to a Jim Crow army, and commit suicide, for a world war that nobody wants but the rich Americans who profit by it.

If war were a matter of careful study and grave decision, of prayerful thought and solemn deliberation, we might take its fearful outbreak as at least no more than human error, soon to be stopped by decency and common sense. But when did you ever vote for war? You who have spent most of your lives in a fighting, murdering world? When did you ever have a chance to decide this matter of maiming and murder? Never! And you never will as long as an executive, of his own initiative, can start a "little police action" which costs the lives and health of over 50,000 American boys, in order that big business can interfere with the governments of Asia.

Of what are we in such deathly fear? Have we been invaded? Has anyone dropped an atom bomb on us? Have we been impoverished or enslaved by foreigners? Is our business failing, and are our millionaires disappearing? Has the rate of profit gone down, is our machinery less cunning, or our natural resources destroyed by strangers? Is there any sign that the United States of America is victim, or can be victim of any foreign country? No! Then of what are we afraid, and why are we trying to guard the earth from Pacific or Atlantic and from the North to the South Pole, unless it be from ourselves?

Our rulers are afraid of an idea; tempted by a vision of power which this idea fights. The power they crave long misled and slaughtered the peoples of Europe and Asia, and now insidiously creeps into our own fever-mad heads; and that is imperialism — world rule over the world. Once this was sought through black slavery; then it was made easy by yellow coolies; then by all "lesser breeds without the law," who could furnish a "white man's burden" and let him strut over the world, and lord it in Asia and Africa, and rule and rule without end, forever and forever. That was the vision of the nineteenth century. The fever of imperialism caught the United States as the nineteenth century died and we choked a few islands out of dying Spain. But these were but small change which whetted our appetite. With the First World War came the vision of an Imperial United States as successor of the empire on which the sun already sets. We rushed so madly at the spoils left by European empire that we brought down our whole industrial system about our own ears.

It would seem that the memory of the great depression of the thirties would convince all thinking men that war is not the path to the millennium, and that what we need is reform of our own system of work and industrial organization, before we attempt to teach the world what to think or how to live.

But what the men of big business ignored was that the industrial system which they were seeking to reinstall had already met a terrible and costly reverse; that modifications of imperialism and monopoly capitalism had already been suggested and tried. Such efforts, comprehended loosely by the name "socialism," were not invented by Russia nor first tried by Russia. On the contrary, socialism is an English, French and German conception and was tried in Russia because that unhappy land was one of the last and worst victims of the capitalist system.

If tomorrow Russia disappeared from the face of the earth, the basic problem facing the modern world would remain: why is it, with the earth's abundance, our mastery of natural forces, and our miraculous technique; with our commerce belting the earth, and goods and services pouring from our stores, factories, ships and warehouses

—why is it that, nevertheless, most human beings are starving to death, dying of preventable disease and too ignorant to know what is the matter, while a small minority are so rich that they cannot spend their income?

That is the problem which faces the world, and Russia was not the first to pose it, nor will she be the last to ask and demand answer. The nineteenth century said that this situation was inevitable and must always remain because of the natural inferiority of most men; the twentieth century knows better. It says that there can be food enough for all; that clothes and shelter for all can be provided; that most disease is preventable and that the overwhelming mass of human beings can be educated; that intelligence, health and decent comfort are not only possible, but should be demanded by all men, planned by all states, and made increasingly effective by all voters in each election.

But the powerful who today own the earth and the fullness thereof, who monopolize its industry and own its press and screen its news, have another answer. They order us to fight an idea; to "contain" and crush any dream of abolishing poverty, disease and ignorance; and to do this by organizing war, murder and destruction on any people who dare to try to plan plenty for all mankind. From the nineteenth century, they attempt to take over imperialism to bribe the workers and thinkers of the most powerful countries by high wage and privilege, in order to build a false and dishonest prosperity on the slavery and degradation, the low wage and disease, of Africa and Asia and the islands of the sea; and to pay the price for this, they demand that you, your sons and daughters, in endless stream, be murdered and crippled in endless wars.

This is why we are fighting or preparing to fight in Europe, Asia and Africa—not against an enemy, but against the idea—against the rising demand of the working classes of the world for better wage, decent housing, regular employment, medical service and schools for all.

It does not answer this worldwide demand to say that we of America have these things in greater abundance than the rest of the world, if our prosperity is based on, or seeks to base itself on, the exploitation and degradation of the rest of mankind. Remember, it is American money that owns more and more of South African mines worked by slave labor; it is American enterprise that fattens off Rhodesian copper; it is American investors who seek to dominate China, India, Korea and Burma; who are throttling the starved workers of the Near East.

Yet is it not clear that such a program is sheer insanity? That no nation, however rich and smart, can conquer this world? Have not Egypt, Assyria, Greece, Rome, Britain and Germany taught us this? And also that no idea based on truth and righteousness can ultimately be suppressed by force and murder?

I never thought I would live to see the day that free speech and freedom of opinion would be so throttled in the United States as it is today. Today in this free country, no man can be sure of earning a living, of escaping slander and personal violence, or even of keeping out of jail unless publicly and repeatedly he proclaims:

- that he hates Russia;
- that he opposes Socialism and Communism;
- that he supports wholeheartedly the war in Korea;
- that he is ready to spend any amount for further war, anywhere or at any time;
- that he is ready to fight the Soviet Union, China and any other country, or all countries together;
- that he believes in the use of the atom bomb or any other weapon of mass destruction, and regards anyone opposed as a traitor;
- that he not only believes in and consents to all these things, but is willing to spy on his neighbors and denounce them if they do not believe as he does.

The mere statement of this creed shows its absolute insanity. What can be done to bring this nation to its senses? Most people answer: nothing; just sit still; bend to the storm; if necessary, lie and join the witch-hunt, swear to God that never, never did you ever sympathize with the Russian peasants' fight to be free; that you never in your life belonged to a liberal organization, or had a friend who did; and if so, you were deceived, deluded and a damned fool.

I want progress; I want education; I want social medicine; I want a living wage and old-age security; I want employment for all and relief for the unemployed and sick; I want public works, public services and public improvements. I want freedom for my people. And because I know and you know that we cannot have these things, and at the same time fight, destroy and kill all around the world in order to make huge profit for big business; for that reason, I take my stand beside the millions in every nation and continent and cry *Peace— No More War!*

A new era of power, held and exercised by the working classes the world over, is dawning, and while its eventual form is not yet clear, its progress cannot be held back by any power of man.

Arena (London), Vol. II, June-July, 1951, pp. 50-54.

24

THE NEGRO AND
THE WARSAW GHETTO

*The following address was delivered by Dr. Du Bois
at the* Jewish Life *"Tribute to the Warsaw Ghetto Fighters,"
at the Hotel Diplomat in New York City on April 15,
1952. Dr. Du Bois emphasized that by acquaintance with
the problems of Jews and other targets of oppression, one
gets "more complete understanding" of the Negro question.*

I have been to Poland three times. The first time was
fifty-nine years ago, when I was a student at the University
of Berlin. I had been talking to my schoolmate, Stanislaus
Ritter von Estreicher. I had been telling him of the race
problem in America, which seemed to me at the time the
only race problem and the greatest social problem of the
world. He brushed it aside. He said, "You know nothing,
really, about real race problems." Then he began to tell
me about the problem of the Poles and particularly of that
part of them who were included in the German empire;
of their limited education; of the refusal to let them speak
their own language; of the few careers that they were allowed to follow; of the continued insult to their culture
and family life.

I was astonished; because race problems at the time
were to me purely problems of color, and principally of
slavery in the United States and near-slavery in Africa.
I promised faithfully that when I went on my vacation
that summer, I would stop to see him in his home at Krakow, Poland, where his father was librarian of the university.

I went down to South Germany through Switzerland to Italy, and then came back by Venice and Vienna and went out through Austria, Czechoslovakia and into German Poland and there, on the way, I had a new experience with a new race problem. I was traveling from Budapest through Hungary to a small town in Galicia, where I planned to spend the night. The cabman looked at me and asked if I wanted to stop *"unter die Juden."* I was a little puzzled, but told him "Yes." So we went to a little Jewish hotel on a small, out-of-the-way street. There I realized another problem of race or religion, I did not know which, which had to do with the treatment and segregation of large numbers of human beings. I went on to Krakow, becoming more and more aware of two problems of human groups, and then came back to the university, not a little puzzled as to my own race problem and its place in the world.

Gradually I became aware of the Jewish problem of the modern world and something of its history. In Poland I learned little because the university and its teachers and students were hardly aware themselves of what this problem was, and how it influenced them, or what its meaning was in their life. In Germany I saw it continually obtruding, but being suppressed and seldom mentioned. I remember once visiting on a social occasion in a small German town. A German student was with me and when I became uneasily aware that all was not going well, he reassured me. He whispered, "They think I may be a Jew. It's not you they object to, it's me." I was astonished. It had never occurred to me until then that any exhibition of race prejudice could be anything but color prejudice. I knew that this young man was pure German, yet his dark hair and handsome face made our friends suspicious. Then I went further to investigate this new phenomenon in my experience.

Thirteen years after that I passed again through Poland and Warsaw. It was in the darkness, both physically and spiritually. Hitler was supreme in Germany where I had been visiting for five months and I sensed the oncoming storm. I passed through Warsaw into the Soviet Union just three years before the horror fell upon that city.

But in Berlin, before I left, I sensed something of the Jewish problem and its growth in the generation since my student days. I went to the Jewish quarter one day and entered a bookstore. It was quiet and empty. After a time a man came into the room and very quietly he asked me what I was looking for. I mentioned certain books and browsed among those he pointed out. He said nothing more nor did I. I felt his suspicion and at last I wandered out. I went that night to a teacher's home. There were a few Americans and several Germans present. The curtains were carefully drawn and then the teacher spoke. He defended the Nazi program in the main—its employment, its housing and roads; but he frankly confessed that he was ashamed of the treatment of the Jews or at least some of them. He blamed some severely but he had friends among them and he was ashamed of their treatment.

Then at midnight I entered Poland. It was dark—dark not only in the smoke, but in the soul of its people, who whispered in the night as we rode slowly through the murk of the railway yards.

Then finally, three years ago I was in Warsaw. I have seen something of human upheaval in this world: the scream and shots of a race riot in Atlanta; the marching of the Ku Klux Klan; the threat of courts and police; the neglect and destruction of human habitation; but nothing in my wildest imagination was equal to what I saw in Warsaw in 1949. I would have said before seeing it that it was impossible for a civilized nation with deep religious convictions and outstanding religious institutions; with literature and art; to treat fellow human beings as Warsaw had been treated. There had been complete, planned and utter destruction. Some streets had been so obliterated that only by using photographs of the past could they tell where the street was. And no one mentioned the total of the dead, the sum of destruction, the story of crippled and insane, the widows and orphans.

The astonishing thing, of course, was the way that in the midst of all these memories of war and destruction, the people were rebuilding the city with an enthusiasm that was simply unbelievable. A city and a nation was literally rising from the dead. Then, one afternoon, I was taken out to the former ghetto. I knew all too little of its story although I had visited ghettos in parts of Europe, particularly in Frankfurt, Germany. Here there was not much to see. There was complete and total waste, and a monument. And the monument brought back again the problem of race and religion, which so long had been my own particular and separate problem. Gradually, from looking and reading, I rebuilt the story of this extraordinary resistance to oppression and wrong in a day of complete frustration, with enemies on every side: a resistance which involved death and destruction for hundreds and hundreds of human beings; a deliberate sacrifice in life for a great ideal in the face of the fact that the sacrifice might be completely in vain.

The result of these three visits, and particularly of my view of the Warsaw ghetto, was not so much clearer understanding of the Jewish problem in the world as it was a real and more complete understanding of the Negro problem. In the first place, the problem of slavery, emancipation, and caste in the United States was no longer in my mind a separate and unique thing as I had so long conceived it. It was not even solely a matter of color and physical and racial characteristics, which was particularly a hard thing for me to learn, since for a lifetime the color line had been a real and efficient cause of misery. It was not merely a matter of religion. I had seen religions of many kinds — I had sat in the Shinto temples of Japan, in the Baptist churches of Georgia, in the Catholic cathedral of Cologne and in Westminster Abbey.

No, the race problem in which I was interested cut across lines of color and physique and belief and status and was a matter of cultural patterns, perverted teaching and human hate and prejudice, which reached all sorts of people and caused endless evil to all men. So that the ghetto of Warsaw helped me to emerge from a certain social provincialism into a broader conception of what the fight against race segregation, religious discrimination, and the oppression by wealth had to become if civilization was going to triumph and broaden in the world.

I remembered now my schoolmate, Stanislaus. He has long been dead and he died refusing to be a stoolpigeon for the Nazis in conquered Poland. He gave his life for a great cause. How broad it eventually became! How much he realized that behind the Polish problem lay the Jewish problem and that all were one crime against civilization, I do not know.

I remember now one scene in Poland over a half century ago. It was of worship in a Catholic church. The peasants were crowded together and were groveling on their knees. They were in utter subjection to a powerful hierarchy. And out of that, today, they have crawled and fought and struggled. They see the light.

My friend, Gabriel D'Arboussier, an African, recently visited Warsaw and wrote: "At the entrance to the city rises an imposing mausoleum erected to the memory of the 40,000 soldiers of the Red Army who fell for the liberation of Warsaw and who are all buried there. This is no cemetery, cut off from the living, but the last resting place of these glorious dead, near whom the living come to sit and ponder the sacrifice of those to whom they owe life. Had I seen nothing else, that mausoleum alone would have taught me enough to understand the Polish people's will to peace and its attachment to the Soviet Union. But there is more to tell and it cannot be too often told: of Poland's thirty-two million inhabitants six and a half million died. There is also Warsaw, 83 percent destroyed and its population reduced from over a million to 22,000, and the poignant spectacle of the flattened ghetto."

But where are we going — whither are we drifting? We are facing war, taxation, hate and cowardice and particularly increasing division of aim and opinion within our own groups. Negroes are dividing by social classes, and selling their souls to those who want war and colonialism, in order to become part of the ruling plutarchy, and encourage their sons to kill "Gooks."[1] Among Jews there is the same dichotomy and inner strife, which forgets the bravery of the Warsaw ghetto and the bones of the thousands of dead who still lie buried in that dust. All this should lead both these groups and others to reassess and reformulate the problems of our day, whose solution belongs to no one group: the stopping of war and preparation for war; increased expenditure for schools better than we have or are likely to have in our present neglect and suppression of education; the curbing of the freedom of industry for the public welfare; and amid all this, the right to think, talk, study, without fear of starvation or jail. This is a present problem of all Americans and becomes the pressing problem of the civilized world.

Jewish Life, April 1952, pp. 14-15.

25

WHAT IS WRONG WITH
THE UNITED STATES?

On May 13, 1952, at Madison Square Garden in New York City, Dr. Du Bois delivered the keynote address at a meeting sponsored by the American Labor Party which launched its 1952 campaign for office of president of the United States. Seventeen thousand persons attended the meeting.

What is wrong with the United States? We are an intelligent, rich and powerful nation. Yet today we are confused and frightened. We fear poverty, unemployment and jail.

We are suspicious not only of enemies but especially of friends. We shrink before the world and are ready to make war on everybody. General Eisenhower has assured us that "we can lick the world" and we are preparing to spend billions of dollars to do it even when we do not know whom to fight or why or how.

Of the thirty-five civilized nations of the world, we and Japan are the only ones which have refused to sign the International Treaty promising not to resort to germ warfare; and it is widely charged that we are now using bacteria in China.

We face today a national election, to exercise the greatest prerogative of citizenship, in order to decide our future policy as to peace and war; trade and commerce; taxation, wages and prices; employment; social progress in housing, flood control, education, sickness and old age; honesty in public service; labor unions and civil rights.

These are tremendous problems before us which we are supposed to settle in broad outline, and yet apparently we will not have real opportunity to pass judgment on these questions.

We are deprived from day to day of knowledge of the real facts. Our sons fight and die and we cannot learn why or how. Deaths by bullets are reported but deaths by freezing and disease are concealed. We are allowed no free discussion on platform or over the radio; in newspapers or periodicals. Nearly every independent thinker has been silenced, while stool pigeons, traitors and professed liars picked by wealth, industry and power, can talk to the nation unhampered and ungagged.

We know that the nation is spending far more money than it is collecting or can collect, and that rising prices, pushed by huge private profits, are putting the cost of living ever beyond a decent standard of living for most of us. Our industry and continued employment depend largely on foreign trade, yet we are stopping foreign trade by cutting down imports and refusing to buy the goods we need from the nations who want to sell. Unless we continued to make weapons and war our economy may utterly collapse. Continually prices are outrunning wages, yet union labor, led too often by reactionary stupid men, is under increasing and coordinated attack, and its energies dissipated by internal division. We are spending millions on misleading advertising to increase private profit in patent medicines, toothpaste and junk. We are faced by increasing graft and stealing and lying in high office, and the highest office is afraid to investigate lest we know the thieves by name.

We are no longer free to travel, to speak our minds. We are money-mad. Greed and wealth have chained the beast of power. Yet, as my dead schoolmate once sang:

> The beast said in his breast
> > Till the mills I grind have ceased
> The riches shall be dust of dust
> > Dry ashes be the feast.

What can we do about it? How can we face and heal our plight? Not by silence, not by fear; not by voting again for the same old parties and going continually over the same mumbo jumbo of meaningless elections. We are boasting we are free when we are not free even to cast our ballots. We are peddling freedom to the world and daring them to oppose it and bribing them kindly to accept it, and dropping death on those who refuse it; while we, the real victims, whose taxes furnish the bribes and whose dead and crippled and insane children furnish the soldiers, sit and ask with vacant faces: for whom shall we vote, which candidate shall we vote for, and if you please, dear candidate—will you kindly please tell us: what the hell do you stand for anyway? Is it too much for us to ask of your Majesty?

Yet we are fooling nobody, not even ourselves. We have no choice. There are no two parties. There is no choice of candidates whether his name is Eisenhower or Taft, Kefauver or Stassen or Warren, Dulles or Dewey, Joe or Charlie McCarthy. [1] All of them listen to their master's voice, the steel trust, the aluminum trust, the rubber combine, the automobile industry; oil, power, plastics, the railroads, tobacco, copper, chemicals and Coca-Cola, telegraph and telephone; liquor, radio and movie—all of the more than two hundred giant corporations which wield the power that owns the press and the magazines, and determines what news the news agencies will print, and what the movies will screen. They are united in that super-congress of which the National Association of Manufacturers is the upper house and the United States Chamber of Commerce is the lower, which are preparing world war to rule mankind and reduce again the worker not simply to slavery but to idiocy.

W. E. B. Du Bois, *An ABC of Color*, Berlin, 1963, pp. 202-05.

26

ONE HUNDRED YEARS
OF NEGRO FREEDOM

In 1953 the campaign was launched by many Negro organizations, especially the NAACP, for full freedom by 1963, the centennial of the Emancipation Proclamation. Early in January, Freedom, *a Negro monthly published in New York City under the editorship of Paul Robeson, sponsored a dinner in connection with the campaign. Dr. Du Bois was the main speaker, and he delivered an address tracing a century of Negro freedom struggles and analyzing some of the major problems facing his people.*

A century ago this mass of intermingled African, American Indian, and European blood was nearly 90 percent slaves, and bought and sold in open market. In the year 1853 particularly, the spirits of their leaders were low, and many of them practically had surrendered the fight for freedom in the United States and looked for hope in migration. Others fought with the white abolitionists led by Garrison and Phillips but they have been almost driven to the wall. The slave owners of the South were triumphant in political power and social philosophy. It was the current scientific opinion that Negroes could not progress and that any attempt to emancipate Negro slaves in the United States meant disaster to black and white.

Contrast this with the situation of 1953. The fifteen million descendants of those Negroes are legally free men. They are, to be sure, subject to certain caste conditions in residence, employment, education and public esteem. Most of their children are in school, and from an illiteracy of over 90 percent certainly three-fourths of the Negroes ten years of age can read and write. Ninety thousand

Negro students are in college, and the number of Negro
Americans who have achieved distinction in the professions, in science and in literature and art is considerable.
Negro ownership of land and property has increased,
while lynching and mob violence against them have
greatly decreased. Their political power is such that in
the election of 1952 they were recognized as having the
balance of power in many cities and states. Of 8,500,000
Negro voters perhaps 3,750,000 voted, or 43 percent as
compared with 60 percent of the nation. This is due, naturally, to the legal and customary disfranchisement of
most Negroes living in the South. From a largely rural
people they have become 50 percent urbanized and have
migrated by millions from the former southern slave states
to the northern and western states. This has greatly increased juvenile delinquency and added to the number of
the poor, unfortunate and sick, which counteract the movement forward of the group in general.

By stressing figures illustrating this change, a story
of almost miraculous progress can be written. I myself
have many times emphasized this progress and compared
it favorably with similar progress of any group of people
at any time. On the other hand, no sooner are statements
of this sort made than there arise curiously contrasting
and contradictory conclusions. Many Americans would
say: "With such a record of progress why is there continued complaint and agitation among Negroes? How
much faster could they reasonably have been expected to
develop?" But the very fact that this nation boasts of its
democracy and freedom emphasizes the failure in the case
of a tenth of its population. Foreigners, people from Europe, especially visitors from Asia and Africa, continually
point out the discrepancies in American democracy.

Indeed, in the greatest study of the American Negro
problem ever made, conducted by the Swede, Gunnar
Myrdal, 1938-42, assisted by native and foreign students,
colored and white, the main conclusion was that the treatment of the Negro is America's greatest failure, and his
almost universal segregation, America's outstanding denial
of its own faith in human equality.[1]

Finally, among Negroes themselves there is a curious

dichotomy in their attitude toward their own history and progress. They are at once proud and ashamed. They have done well but could have done better if they had not been deliberately retarded. They see immigrant groups like the Irish, Italians and Slavs surpass them continually in accomplishment and preferment mainly because they are white.

On the other hand, there are large and increasing numbers of Negroes who are not complaining because they personally are content; their comfort may be due to their own exertions; it may be due to exceptional circumstances; it may be due to winking at color discrimination by whites or to exploitation of fellow Negroes by themselves. In any case, they are content and uncomplaining. They have adequate incomes for their standard of living and that standard as compared with the world average is reasonably high. They do not complain and they do not countenance complaint from other Negroes. They admit discrimination but point out the changes and progress. They are apt to think success is personal and failure racial.

Nevertheless, within the Negro group there certainly are those who do complain; who point to failure due to racial discrimination and not to personal fault; who point to poor schools and low wages and scarcity of good homes and jobs, and deny that the present situation is generally good or that the average is bettering so fast that radical demand for improvement should be decried.

In the midst of such contradictions it is not easy for anyone to make a satisfactory answer to the question as to how great progress the struggle for Negro freedom has made in the last century, and whether or not the progress should be regarded as satisfactory.

There are three sorts of comparisons that could be made and are made and which confuse the final answer. For a long time it has been the custom of the United States Census to compare the condition of Negroes with the corresponding facts concerning the white population. This of course is a crude and unfair comparison. There is not much to be learned by comparing a group of less than a century removed from slavery and still suffering grave social and economic discrimination with the mass of the white citizens. A much more illuminating comparison can be made by studying the social and economic classes within the Negro group. Of course the most valuable comparison would be that contrasting the group with itself at different times and places.

This kind of study of the American Negro has not been adequately done. It was started at Atlanta University in 1897 and for thirteen years investigations which made a study of the inner development of the American Negro possible were carried on by Negro scholars. It was partially pursued further at Fisk University and at Howard University, but there was no real concentration of effort on the American Negro group, and Negroes gradually lost leadership and direction in this field.

To supply this lack I tried in 1940 to rehabilitate the Atlanta University studies on a broader scale, and to interest some fifty colored institutions in the southern states in a concentrated series of social studies which might have produced the most interesting social experiment in the modern world. This project was allowed to lapse when I was retired.

In addition to the comparison between the American Negro group and the white group and the more significant comparison of the Negro group with itself at different times and places, there is also an increasingly more significant comparison of the American Negro group with other groups in the world; as for instance with various parts of Africa and with the nations of Asia, the peoples of the South Sea islands, the West Indies, South and Central America. These comparisons are important because they point out the differences between the Negro group and these other groups and the comparative influence of different environments and social developments.

Such attempts, however, bring up the question as to what the American Negro group is and with what it can be rationally compared. Is it a nation, a closed economy, a cultural unity or what? It is certainly not a nation, for its political power is limited and seldom exercised as a unit. It is not a closed economy but part of the economy of the whole nation and becoming more and more integrated. It is proportionately more largely engaged in agriculture, domestic service and common labor, and that increases its dependence on the national economy. There is some evidence of group economy where Negro professional men, businessmen and artisans serve primarily a Negro group; but it is not known how this development is growing in comparison with the general picture.

One thing is certain: the economic survival of the Negro in the South depends today on close union with the white workers, so as to present a united front against the tremendous growth of monopoly capital in the South today. This Negro group inherited and has formed a group culture with some customs, language dialects, with a growing literature and other works of art. Yet as this goes, there is increasing integration with the American culture until it is difficult to say how far there is today a distinct American Negro culture and in what direction it will probably grow.

When we compare American Negroes with other groups we are not comparing nations, nor even cultural groups; since American Negroes do not form a nation and are not likely to if their present increasingly successful fight for political integration succeeds. They will exercise political power but not as a unit, since that would contradict their fight against segregation. They do not even form a complete cultural unit, although by reason of suffering and discrimination, and by historic artistic gifts, such a culture may be deliberately cultivated and in the end will unify the Negro with other groups rather than divide them. Negro, Russian, and Irish art can flourish in the same state side by side.

The most illuminating comparison of Negro and other groups is to regard the American Negro as mainly a group of workers developing toward full political democracy in the same national government, but with a minimum of class division into exploiting employers and poor laboring classes. This working group can be compared with the working classes of other nations. But even here we must understand that the exploiting class is beginning to appear among Negroes. Its extreme development must be opposed.

How the political aspect will develop is not clear. The old idea of mass migration of Negroes to found a foreign state is unlikely to be renewed. The newer idea of an American Negro state within the United States is both improbable and undesirable. It contradicts our present effort at complete integration and also the modern tendency toward fewer rather than more separate political states with state antagonisms, hatreds and war. Cultural units may, on the other hand, develop and grow to the advantage of all.

Comparisons show that the American Negro compared with the main working groups of the world stands relatively high. His literacy is nearer to Europe than that of Asia and Africa, and far exceeds South America and the West Indies. His economic situation is far better than that of India, China, the Middle East, or any part of Africa.

Let us now turn to the question as to just what the present situation of the American Negro is, so far as it can be reduced to understandable terms. In physique, including health, reproduction and family life, the Negro is standing up well and is disappointing those prophets of doom who formerly believed that no group of Negroes in competition with the people of a white nation could survive. The Negro has survived and multiplied, and while his health is below the average of the favored nation, it is above the average of most comparable groups; and what is of greater importance, it is and for a hundred years has been steadily improving. The expectation of life has notably increased and in view of world conditions can be called above normal.

All the factors of survival, however, have been affected by the urbanization of the Negro, his industrialization and the problem of occupation. The present economic condition of American Negroes is uncertain. There is serfdom on southern plantations, lower wage differential throughout the South, and while the Negro is widely employed in industry, there is discrimination in pay even in the North, and tardiness in upgrading. He is widely employed as laborer and servant at wages too low for an American standard of living. Here again, however, he is pushing forward. The national FEPC law, while it lasted, and the few state and city laws are giving him legal help, and nearly every Negro family can look back on lower living conditions than it now enjoys.

That means, however, that the present conditions are bad in the country districts and in the city slums. In the higher grades of employment, in professions, arts and sciences, there is still lack of opportunity for Negroes and poor preparation offered; there is difference in opportunity for apprenticeship, not only in technique but in science and art. All of these things, though difficult to measure, are real and have much to do with the pessimistic attitude of most American Negroes.

Fundamental, of course, to all this, is the matter of education. Most Negro school children go to separate schools, and the Negro schools are poorer than the white schools, the differences in appropriations sometimes being fantastic and nearly always considerable. This means a vast difference of opportunity for preparation for better work and in general intelligence. It is one of the greatest hindrances of the Negro.

Then there is the matter of civil, social and political rights. They cannot be easily separated, and relate in general to the place that the black man occupies in daily American life. There is no question as to the social discrimination against these fifteen million Americans. They are either not legally allowed or unwelcome in most areas of civil life, whether it be hotels, churches, public meetings, restaurants, attendance at social functions or exercising political rights. Negroes are still widely discriminated against in voting throughout the South where more than 60 per cent of them still live.

There are other discriminations which are not so much of pressing importance as of continuous insult and psychological degradation. In twenty-nine states of the United States, for instance, marriages between whites and Negroes are automatically void, and "miscegenation" is a crime. Moreover, just what a "Negro" is under this definition, is a matter of special legislation in twenty states. Naturally, most colored people do not marry most white people and have no particular plans on the subject; but it is a continual insult to have this matter of marriage a question of statute, and sometimes of insulting legal action. This attacks a fundamental human right.

There are also all kinds of laws on ways and places where colored and white people may meet; on trains and buses, in elevators, in hotels, in public assemblies. In most cases such laws are for the most part confined to the sixteen former slave states, and vary there from custom to fierce enforcement; but where law is silent, custom intervenes. It makes the life of a black American often a nightmare—always in uncertainty, anywhere in the nation.

The Negro problem is thus on the whole a question of what has mainly been called "social equality": how far is a person of Negro descent, whether he shows it in appearance or not (indeed whether he knows it or not), liable to special treatment and particularly to insult and segregation because of that fact? In no other modern civilized country are persons subject to such caste conditions as in the United States except in the Union of South Africa.

When now we ask the question as to how soon this kind of discrimination, customary and legal, is going to disappear, considering what has happened in the last hundred years, naturally no definite answer can be given. It will, of course, gradually disappear if civilization persists, and as Negroes advance, organize and insist. It will disappear more quickly under definite statute law, than it will if left to the inertia of slowly fading custom. The color line will fade away not only by slow, natural evolution but by determined effort—the more quickly, as that effort is accelerated, and we work for:

The abolition of "Jim Crow" laws of caste, like prohibition of intermarriage, segregated travel, etc.

The passage of national and state FEPC laws.

Increasing cooperation between white and colored union labor, especially in the South, until complete integration is reached without color or race discrimination.

Universal suffrage and doing away with the "rotten borough" system.

The socialization of wealth by more suitable distribution of the results of labor.

Universal free education of the young, without segregation by religion, race, color or wealth; under the control of the state, with technical and higher learning according to wish and gift; and with systematic adult education.

Freedom, New York, January 1953.

27

ON THE FUTURE OF
THE AMERICAN NEGRO

In 1953, at the age of eighty-five, Dr. Du Bois toured the United States and publicly addressed tens of thousands. Two years before, he had been indicted, tried and acquitted on the charge of "unregistered foreign agent" in connection with leadership of the Peace Information Center. He spoke during the high point of McCarthyism, and his courage and confidence gave heart to many Americans and brought new allies to the fight against the witch-hunters. Among other speeches, Dr. Du Bois delivered the following address in several cities on this tour.

I find that audiences are fond of asking speakers to talk about the future, and most speakers are only too willing to accede to this request, since there is no immediate danger that their prophecies will be contradicted by facts. Usually, however, I avoid this proffered temptation, since my attempts at prophecy in the last half century have not been conspicuously successful. Today, therefore, I am not going to tell you what will happen in the future, because I do not know. But I am going to emphasize certain present facts and tendencies of which I am afraid you are not fully aware.

Social problems change more often and in more ways than physical problems because of the unpredictable variations in human feelings and choices. Probably most of these emotions and conclusions are subject more or less indirectly to the same physical laws as those which dominate sticks and stones. But there is enough of volition to make it necessary for persons who are studying a human problem or trying to conduct their action in accordance with its present manifestations, to keep a wary eye on changes and current facts.

For instance, in the United States during the young manhood of Frederick Douglass the Negro problem was the problem of slavery. There were, of course, minor and connected problems, but they were all subjected to the main problem of human freedom. Then suddenly, between 1863 and 1876 the Negro problem became a problem of political enfranchisement and party government, which rapidly descended into race war, leading to temporary attempts to grapple with problems of work and education, but finally ending in practical disfranchisement of the Negro race in 1876. From 1876 until our day, the race problem in the United States has been primarily a struggle to regain the right to vote, in the midst of caste discrimination, changing slowly but definitely to a problem of the right to work and to be trained for work at all levels; and to a struggle for broad civil and social rights.

Most of you, I think, assume that this is still the Negro problem, but you must be warned that it is not wholly or mainly that; and the reason that it is not is because of the fundamental changes now spreading over the world. Whereas in the nineteenth century the world thought that progress and emancipation were coming from popular education and universal suffrage, we now know that more fundamental than these important rights is the economic organization of the world; that is, the way in which the labor of human beings is organized to satisfy human needs. This question is so fundamental that all other questions of political power, education and human happiness depend upon it. This is the basic reason for the rise of philanthropy, socialism, and the attempt at complete realization of socialism through communism. It is immaterial whether or not you like or accept socialism or communism. The absolute compulsion of your facing the problem which they try to solve is inescapable.

While I am sure most of you realize this worldwide change of emphasis, I doubt if you see how this affects the Negro problem, because most American Negroes of education and property have long since oversimplified their problem and tried to separate it from all other social problems. They conceive that their fight is simply to have the same rights and privileges as other American citizens. They do not for a moment stop to question how far the organization of work and distribution of wealth in America is perfect, nor do they for a moment conceive that the economic organization of America may have fundamental injustices and shortcomings which seriously affect not only Negroes, but the world.

Just as Booker T. Washington in his day assumed that American ideals were complete and right, and that all we had to do was to fight to imitate and attain them, so today we Negroes are largely quite swept away by the miracles of American industry, the huge accumulation of wealth, and the conspicuous expenditure which we find about us. Our idea of heaven is to be rich Americans, to make the kind of show in home, dress and automobiles that is so popular in America, and to suffer, in our effort to be able to do these things, no discrimination on account of race or color.

This is dangerously shortsighted. We American Negroes are part of the working force of the world. Not only do we represent an important segment of the American working class, but also of the working class of Europe, Asia and Africa and of the other Americas. In this respect we occupy a strategic place in that a large and growing segment of us have on the whole better training than the mass of the world's workers outside of the United States and Europe; and secondly because we are in such direct touch with the world's greatest industrial organization that we can easily imitate its methods and share its gains and repeat its fatal mistakes.

We must therefore see our duty of joining and cooperating with that part of the world's population which is going forward toward a better economic organization, and in not yielding to the temptation of joining our interests with those who are using their power and advantages to make industry serve their selfish interests and distorted ideals.

I remember once in Charleston, South Carolina, when a well-educated Negro pointed out to me the tenement houses which he was renting to poor workers at huge profit. In Atlanta I have seen an insurance society bought by a Negro group from whites, which was cheating and stealing from the workers with exactly the same methods that the white company had used, and piling up fortunes for young colored men. In fact, the more widely and successfully colored businessmen follow the methods of white businessmen, the more many of us regard them as unusually successful.

All these considerations affect and must, in the future more largely than now, affect what we call now the Negro problem. And any assessment of the future aspects of this problem must take the matters which I have emphasized into serious and careful consideration.

There is today in America a confusion of mind so tragic and so misleading that our whole thought and philosophy is distorted. At the very time that economics, that is, the study of work and income, is of foremost importance for our well-being, economics is not being studied in our schools. Neither in the elementary schools nor in colleges are students learning about the philosophy of money and exchange, production and trade, wealth and saving. Our university students are pouring into chemistry and physics, and deserting history and sociology. Why? Because to us the basic problem is how large an income can we get; how much money we can control; what careers for our children will insure them the most wealth.

The object of our ambition is rising to higher and higher income brackets; and what we see as progress is escaping from manual labor to white-collar jobs; thence to employing others to work for us; then to owning so much property that we need not work ourselves, so that we may sit in stark idleness and dissipation, having never learned anything to do except to arrange to have nothing to do. From this contradiction arises the strange paradox that poverty in the worker must be perpetual in order that he be compelled to work for the rich.

To most Americans this paradox is at once true and impossible. They sit dumb and bemused by it. Yet a little thought, a little clear thinking in the home and the elementary schools, a minimum of leadership from the universities where past experience could sit beside present knowledge, and our eyes could see and our deaf ears hear. What is *life* but the attempt of human beings to be happy and contented in a world which with all its ills has a mass of sun and waters, trees and flowers, beauty and love? To realize this at its highest we need food, clothes and shelter. We need health of body and balance of mind. We want to know what this world is, how its wonderful laws act, who its peoples are, how they think and act, and how what they have done in years and ages past may guide us today. We want to see, realize and conceive beauty in form and line and color. We want to know our own souls and the myriad-sided souls of others, and then to imagine what might be if what is should grow to what we wish. This is *life*, and this is the end and fairy tale of *life*. We know this, and yet we sit dumb and muddled before it, seeing the world as a twisted contradiction.

Yet the problem is simple. We have a rich land: earth and water, minerals and vegetables of every sort; breathtaking scenery in mountain, ocean, river and vale. We have combed the races of earth for strength, intelligence and daring. All that is needed is that each of us do all we can first to supply our own wants in food and shelter, health and learning; but more than that: that we do for others what they need done and cannot do for themselves and yet which must be done, lest *we* suffer. Beyond that there are many tasks which all working together can do faster and better than many working apart. All for one and one for all is an axiom of life, and to refuse to let all work in common would be as silly as to let no one work alone.

All this is clear and true, and yet it is blinded in our eyes. The object of work for many is *not* to work. The end of labor is not to do what must be done but to get somebody else to do it. The wealth of the nation—the land and water, the coal and oil, the iron and aluminum —ought not belong to the nation some say, but to those who by chance or cheating have legal power to make you pay their price for what God gave them. Even if ten or ten thousand men combine and in sweated sacrifice make steel, wheat, corn, meat or shoes, the result of the combined labor belongs to one or a few of them while the others scramble to keep from starving.

What has gone wrong? It is clear the workers do not understand the meaning of work. Work is service, not gain. The object of work is life, not income. The reward of production is plenty, not private fortune. We should measure the prosperity of a nation not by the number of millionaires but by the absence of poverty, the prevalence of health, the efficiency of the public schools, and the number of people who can and do read worthwhile books.

Toward all this we strive, but instead of marching breast-forward[1] we stagger and wander, thinking that food is raised not to eat but to sell at a good profit; that houses are built not to shelter the masses but to make real-estate agents rich; and solemnly declaring that without private profit there can be no food nor homes. All this is ridiculous. It has been disproven centuries ago. The greatest thinkers of every age have inveighed against concentration of wealth in the hands of the few and against the poverty, disease and ignorance of the masses of men.

We have tried every method of reform. A favorite effort was force by war, but the loot stolen by murder went to the generals not to the soldiers. We tried through religion to lead men to sacrifice and right treatment of their fellow men. But the priests too often stole the fruits of sacrifice and concealed the truth.

In the seventeenth century of our modern European era, we sought leadership in science, and dreamed that justice might rule through natural law. But we misinterpreted law to mean that most men were slaves and white Europeans were of right masters of the world. In the eighteenth century we turned toward the ballot in the hands of the worker to force a just division of the fruits of labor among the toilers. But the capitalists, fattening on black slavery and land monopoly and on private monopoly of capital, forced the modern worker into a new slavery which built a new civilization of the world with colored

slaves at the bottom, white serfs between, and the power
still in the hands of the rich.

But one consideration halted this plan. The serfs and
even the slaves had begun to think. Some bits of education
had stimulated them and some of the real scientists of
the world began to use their knowledge for the masses
and not solely for ruling classes. It became more and
more a matter of straight thinking. What is work? It is
what all must contribute to the common good. No man
in this world has a right to be idle. It is the bounden
duty of each to contribute his best to the well-being of all.
Of what men gain or do by their efforts all have a right
to share, not to the extent of all they want, but certainly
to the extent which they finally need. We feared yesterday
that if all the reasonable needs of all men were met most
would still starve. We know better than that today. All
may eat and none need starve unless some insist on cake
when others have no bread. And that, says modern justice,
is crime even if the starving man be Negro, Mexican or
Korean.

From this program, even from any attempt to realize
it in any way, many of the most powerful nations today
and many influential persons not only are opposed, but
threaten world war on nations and hell and damnation
on people who even dare think, much less talk, of a world
without poverty, ignorance and disease. Of attempts to
realize such a world, organized civilization deliberately
lies.

Let me cite one instance: England a few years ago
adopted social medicine and arranged that every Englishman should get free medical attention, hospitalization,
medicine and dental care. It was a desperately needed
reform. There is no reason on earth why such a measure
should not be characteristic of every civilized nation. Yet
every disaster was predicted, and every lie scattered to
stop it. It was tried in Britain. It was a marked success.
Even world reaction has not dared even essay to displace
it. The utmost that Churchill attempted was to restore
a small payment for false teeth! Despite the marked success
of this simple act of justice to human citizens, the physi-

cians of the United States launched an outrageous propaganda, backed by money, advertising and lecturing, until every ordinary American is firmly convinced that social medicine in England is a failure and that any step toward it in America would be *revolution!* Even Negro physicians, administering to a sick and diseased people who need social medicine more than any part of this nation, have with but a few honorable exceptions lined themselves with those "distinguished" white Americans fighting to defend disease and death.

This brings me to the crux of my message. We Negroes are not fighting tonight against slavery. That fight is won. We are not fighting in vain for the ballot. We hold the balance of political power in the North, and either we get the vote in the South or we come North and get it here. But we are fighting and fighting desperately the economic battle for the right to work and to get from our work food, housing, education, health and a chance to live as human beings. But in this fight we are not alone. With us stand and must stand whether they will or not, the white workers of America and of the world. The continuation of a colonial world of slaves and serfs cheek by jowl with a free world of workers with modern technique is no longer possible. The effort to achieve this by yelling "Communism" and by propelling this nation to pour death and degradation on helpless Korea and to seek in every way to enslave China must and will fail.

You as voters and intelligent citizens must force *peace* on the professional soldiers and the business leaders who make fortunes on war and murder, and you must let the world know that this is your simple and unwavering program: the abolition of poverty, disease and ignorance the world over among women and men of all races, religions and colors. To accomplish this by just control of concentrated wealth and the overthrow of monopoly. To insure that income depends on work and not on privilege or chance.

That *freedom* is the heritage of man and by freedom we do not mean freedom from the laws of nature, but freedom to think and believe, to express our thoughts and dream our dreams, and to maintain our rights against secret police, witch-hunters or any other sort of modern fool or tyrant.

Work and ever-increasing categories of work must be carried on for the common good: work like forest preservation and flood control, the suppression of epidemics, research into disease, the broad planning of cities, the allocation and integration of industry. If all this must be done for the good of all it cannot be done by private initiative. It cannot be carried on for private profit. It must be planned. It must be conducted under discipline, and any set of social leaders who try to stop this social progress are enemies of mankind and destroyers of human culture.

The four freedoms come not by slavery to corporations and monopoly of press, cinema, radio and television, but by united social effort for the common good so that decently fed, healthy and intelligent people can be sure of work, not afraid of old age, and hold high their heads to think and say what they damn please without fear of liars, informers, or a sneaking FBI.

This is the life and the conception of life which today is being denied. Instead of regarding work as honorable, and necessary, and its object human service, we look on work as something to avoid, and its object as a private profit and so far as possible profit for the man who does not do the work. Most Americans believe that without the incentive of private profit, industry would collapse. No! The object of work is what it does for human beings and in all the long history of mankind this has been the open and avowed end of human toil.

It is only in the curious interval of modern history marked by the discovery of America and the theft of capital monopolized by force and used to enslave most of mankind to work for the few, that a theory of life has arisen which reduces the people of Asia, Africa and the islands to toil for the wealth of Europe and North America; and even in these lands, makes most workers, although better paid than colored workers, yet too poor to be healthy and intelligent.

When, then, modern world revolution started, of which

hat of Russia is but a part, revolution which has changed he face of industry in every modern nation, here in America there has started a desperate effort to lead this nation nto witch-hunting and world war, to stop this world rend toward abolition of labor exploitation and a real rotherhood of man, and to abolish forever the vulgar ole of private wealth. Thus the peace movement epitomizes in itself the world uplift today and of this American Negroes must become increasingly aware if they do not vant to fall behind progress and hold back the march of nankind.

This does not call for force nor revolution. It does call or courage even to the loss of jobs; for daring to think and guts at least to listen; to the refusal to mistake money nade by gamblers either at policy or on the stock market, or display of clothes or homes as progress. Progress s *peace*, and peace is time for food, homes for love, 1ealth for happiness, and books to read.

> Awake, awake,
> Put on thy strength, O Zion,
> Put on thy beautiful robes.

Freedomways, First Quarter, 1965, pp. 117-24.

28

TWO HUNDRED YEARS
OF SEGREGATED SCHOOLS

In a masterly address, delivered in February 1955, less than a year after the Supreme Court decision of May, 1954, Dr. Du Bois traced the history of segregated education in the United States and analyzed the significance of the court decision.

The African slave in America had tried physical force against oppression from the time of Columbus to the day of Nat Turner. In every island and every slave state, as Herbert Aptheker[1] has shown us, there were hundreds of slave revolts which prove, as Haitian historians say, that the French Revolution did not spread from France to the West Indies but from the West Indies to France. Negro revolt under the Maroons culminated in Haiti where Britain, France and Spain were worsted and the United States was frightened into stopping the slave trade. The United States then got the territory west of the Mississippi as a gift.

Nevertheless, against force wielded by slaves, greater force brought to bear by organization and arms in white America kept the shackles riveted on many of the Negroes. These Negroes therefore became determined to achieve freedom by brain if not by muscle.

In the early eighteenth century two free Negroes of Massachusetts built schools and opened them to all who would attend. Then Negroes had schools furnished for them in New York, Philadelphia and Cincinnati. Teachers first were white and funds came from missionary organi-

:ations like the British Society for the Propagation of he Gospel and from individual philanthropists like Thomas Bray and Anthony Benezet. Sometimes Negroes ook over the teaching, like Katy Ferguson who established the Sunday Schools in New York for white and :olored; and John Chavis of North Carolina, who taught some of the most distinguished whites.

In the early nineteenth century free Negroes conducted schools in New York, Charleston, Savannah, New Orleans and elsewhere. As free public schools became common n the North, a few Negroes entered here and there, but he barriers closed against them and they began to fight. Alexander Crummel and two companions secured admission to a New Hampshire semiprivate school but enraged whites dragged the schoolhouse into a swamp. Prudence Crandall received a colored girl into her seminary in New Haven and was crucified in spirit and property. By 1855, ed by William C. Nell, the segregated school system of Massachusetts was abolished.

Then there grew up later in the century distinct Negro public-school systems, supported by the state, usually with colored principals but not as well equipped as the white schools. These systems spread in northern cities like New York, Philadelphia and Cincinnati. Private higher schools also were established for Negroes, especially by churches. Lincoln in Pennsylvania, run by white Presbyterians, and Wilberforce in Ohio, run by colored Methodists, gave secondary school instruction and some college work about 1854. In 1850 there were 4,000 colored children in school in the South and 22,000 in the North.

After emancipation there arose a complete Negro public-school system in Washington and in several other cities; while in the South Negro voters demanded a public-school system of the reluctant whites. The Civil War and emancipation also brought Negro schools under the Freedmen's Bureau and northern missions. This system, which covered much of the South, became the southern system of free public education under the Reconstruction governments.

As I have written elsewhere, "The first great mass movement for public education at the expense of the state in

the South came from Negroes. Many white leaders before
the war had advocated general education for white children but few had been listened to. Schools for indigents
and pauper white children were supported here and there
and more or less spasmodically. Some states had elaborate plans but they were not carried out. Public education
for all at public expense was, in the South, a Negro idea."[2]

The question of separating races in these schools was
not at first regarded as important. Negroes wanted education on any terms. In theory of course they knew that the
mixed school was the democratic ideal and they were
sure that the cost of a double system would eventually
force a mixed system. They accepted temporarily separate
schools, therefore, without much objection.

The action of the states varied. With Reconstruction,
public schools were opened in Charleston, South Carolina,
without distinction of color. Twenty-five of the forty-two
teachers were colored. The South Carolina Act of 1870
for a system of free schools was the most complete legislation that the state had ever enacted. Textbooks were
provided at cost or free to the poor but the schools were
separated by race.

In Louisiana, by the Constitution of 1863 all children
were admitted to schools regardless of color. That prevailed until 1877, although often by administrative action
colored children were kept out of white schools. Finally
segregated schools prevailed. In Mississippi, separate
schools by race were demanded in 1875. In Florida, the
colored superintendent, Jonathan E. Gibbs, established
schools which at first were mixed but afterward they became by law separated by color.

The state system of schools for North Carolina in 1869
called for separation by race. In Virginia the constitution
did not provide for separate schools but laws passed in
1869 separated the schools by color. In the District of
Columbia, Negroes from 1807 ran self-supported schools.
In 1864 public schools were provided with separate and
poorer schools for Negroes. By 1867 the Negro schools
began to receive a proportionate share of the funds and
there came two separate systems, white and colored, each
with its own superintendent. About 1890 the system be-

came unified, with a colored assistant superintendent in charge of the schools for Negroes.

Gradually the South, backed by the dictates of the Supreme Court, settled down to a system of public education with separation of whites and Negroes. There were separate buildings and facilities. Teachers in colored schools were usually colored, although in Charleston and Richmond southern white teachers were long retained, to the disgust of Negroes and retardation of Negro children. The superintendence of the colored systems was entirely in the hands of the whites, save in a few cases of powerless local colored trustees. The white school authorities could allocate the school funds as they pleased and often did not have to report even to the federal government on federal funds.

There came into use a custom, encouraged by the Southern Education Board and its successor, the General Education Board, where discrimination against Negroes was excused, with the dogma of "first educate the whites and later the Negroes." This changed soon to deliberately poorer and cheaper Negro schools. Then the South moved North and planted "Jim Crow" in schools in localities in twenty northern states. This situation finally became so great a national disgrace that Negroes and many whites began systematically to complain.

It long seemed useless to bring the matter to the courts. When the Supreme Court declared in 1896 that separate but equal schools meant separate but not equal;[3] and when later to the astonishment even of the white South decreed that the city of Augusta, Georgia, could provide an elaborate high school and night schools for whites and none for Negroes, the Negroes were in despair for years. They were reduced to begging local white school authorities for some pretense of decent treatment and only in case of federal appropriations to demand directly from Congress equal shares.

As Negro voting increased, Congress got an improved sense of hearing. First, Negroes secured some increase of justice in the distribution and administration of federal funds. The shares of the Negro Land Grant colleges began slowly to increase and the crisis came in the matter of state-supported professional education. The prohibitive and impossible cost of a double system of public elementary schools had long been clear. Secondary public-school education for Negroes was even more idiotic and professional education nonexistent.

Then a Negro in Missouri in 1936 sued for a chance at training in law, and the Supreme Court in an unexpected moment of sanity gave him a favorable verdict in 1938. The Bourbon South began to move. They increased the inadequate scholarships for Negro professional students to study in states where the school systems were more civilized.

The National Association for Advancement of Colored People now began to take notice. For a time it confined its demands to equal school facilities and equal salaries. Then its work was divided in two parts, one of which, with a separate office, funds, and authority, addressed itself under Arthur Spingarn and Thurgood Marshall to the question of discrimination as such. The South rushed to reform its lines. Whites surrendered a large part of the federal funds which, with the connivance of northern white philanthropy, they had stolen from Negroes for twenty-five years and more. They tried hard to induce Negroes to consent to "regional" instead of state professional schools; and they finally admitted a few Negro students to southern white professional schools about which vast advertisement was spread abroad.

But the Spingarn-Marshall team proceeded to challenge the entire race-segregation system on the grounds of unconstitutionality. Few dreamed that the Supreme Court, after recently curtailing freedom of speech and instituting thought control, dare give the Negro the justice denied him in education for seventy-five years!

Many southern states had hurriedly begun to increase their appropriations for Negro public schools. The new Ford Foundation hired a southern white newspaper man to write a book showing how marvellous the new southern support of Negro public schools was becoming — indeed, he implied, it looked as though they would soon become equal to the white! Right on his head fell the decision of May 17, 1954, and to top it all, it was unanimous; race segregation in public schools was declared unconstitutional. [4]

Of course it has not yet been implemented and South Carolina, Georgia and Mississippi, with the highest illiteracy in the nation, are ready to secede from the union when it is. At best it will be a generation before the segregated Negro public school entirely disappears. But considering the worldwide advertisement that the United States has at last started to become a democracy without a color line, it is going to be difficult for the South and the northern copperheads to treat the separate school decision as they have treated Negro disfranchisement since 1876.

Nevertheless this decision, even with its delayed implementation and in accordance with the widespread American contempt of law—the decision faces Negroes with a cruel dilemma. They want their children educated. That is a must, else they continue in semislavery. Not even the propaganda of Booker T. Washington with his backing from wealth and fame could bribe black America from this determination. Here they still stand; God helping them, they can do nothing else.

Yet with successfully mixed schools they know what their children must suffer for years from southern white teachers, from white hoodlums who sit beside them and under school authorities from janitors to superintendents, who hate and despise them. They know, dear God, how they know! Yet they also know that they themselves must accept this verdict and even insist on it. They dare do nothing else, for equality is what they have demanded for 250 years and now that a further push has been achieved with dirty accompaniments, they must accept it in justice to generations to come, white and black. They must eventually surrender race "solidarity" and the idea of American Negro culture to the concept of world humanity, above race and nation. This is the price of liberty. This is the cost of oppression.

The best of the Negro teachers will largely go because they will not and cannot teach what many white folks will long want taught. Much teaching of Negro history will leave the school and with it that brave story of Negro resistance. This teaching will be taught more largely in the home or in the church where, under current Christian custom, segregation by race and class will remain until the last possible moment.

Despite all this we Negroes will stand fast and pull through. Some of our literature will for a season descend into the "white folks' n-----" type, with fulsome praise of what "good white folk" have done for us. Our leadership in social studies may well succumb to money which millionaires will drop into the laps of young white southern "scholars" and subservient blacks to undertake the study of Negroes, which Negro scholars began.

Yet we will survive. The labor unions are open now for us as never before and beginning to receive us not with condescension but in brotherhood. Europe is listening to us and not so exclusively to the "professional" whites to tell them about kind slave drivers and "black mammies." Asia has risen to her feet and taken her stand against white supremacy: and finally Africa too, despite American dollars, artillery and atom bombs imported to back Malan. It's just one more long battle, but we are ready to fight it.

"Jewish Life" Anthology, *1946-1956*, New York, 1956, pp. 201-06.

29

IF EUGENE DEBS RETURNED

On November 28, 1955, a Debs Centennial celebration to honor the great leader of the Socialist Party from 1900 to his death in 1924 occurred in a number of cities. In New York the Debs Centennial Meeting was held at the Fraternal Clubhouse under the sponsorship of the editors of the Monthly Review, National Guardian, I. F. Stone's Weekly, *and the* American Socialist. *More than five hundred persons attended and heard speeches by Dr. Du Bois, Clifford T. McAvoy, I. F. Stone, Bert Cochran, Leo Huberman, and James Aronson, Executive Editor of the* National Guardian. *All of the speakers dealt with the meaning of the Debs heritage and the current problems of socialism and progressivism. Here is Dr. Du Bois's speech.*

In the year 1920 when 919,000 American voters wanted Eugene Debs to be president of the United States,[1] the socialist platform on which he ran demanded in general terms that eventually the ownership of the means of production be transferred from private to public control. The steps toward this end were not altogether agreed upon. But Debs demanded the supreme power of the workers "as the one class that can and will bring permanent peace to the world." He declared that then "we shall transfer the title deeds of the railroads, the telegraph lines, the mines, mills and great industries to the people in their collective capacity; we shall take possession of all these social utilities in the name of the people. We shall then have industrial democracy. We shall be a free nation whose government is *of* and *by* and *for* the people."

If tonight Mr. Debs should saunter back to celebrate with us this, his one-hundredth birthday, he would feel considerable gratification at the progress of his cause in thirty-five years. Capital is still mainly in private hands but not entirely. Increasing public control of capital is the rule in the United States, while over most of the world public ownership is rapidly increasing. In our country public regulation of utilities, including railroads, water power and communications, has increased. We direct private business in numerous instances; we tax wealth in new ways, we defend the right of labor to organize and we pay out $1,500 million a year in social insurance. This is not yet socialism, but it is far from the uncontested rule of wealth.

Eugene Debs, however, being an astute man and a logical thinker, would not be inclined to spend his birthday in celebrating the triumph of socialism in the United States. He would, on the contrary, see clearly that this nation, despite its advances toward socialism, is spending more money utterly to destroy socialism than it spends on education, health and general social uplift together.

He would realize with distress that advance toward the objects of socialism does not necessarily mean that the socialist state is at hand. Socialism includes planned production and distribution of wealth. But a completely socialistic result depends on who does the planning and for what ends. A state socialism planned by the rich for their own survival is quite possible, but it is far from the state where the rule rests in the hands of those who produce wealth and services and whose aim is the welfare of the mass of the people.

If Mr. Debs, during his absence from this earthly scene, has followed events of which we are too painfully aware, he will know that not all that is called socialism is socialistic in the sense that he used to understand it. He will know of Hitler's National Socialism, which, indeed, built a magnificent system of roads and excellent public housing, controlled finance and wages, owned railroads, telegraphs and telephones and yet was *not* socialism as Debs envisioned it. He would note that widespread socialist methods in Britain, France, Holland and Belgium have not prevented these nations from exploiting labor in Europe, Asia, Africa and America and that their own laboring classes have been willing to base their increased wage and higher standard of living on the poverty, ignorance and disease of most of the working people of the world. This again can hardly be called socialism, and Debs would know that socialistic methods in the United States have succeeded in staving off financial collapse and may continue to do this for a considerable time, but that this social effort is for and by big business and financial monopoly and not for the farm and the shop. It bribes organized labor with high wages built on war industry and by this very act threatens the welfare of the mass of the people of the world.

The matter which would, I think, bother Eugene Debs most in the present scene would be the failure of democracy to change all this. If he arrived in time to look in on the polling places during our recent election, he would have seen with dismay that most Americans who have the right to vote do not make any effort to use it. It is unusual for a majority of voters to attend elections, not to mention the millions legally disfranchised by color and poverty.

Now, the socialism of Eugene Debs was founded on the democratic state in which the law of the land was to be determined by the will of the people. If and when this prerequisite of the socialist state failed, I am sure that Mr. Debs, like Charlie Chaplin, would not think of returning to America, even for this celebration.

If then, Mr. Debs is nonplussed by the apathy of voters, he would learn in any barroom, barbershop or prayer meeting, or even in the subway, that the reason lay in the fact that Americans have had no chance lately to vote on the matters in which they have the greatest interest. We have not had a chance to vote on peace or war, and will not next year, if we must choose between Eisenhower and Stevenson, or Nixon and Harriman. We have never voted on universal military service. We never voted to spend more than half our income on war;

we never voted to make war in Korea. We never voted to beg, borrow or steal one hundred military bases all over the world to overthrow communism.

Why then should we vote if we cannot vote on matters which seem of greatest importance to us?

Mr. Debs's reaction would be: If this be true, then it is our own fault that we have not talked to the people. He would say: Tell them the truth! Publish books and pamphlets; agitate! And then if Eugene Debs, forgetting that he is dead, should attempt to hire a hall, or stage a mass meeting on Union Square, or get time on radio or television, or get a book on the shelves of the public library, he would find himself guilty of subversion, proven a Communist quite unnecessarily by Budenz, Bentley and Philbrick, Inc.,[2] and since the courts have almost said that all Communists are criminals set to bring on violent revolution, Debs would soon be back in the very jail where imprisonment had already killed him.[3]

But naturally, before Debs started on this impossible effort, we his friends and admirers would have coached him on the facts of life as we know them in this our America of today. It is not only true that Johnnie does not learn to read, but even if he could read he would have difficulty in reading the truth; that the vast monopolies which collect news from all over the world omit what they do not want known, distort what they submit and often deliberately lie about the rest.

"But," I imagine Debs saying, waxing a bit hysterical, "why do not people insist on knowing the facts?" Our only answer would be that since we have become a nation of the rich, run by the rich for the rich (a statement which Mr. Stevenson says he did not originate but merely quoted) the voters do not and cannot know that their best interests are not paramount aims of government; that as their education deteriorates during this the most illiterate government we have endured since Jackson, as their news becomes tainted, suppressed and slanted, it is increasingly difficult for science and goodwill to usher in the state where the welfare of the mass of the people is the aim of government, where capital is owned by the people, where private profit is *never* the sole object of industry and where exploitation of labor is always a crime. We are no longer a democracy free to think, but a frightened people scared of the socialism and communism which we dare not know nor study. We are threatened by mounting crime and facing jails not only of criminals but increasingly of honest men whose fault is that they believe in the socialism for which Debs gave his life.

In the midst of this losing of our moral and intellectual integrity we are permitting almost unchallenged a concentrated power of industry and commerce and a monopoly of wealth and natural resources which is not only a threat to the United States but so great a threat to the world that the world with increasing unanimity is resenting it and organizing to oppose it. However, we could assure Mr. Debs that at times public opinion bursts the bonds of organized politics and wealth-control, and screams. We would for instance today be in the midst of a third and fatal world war if Nixon and Knowland had not been stopped in their tracks by an extraordinary avalanche of letters which made even the dumbest politicians in Washington realize that the nation wanted peace even if they got no chance to vote for it.

But this, Debs would say correctly, is not enough. It may come after some outrageous occurrence. However, for the long run and the continuing education of the people, Debs must learn that few reputable publishers today will take any book that deviates from respectable lines of thought as laid down by the National Association of Manufacturers; that no reputable bookstore will carry books advocating *or not attacking* communism; that public libraries will neither buy nor place books of which the FBI does not approve, and that none of our leading literary journals would mention a book by Debs himself should it appear today with a Heavenly imprint. Debs would learn with distress that the tendency apparent in his day of the readers of newspapers and magazines refusing to pay for the full cost of what they read has today sunk to the place where they expect to have their news and literature furnished them free and with pictures and gifts by the purveyors of tobacco, neckties and toothpaste.

If Debs were still able to listen, he would learn that our

representatives in Congress and legislature, our scientists, our preachers, teachers and students are afraid to think or talk lest they starve or disgrace their families and friends. Thus our basic culture patterns are vitiated.

To which Debs would reply: Those who believe in truth and know from slavery, poverty and crime what falsehood can do, must if possible save the truth from burial. Such action is not mere almsgiving, it is a great crusade. Without unpaid crusaders and unknighted chivalry we plunge back into new Dark Ages, where "Guys and Dolls" regale us with a crap game in a sewer.

And so Eugene Debs, returning with both sorrow and relief to the blessed peace of Heaven or the genial warmth of Hell (this depending on whether one reads the *Times* or *The Worker*) will, I imagine, after a season of rest and reflection, look carefully about and say:

"What really I fear for America is not merely loss of freedom, degeneration of schools, failure of the free press or failure of democracy. These, reason in time will combat. Rather I fear the threat of insanity; the loss of ability to reason. You'd hardly believe this," he'd say, "but intelligent Americans cannot today see the direct connection between war, murder, lying, stealing, and juvenile crime. Their leaders actually propose to gain peace by war, to stop poverty by making the rich richer and to prevent force and violence by preparing force and violence on a scale of which the world never before dreamed anywhere at any time."

"And furthermore, (this you will never believe, but I swear it's true)" says Debs, "the man who succeeded me as leader of socialism in the United States and ran on the Socialist ticket for president five times, is today the most bitter and hysterical enemy of the only governments on earth which approach complete socialism.[4] Brethren, I firmly believe that what my country needs today above all else, is more and better insane asylums strategically placed."

American Socialist, January 1956, pp. 10-11.

30

ADVICE TO A GREAT-GRANDSON

On his ninetieth birthday, Dr. Du Bois's friends invited his well-wishers to a party at the Roosevelt Hotel. No body of sponsors could be found willing to lend their names to an occasion honoring one of America's greatest sons, the outstanding American intellectual of the twentieth century, and one of the leading world figures of his day. Dr. Du Bois had been accused of being a subversive supporter of peace and socialism, and in the year 1958 in the United States such an accusation was enough to frighten leading black and white Americans who inwardly must have felt ashamed of their fear. However, Angus Cameron, a novelist, progressive book publisher, and editor eagerly accepted the invitation to act as chairman, and Eslanda Robeson, wife of Paul Robeson, as treasurer. Two thousand persons were present including Dr. Du Bois's great-grandson, who, he noted later, "behaved with exemplary decorum." Dr. Du Bois addressed his remarks to his great-grandson.

The most distinguished guest of this festive occasion is none other than my great-grandson, Arthur Edward McFarlane II, who was born this last Christmas Day. He had kindly consented to permit me to read to you a bit of advice which, as he remarked with a sigh of resignation, great-grandparents are supposed usually to inflict on the helpless young. This then is my word of advice.

As men go, I have had a reasonably happy and successful life, I have had enough to eat and drink, have been suitably clothed and, as you see, have had many friends. But the thing which has been the secret of whatever I have done is the fact that I have been able to earn a living by doing the work which I wanted to do and work that the world needed done.

I want to stress this. You will soon learn, my dear young man, that most human beings spend their lives doing work which they hate and work which the world does not need. It is therefore of prime importance that you early learn what you want to do; how you are fit to do it and whether or not the world needs this service. Here, in the next twenty years, your parents can be of use to you. You will soon begin to wonder just what parents are for besides interfering with your natural wishes. Let me therefore tell you: parents and their parents are inflicted upon you in order to show what kind of person you are; what sort of world you live in and what the persons who dwell here need for their happiness and well-being.

Right here, my esteemed great-grandson, may I ask you to stick a pin. You will find it the fashion in the America where eventually you will live and work to judge that life's work by the amount of money it brings you. This is a grave mistake. The return from your work must be the satisfaction which that work brings you and the world's need of that work. With this, life is heaven, or as near heaven as you can get. Without this — with work which you despise, which bores you and which the world does not need — this life is hell. And believe me, many a $25,000-a-year executive is living in just such a hell today.

Income is not greenbacks, it is satisfaction; it is creation; it is beauty. It is the supreme sense of a world of men going forward, lurch and stagger though it may, but slowly, inevitably going forward, and you, you yourself with your hand on the wheels. Make this choice, then, my son. Never hesitate, never falter.

And now comes the word of warning: the satisfaction with your work even at best will never be complete, since nothing on earth can be perfect. The forward pace of the world which you are pushing will be painfully slow. But what of that: the difference between a hundred and a thousand years is less than you now think. But doing what must be done, that is eternal even when it walks with poverty.

National Guardian, March 5, 1958.

31

TRIBUTE TO PAUL ROBESON

On April 9, 1958, Paul Robeson celebrated his sixtieth birthday. Although he had gained fame as a scholar and athlete at Rutgers University where he was an "All-American" football player and was elected to Phi Beta Kappa in his junior year, and though after graduating from Columbia Law School with honors, he had gone on to gain renown in the theatre and in the concert hall as a baritone, there were few among leaders in American society, black or white, who were willing to do Robeson honor on his birthday. For he had committed the unpardonable sin of standing up firmly for the full rights of his people, had championed the cause of socialism and peace, and defended the Soviet Union and other socialist countries and the independent struggles of the African people. The State Department had canceled his passport, and concert halls and the airwaves were closed to him. But Robeson refused to be silenced, and when worldwide protests forced the State Department to remove the ban on his right to travel, he had gone abroad making a triumphal tour of England, the Continent, and the Soviet Union.

Dr. Du Bois, who himself had experienced the consequences of speaking up for full freedom for his people, for peace and socialism, was a distinguished speaker at Robeson's sixtieth birthday.

The persecution of Paul Robeson by the government and people of the United States during the last nine years has been one of the most contemptible happenings in modern history. Robeson has done nothing to hurt or defame this nation. He is, as all know, one of the most charming, charitable and loving of men. There is no person on earth who ever heard Robeson slander or even attack the land of his birth. Yet he had reason to despise America. He was a black man; the son of black folk whom Americans had stolen and enslaved. Even after his people's hard won and justly earned freedom, America made their lot as near a hell on earth as was possible. They discouraged, starved and insulted them. They sneered at helpless black children. Someone once said that the best punishment for Hitler would be to paint him black and send him to the United States. This was no joke. To struggle up as a black boy in America; to meet jeers and blows; to meet insult with silence and discrimination with a smile; to sit with fellow students who hated you and work and play for the honor of a college that disowned you—all this was America for Paul Robeson. Yet he fought the good fight; he was despised and rejected of men; a man of sorrows and acquainted with grief and we hid as it were our faces from him; he was despised and we esteemed him not.

Why? Why? Not because he attacked this country. Search Britain and France, the Soviet Union and Scandinavia for a word of his against America. What then was his crime? It was that while he did not rail at America he did praise the Soviet Union; and he did that because it treated him like a man and not like a dog; because he and his family for the first time in life were welcomed like human beings and he was honored as a great man. The children of Russia clung to him, the women kissed him; the workers greeted him; the state named mountains after him. He loved their homage. His eyes were filled with tears and his heart with thanks. Never before had he received such treatment. In America he was a "nigger"; in Britain he was tolerated; in France he was cheered; in the Soviet Union he was loved for the great artist that he is. He loved the Soviet Union in turn. He believed that every black man with blood in his veins would with him love the nation which first outlawed the color line.

I saw him when he voiced this. It was in Paris in 1949

at the greatest rally for world peace this world ever witnessed. Thousands of persons from all the world filled the Salle Pleyel from floor to rafters. Robeson hurried in, magnificent in height and breadth, weary from circling Europe with song. The audience rose to a man and the walls thundered. Robeson said that his people wanted peace and "would never fight the Soviet Union." I joined with the thousands in wild acclaim.

This, for America, was his crime. He might hate anybody. He might join in murder around the world. But for him to declare that he loved the Soviet Union and would not join in war against it—that was the highest crime that the United States recognized. For that, they slandered Robeson; they tried to kill him at Peekskill; [1] they prevented him from hiring halls in which to sing; they prevented him from travel and refused him a passport. His college, Rutgers, lied about him and dishonored him. And above all, his own people, American Negroes, joined in hounding one of their greatest artists—not all, but even men like Langston Hughes, who wrote of Negro musicians and deliberately omitted Robeson's name[2]—Robeson who more than any living man has spread the pure Negro folk song over the civilized world. Yet has Paul Robeson kept his soul and stood his ground. Still he loves and honors the Soviet Union. Still he has hope for America. Still he asserts his faith in God. But we—what can we say or do; nothing but hang our heads in endless shame.

The Autobiography of W. E. B. Du Bois: A Soliloquy on Viewing My Life from the Last Decade of its First Century, New York, 1968, pp. 396-97.

32

THE NEGRO AND SOCIALISM

In 1958 Dr. Du Bois spoke at a symposium entitled, "Toward a Socialist America," and delivered a paper on "The Negro and Socialism." Later, the papers were published under the editorship of Helen Alfred. Dr. Du Bois's paper sums up his thinking on socialism for over half a century since he was attracted to socialism as early as 1904.

The United States, which would like to be regarded as a democracy devoted to peace, finds itself today making the greatest preparations for war of any nation on earth and holding elections where citizens have no opportunity to vote for the policies which they prefer.

What are the causes of this contradictory situation? First, we know that our main reason in preparing for war is the fact that slowly but surely socialism has spread over the world and become a workable form of government. Today for the first time in history the majority of mankind live under socialist regimes, either complete socialism as in the Soviet Union and China, or partial socialism as in India and Scandinavia. Most Americans profess to believe that this spread of socialism is mainly the result of a conspiracy led by the Soviet Union and abetted by a section of American citizens. For fear of this group, we have curtailed democratic government, limited civil liberties, and planned war on a gigantic scale.

The spread of socialism in the last one hundred years is unquestionably a fact. It stemmed from growing protest against that tremendous expansion of business enterprise which followed the· French Revolution. This private initiative and economic anarchy resulted in the factory system, which stemmed from the American slave trade, the sugar empire and the Cotton Kingdom. All this was concurrent with such suffering and degradation among the laboring masses that by the end of the nineteenth century there was hardly a man of thought and feeling, scarcely a scientist nor an artist, who did not believe that socialism must eventually supplant unbridled private capitalism, or civilization would die.

All over the earth since the Civil War in America, socialism has grown and spread and become more and more definite. It has emerged from dream and doctrinaire fantasy such as characterized Fourier and Saint-Simon into the rounded doctrine of Karl Marx and finally into the socialist states of Lenin and Mao Tse-tung. In all this struggling advance lay the central idea that men must work for a living, but that the results of their work must not mainly be to support privileged persons and concentrate power in the hands of the owners of wealth; that the welfare of the mass of people should be the main object of government.

To ensure this end the conviction grew that government must increasingly be controlled by the governed; that the mass of people, increasing in intelligence, with incomes sufficient to live a good and healthy life, should control all government, and that they would be able to do this by the spread of science and scientific technique, access to truth, the use of reason, and freedom of thought and of creative impulse in art and literature.

The difficulty of accomplishing this lay in the current culture patterns — in repressive religious dogmas, and in the long inculcated belief that nothing better than private ownership and control of capital could be planned, with human nature as it is.

Democratic control, therefore, while it increased, tended to be narrowly political rather than economic. It had to do with the selection of officials rather than with work and income. Discovery of new natural forces and of increased use of machines with intricate industrial techniques tended to put land, labor, and the ownership of capital and wealth into control of the few who were fortunate or aggressive or unscrupulous and to emphasize a belief that, while the mass of citizens might share in government by electing officials to administer law, and legislators might make laws in certain areas of government, the people could not control industry or limit income.

As science increased its mastery of nature and as industry began to use world trade to expand markets, an entirely new problem of government arose. Industry realized that, unless industrial organization largely controlled government, it could not control land and labor, monopolize materials, set prices in the world market, and regulate credit and currency. For this purpose new and integrated world industry arose called "big business"—a misleading misnomer. Its significance lay not simply in its size. It was not just little shops grown larger. It was an organized supergovernment of mankind in matters of work and wages, directed with science and skill for the private profit of individuals. It could not be controlled by popular vote unless that vote was intelligent, experienced, and cast by persons essentially equal in income and power. The overwhelming majority of mankind was still ignorant, sick and poverty-stricken.

Repeated and varying devices for keeping and increasing democratic control over industry and wealth were regularly rendered useless by the superior training and moral unscrupulousness of the owners of wealth, as against the ignorance and inexperience of the voters. Bribery of the poorer voters; threats and even violence; fear of the future and organized conspiracy of the interested few against the unorganized many; lying and deftly spread propaganda used race hate, religious dogma and differing family and class interests to ruin democracy. In our own day we have seen that the income tax, designed to place the burden of government expense on property owners in ratio to income, actually lays the heaviest weight of taxation on the low-income classes, while the rich individuals and corporations escape with the least proportion of taxes.

When the American farmers and workers revolted against

the beginnings of the British colonial system and set out
to establish a republic of free and equal citizens, it seemed
to most thinking people that a new era in the development
of Western civilization had begun. Here, beyond the privilege of titled Europe, beyond the deep-seated conditioning
of the masses to hereditary inequality and subservience to
luxury and display, was to arise a nation of equal men.
That equality was to be based on economic opportunity
which, as Karl Marx later preached, was the only real
equality.

But unfortunately while the United States proclaimed,
it never adopted complete equality. First, it prolonged the
European recognition of property as more significant than
manhood. Then it discovered that theft of land from the
Indians was not murder but a method of progress. Next,
America reduced the African labor, which rising British
commerce had forced on her, to slave status and gained
thereby such fabulous income from tobacco, sugar and
cotton that Europe became the center of triumphant private capitalism, and the United States its handmaid to
furnish free land and cheap labor.

This nation had to fight a Civil War to prevent all
American labor from becoming half enslaved. Thus, from
1620 when the Puritans landed until 1865 when slavery
was abolished, there was no complete democracy in the
United States. This was not only because a large part of
the laboring class was enslaved, but also because white
labor was in competition with slaves and thus itself not
really free.

In the late nineteenth and twentieth centuries, while socialism advanced in the leading European nations and
in North America, in most of the world European monopoly of wealth and technique—strengthened by theories of
the natural inferiority of most human beings—led to the
assumed right of western Europe to rule the world for the
benefit and amusement of white people. This theory of
world domination was hidden behind the rise of the Western working classes, and helped keep democracy and social progress from eastern Europe, Asia, and Africa; from
Central and South America, and the islands of the seven
seas.

In western Europe a labor movement, and popular education kept forcing increasing numbers of the workers and of the middle classes into a larger share of economic power. But on the other hand, the mass of colored labor, and white labor in backward Latin and Slavic lands, were reduced to subordinate social status so that increased profit from their land and labor helped to maintain the high profits and high wages of industry in western Europe and North America. Also it was easy there to hire white soldiers to keep "niggers," "chinks," "dagoes," and "hunkies" in their places. This was the essence of colonial imperialism. It was industry organized on a world scale, and holding most of mankind in such economic subjection as would return the largest profit to the owners of wealth.

Meantime, the new effort to achieve socialism fathered by Karl Marx and his successors, increased. It declared that even before the mass of workers were intelligent and experienced enough themselves to conduct modern industry, industrial guidance might be furnished them by a dictatorship of their own intelligent and devoted leaders. As knowledge and efficiency increased, democracy would spread among the masses and they would become capable of conducting a modern welfare state. This social program the world governed by owners of capital regarded as impossible without the dictatorship falling out of their well-meaning hands and into the hands of demagogues. Every sort of force was employed to stop even the attempt to set up such states. Yet the First World War, caused by rivalry over the ownership of colonies, resulted in the effort to start a complete socialist state in Russia; and after the Second World War, arising from the same causes as the first, a similar attempt was made in China.

Despite wide and repeated opposition, which used every despicable and criminal method possible, both of these states have become so successful and strong that their overthrow by outside force or inner revolt does not today seem at all likely. Also and meantime, in all leading countries, socialistic legislation steadily increased. It did not creep. It advanced with powerful strides.

This development has emphasized the fight between beleaguered private capitalism and advancing socialism, the

Communists pointing out the unnecessary lag of socialization in Western lands and the capitalists accusing communism of undemocratic dictatorship.

In order to fight socialism super big business, as contrasted with ordinary small-business enterprise, had to become itself socialism in reverse. If public welfare instead
of private profit became its object, if public officials sup-
planted private owners, socialistic government would be
in control of industry. However, those Americans who
hope that the welfare state will thus be realized under a
system of private capital are today having the carpet
pulled from beneath their feet by the recession of democracy in the United States. This has come about by the
repudiation of socialism by organized labor and the consequent refusal of the labor vote to follow even the goals
of the New Deal. This surrender of labor has been led by
the new industrial South, with favorable climate, cheap
labor, and half that labor disfranchised and most of it
unorganized. The mass of southerners do not vote. In
the congressional district where the black boy Till [1] was
murdered, there live 400,000 Negroes and 300,000 whites.
Yet only 7,000 voters went to the polls to elect the present
congressman. The disfranchisement of the black half of
the labor vote in the South keeps Negroes poor, sick,
and ignorant. But it also hurts white labor by making
democratic government unworkable so long as the South
has from three to ten times the voting power of the North
and West.

Because of this illegal and systematic disfranchisement,
a majority of American voters can often be outvoted by
a minority. Laws like the McCarran and Smith Act [2] can
become illegal statutes, because a minority of voters can
prevail over a majority. Figures to prove this are easy to
adduce, but I only mention now the fact that former Senator Lehman of New York represented the vote of five
million citizens who went to the polls, while Senator Eastland of Mississippi represented less than 150,000 voters.
Yet Eastland was far more powerful than Lehman.

This loss of democratic control of the government of
our nation can be even more clearly demonstrated. There

was no effective candidate for the presidency in the last national election who stood pledged for peace, disarmament, abolition of the draft, lower taxes, recognition of the right of the Soviet Union and China to have the government which they choose and for stopping our effort to force other nations to do as we want them to do. Not only did we have no chance to decide our foreign policy, but we were equally helpless in deciding our course in domestic affairs. Our system of education is falling to pieces. We need teachers and schoolhouses by the millions, but we cannot have them if we continue making weapons at the present rate and setting our youth to learning death and destruction instead of building, healing, and teaching.

Is this curtailment of democracy the result of knowledge and discussion? On the contrary, knowledge and discussion are today so far curtailed that most men do not even attempt to express their opinions, lest they be accused of treason or conspiracy.

Why is this?

At the very time when the colonial peoples were trying desperately to have food and freedom, powerful Americans became obsessed by the ambition to have North America replace Britain as the empire upon which the sun never dared to set. They demanded high profits and high wages even if the rest of the world starved. In order to restore world rule of organized industry, shaken by war and depression, the United States prefers preparation for universal and continuous world war, until a colonial imperialism in some form is restored under our leadership.

To this program most people of the United States have submitted. How was such submission brought about? Such a national policy found unexpected support in our long-encouraged prejudice against people with black or colored skins and against all groups of foreign-born who were not of Anglo-Saxon descent. This provincial point of view, repudiated by science and religion, still remains in America a living and powerful motive guiding our lives and likes. This support of the colonial system by American race prejudice has resulted in our present program of war. How was this accomplished? How have the majority of

American people been convinced that preparation for war, suspension of civil liberties and curtailment of democracy are our best paths to progress?

America is an intelligent nation, despite large illiterate groups and the lack of an integrated background of culture. We still have large numbers of the poor and sick, but our average income is far higher than that of most nations. This nation wants to do right, as evidenced by a plethora of churches and a wide and loud profession of religion. If any country is ready for increase of democracy, it is the United States. Yet we are preparing our sons for war because we actually have been induced to believe that the Soviet Union is behind a worldwide criminal conspiracy to destroy the United States and that socialism is the result. The statement is so fantastic that most foreign peoples cannot conceive how it can be true that we really accept this fairy tale.

To restore our lost opportunity to make huge profit on private investment in Russia, the Balkans, and particularly in China, big business has restricted and guided public access to truth. It has dominated newsgathering, monopolized the press and limited publishing. By fear of losing employment, by secret police and high pay to informers, often confessed liars; by control of education and limitation of radio and television and censorship of the drama — by all these methods and others, the public opinion of the nation has been forced into one iron channel of disaster.

In order to let the nation return to normal sanity we must realize that socialism is not a crime nor a conspiracy, but the path of progress toward which the feet of all mankind are set. Some of the greatest intellectual leaders of our era have been advocates of socialism: Charles Kingsley, Leo Tolstoi, Edward Bellamy, William Morris, Henry George, Robert Owen, Bernard Shaw, Sidney and Beatrice Webb, Keir Hardie, H. G. Wells, Harold Laski. The footsteps of the long oppressed and staggering masses are not always straight and sure, but their mistakes can never cause the misery and distress which the factory system caused in Europe, colonial imperialism caused in Asia and Africa, and which slavery, lynching, disfranchisement, and Jim Crow legislation have caused in the United States.

Our way out of this impasse is straight and clear and as old as the struggle of freedom for the mind of man: Americans must face the facts at all costs. Walking with determination through a morass of deliberate distortion, we must insist on the right to know the truth, to discuss it and to listen to its interpretation by men of intelligence and honesty; we must restore to all citizens their civil rights and the right to vote, no matter whether they are Negroes, Communists, or naturalized foreign-born. We must insist that our foreign policy as well as our domestic problems and especially our problem of industry, be subjects on which we shall have the right to vote.

Meantime, we are prisoners of propaganda. The people of the United States have become completely sold to that method of conducting industry which has been so powerful and triumphant in the world for two centuries that Americans regard it as the only normal way of life. We regard the making of things and their purchase and sale for private profit as the chief end of living. We look on painting and poetry as harmless play. We regard literature as valuable only as handmaiden to industry. We teach business as a science when it is only an art of legal theft. We regard advertising as a profession even when it teaches the best way to lie. We consider the unselfish sacrifice of one to the progress of all as wasted effort. Wealth is the height of human ambition even when we have no idea of how to spend it, except to make more wealth or to waste it in harmful or useless ostentation. We want high profits and high wages even if most of the world starves.

Putting aside questions of right, and suspecting all our neighbors of being as selfish as we ourselves are, we have adopted a creed of wholesale selfishness. We believe that, if all people work for their own selfish advantage, the whole world will be the best of possible worlds. This is the rat race upon which we are set, and we are suspicious and afraid of folk who oppose this program and plead for the old kindliness, the new use of power and machine for the good of the unfortunate and the welfare of all the world of every race and color. We can and do give charity abundantly, particularly when we are giving away money or things which we cannot ourselves use. We give to beggars but we hate the beggars who recoil from begging. This is what stands back of our murderous war preparation as well as back of our endless itch to be rich. At any cost, or in any way, this is our reason for living; gambling on radio, on stock exchange or on race track is our way of life.

The power of wealth and private industry extends itself over education, literature and art, and we live in fear, with a deliberately low standard of culture, lest democracy displace monopoly of wealth in the control of the state.

One of the devastating effects of our current education on our youth is the training of them by military officials. They are indoctrinated by propaganda against socialism, by ridicule for their attachment to their mothers, and with disrespect for all women. They learn to kill and destroy, and force as a social method of progress is extolled. Small wonder that what we call "juvenile delinquency" increases among us.

One of the contradictions of our day is our argument about the distribution of property and the relative size of incomes, at a time when secrecy as to the truth about these matters is a matter of official compulsion, and most carefully guarded on the ground that a man's income is his private business and the ownership of property concerns the owner primarily. These propositions are false and ridiculous. The distribution of income is a public affair since it is increasingly the result of public function. Property is a matter of state control, permitted to rest in private hands only so long as it is of public benefit that it should so rest. For any reasonable thought or action concerning property, there should come first open information as to its ownership. Without that, no science or ethic of wealth is possible. We can only guess madly and conclude erroneously. Taking the meager guesswork of the United States Census, as some approximation of the truth: it is clear that the poor are still with us in this rich land.

There are nearly 40 percent of our families who receive less than $2,000 a year and over 6,000,000 of our 46,500,000 families receive less than $500. In addition to this there is a psychological poverty, in some ways more frightening than actual lack of income: there are the great number of artisans, white-collar workers and professional men who could live plainly on their incomes but who skimp and borrow and gamble, and sometimes steal to "keep up with the Joneses"; who drive a car and spend too little on food and medicine; who buy fur coats and crowd into one room. American culture is made uneasy and insane by the millions among us who expect in some way to get flamboyantly rich and cannot be satisfied with that simple life which all experience teaches is the finest and best.

Especially must American Negroes, awaking from their present fear and lethargy, reassert that leadership in the American world of culture which Phillis Wheatley began in the eighteenth century, Frederick Douglass led in the nineteenth, and James Weldon Johnson and Carter Woodson advanced in the twentieth. American Negroes must study socialism, its rise in Europe and Asia, and its peculiar suitability for the emancipation of Africa. They must realize that no system of reform offers the American Negro such real emancipation as socialism. The capitalism which so long ruled Europe and North America was founded on Negro slavery in America, and that slavery will never completely disappear so long as private capitalism continues to survive.

The fight to preserve racial segregation along the color line in the United States only helps to drive the American Negro that much faster into the arms of socialism. The movement of the whole nation toward the welfare state, and away from the concept of private profit as the only object of industry, is bound to show itself sooner or later in the whole nation. But if the Negro tenth of the nation is forced ahead by color discrimination, the socialization of the nation will come that much sooner.

Consider the situation: there are today about sixteen million Americans of admitted Negro descent. They are by reason of this descent subjected to public insult, loss of opportunity to work according to ability or to receive wages level with white workers; most of these people are disfranchised and segregated in education, travel, civil rights and public recreation. Ten million of these Negroes are poor, receiving less than $50 a week per family. Half of them cannot read or write. They live mostly in the rural districts and small towns of the former slave states whence their efforts to escape are hindered by law, mob violence, and scarcity of places of refuge which welcome them or give them work or places to live.

Above this depressed ten million are four million Negroes who are economically insecure and on the edge of poverty. They work as laborers and servants in the towns and cities. They can read and write, but among them are a class of criminals. Next come one and a half million middle-class Negroes living in cities. They have education and property and are engaged in semiskilled work and white-collar jobs. Many are trained in the better-paid work of personal service, some are teachers and ministers of religion. Out of this group have come the leading intelligentsia. At the economic apex of this middle economic group are a half million Negroes who are well-to-do, receiving at least $10,000 a year. They are professional and business men, civil servants and public entertainers. They have good, sometimes elaborate homes, motor cars and servants. They live mostly in the larger cities.

When discussing American Negroes, one must distinguish among these classes. Southerners raving about the degradation of Negroes are usually talking about their disfranchised and exploited serfs. Negroes talking of their progress are usually referring to their bourgeoisie. But the Negro intelligentsia must ask how it happens that in free, rich America so many Negroes must be poor, sick and ignorant while in Communist Russia, peasants who were emancipated at nearly the same time as Negroes, live without poverty, with universal education and national attack on disease? Why is it that the Chinese coolie, who recently was as low as the Negro slave, is today a man in his own country, with bloodsucking whites driven out? Every effort is made in America to suppress this line of thought among Negroes; but as thought in America regains its lost freedom, as democracy begins to replace plutocracy, the social thought of the nation will find increasing support from Negroes.

Even before such freedom comes, the segregated Negro

group will increasingly be forced toward socialistic methods to solve their inner problems. They will unite in boycotts as in Montgomery, Alabama; they will turn to conumers' cooperation; a new Negro literature must soon burst out of prison bonds and it will find in socialism practically its only voice. Negro schools and colleges, so long as students are excluded from public education, will become centers of thought where the Soviet Union and China cannot escape intelligent discussion.

The modern rise of Africans in the twentieth century to self-expression and organized demand for autonomy and freedom was due in large part to the Pan-African movement started by American Negroes. Today every part of Africa has a national congress fighting for the ends which the Pan-African movement started in 1919. Further leadership of Africa by black America has been stopped — but too late. Already the Africans have their own leaders, and these leaders like Nkrumah and Azikiwe are quite aware of the Soviet Union and China and are building their new nations on socialist lines.

Moreover as the mass of the colored peoples of the world move toward socialism in Asia and Africa, it is inevitable that they influence American Negroes. I had long hoped that American Negroes would lead this procession because of their chances for education. But "philanthropy," disguised in bribes, and "religion" cloaked in hypocrisy, strangled Negro education and stilled the voices of prophets. The yellow, brown and black thinkers of Asia have forged ahead. But nevertheless the black folk of America will hear their voices and, what is more compelling, will see their outstanding success. On March 6, 1957, when ancient Ghana was reborn in West Africa, American Negroes realized how far toward socialism this group of black folk had gone. Soon, too, socialism in the black Sudan, in East Africa, the Belgian Congo and South Africa will place the black world in the train of Soviet Russia, China, and India and tear loose from the allegiance, which American Negroes now try to profess, to the dictatorship of wealth in the United States.

One thing and one alone keeps socialism from growing even more rapidly than it is — that is fear of war and especially of attack by the Soviet Union and China. Most of our vast national income is being spent for preparation for such war and we have but small funds left for education, health and water development and control which we so sorely need. The frantic and continual cultivation of the national fear goes on just as the danger of war decreases. The class structure of our nation grows tremendously at the very time that our propagandists are fiercely denying it. We have a privileged class of men with more income than they can possibly spend and more power than they can hire brains to use. In the guise of idle rich, with trained executives and with a vast and useless military organization throwing away the taxes piled on the workers, this ruling clique outrivals the aristocracy of George III or Louis XIV. We have a middle class of white collar workers, technicians, artisans, artists, professional men and teachers able to live in comfort so long as they restrict their thought and planning, and deceive themselves in thinking they will sometime join the "independently" rich.

Our last presidential election was a farce. We had no chance to vote for the questions in which we were really interested: peace, disarmament, the draft, unfair taxation, race bias, education, social medicine, and flood control. On the contrary we had before us one ticket under two names and the nominees shadowboxed with false fanfare and advertisement for the same policies, with infinitesimal shades of difference and with spurious earnestness. Small wonder that half of the American voters stayed home.

Thus it is clear today that the salvation of American Negroes lies in socialism. They should support all measures and men who favor the welfare state; they should vote for government ownership of capital in industry; they should favor strict regulation of corporations or their public ownership; they should vote to prevent monopoly from controlling the press and the publishing of opinions. They should favor public ownership and control of water, electric, and atomic power; they should stand for a clean ballot, the encouragement of third parties, independent candidates, and the elimination of graft and gambling on television and even in churches.

The question of the method by which the socialist state

an be achieved must be worked out by experiment and reason and not by dogma. Whether or not methods which were right and clear in Russia and China fit our circumstances is for our intelligence to decide. The atom bomb has revolutionized our thought. Peace is not only preferable today, it is increasingly inevitable. Passive resistance is not the end of action, but the beginning. After refusing to fight, there is the question of how to live. The Negro church which stops discrimination against bus riders must next see how those riders can earn a decent living and not remain helplessly exploited by those who own busses and make Jim Crow laws. This may well be a difficult program, but it is the only one.

Helen Alfred, editor, *Toward a Socialist America*, New York, 1958, pp. 179-91.

33

AFRICA AWAKE!

In December 1958, Dr. Du Bois sent the following message to the Accra Conference of African States. It was read to the conference by Shirley Graham Du Bois, Dr. Du Bois's wife, who was the only non-African permitted to address the gathering.

My only role in this meeting is one of advice from one who has lived long, who has studied Africa and has seen the modern world. I had hoped to deliver this word in person, but this was not possible. I have therefore asked my wife, Shirley Graham, to read it to you. It is simple and direct. In this great crisis of the world's history, when standing on the highest peaks of human accomplishment we look forward to peace and backward to war; when we look up to heaven and down to hell, let us mince no words. We face triumph or tragedy without alternative. Africa, ancient Africa has been called by the world and has lifted up her hands! Which way shall Africa go? First I would emphasize the fact that today Africa has no choice between private capitalism and socialism. The whole world including capitalist countries, is moving toward socialism inevitably, inexorably. You can choose between blocs of military alliance, you can choose between groups of political union, you cannot choose between socialism and private capitalism, because private ownership of capital is doomed.

But what is socialism? It is disciplined economy and

political organization in which the first duty of a citizen is to serve the state; and the state is not a selected aristocracy, or a group of self-seeking oligarchs who have seized wealth and power. No! The mass of workers with hand and brain are the ones whose collective destiny is the chief object of all effort. Gradually, every state is coming to this concept of its aim. The great Communist states like the Soviet Union and China have surrendered completely to this idea. The Scandinavian states have yielded partially; Britain has yielded in some respects, France in part and even the United States adopted the New Deal which was largely socialistic, even though today further American socialism is held at bay by sixty great groups of corporations who control individual capitalists and the trade-union leaders.

On the other hand, the African tribe, whence all of you sprung, was communistic in its very beginnings. No tribesman was free. All were servants of the tribe of whom the chief was father and voice. Read of the West Coast trade as described by [J.E.] Casely-Hayford: There is small trace of private enterprise or individual initiative. It was the tribe which carried on trade through individuals, and the chief was the mouthpiece of the common will.

Here then, my brothers, you face your great decision: will you for temporary advantage—for automobiles, refrigerators and Paris gowns—spend your income in paying interest on borrowed funds, or will you sacrifice present comfort and the chance to shine before your neighbors in order to educate your children, develop such industry as best serves the great mass of people and makes your country strong in ability, self-support and self-defense? Such union of effort for strength calls for sacrifice and self-denial, while the capital offered you at high price by the colonial powers like France, Britain, Holland, Belgium, and the United States, will prolong fatal colonial imperialism, from which you have suffered slavery, serfdom and colonialism. You are not helpless. You are the buyers of capital goods, and to continue existence as sellers of capital, the great nations, former owners of the world, must sell or face bankruptcy. You are not compelled to buy all they offer now. You can wait. You can starve a while longer rather than sell your great heritage for a mass of Western capitalistic pottage.

You can not only beat down the price of capital as offered by the united and monopolized Western private capitalists, but at last today you can compare their offers with those of socialist countries like the Soviet Union and China, which with infinite sacrifice and pouring out of blood and tears are at last able to offer weak nations needed capital on better terms than the West. The supply which socialist nations can at present spare is small as compared with that of the bloated monopolies of the West, but it is large and rapidly growing. Its acceptance involves no bonds which a free Africa may not safely assume. It certainly does not involve slavery and colonial control which is the price which the West has demanded, and still demands. Today she offers a compromise, but one of which you must beware: she offers to let some of your smarter and less scrupulous leaders become fellow capitalists with the white exploiters, if in turn they induce the nation's masses to pay the awful cost. This has happened in the West Indies and in South America. This may yet happen in the Middle East and Eastern Asia. Strive against it with every fiber of your bodies and souls. A body of local private capitalists, even if they are black, can never free Africa; they will simply sell it into new slavery to old masters overseas.

As I have said, this is a call for sacrifice. Great Goethe sang, *"Entbehren sollst du, sollst entbehren"*—"Thou shalt forego, shalt do without." If Africa unites, it will be because each part, each nation, each tribe gives up a part of its heritage for the good of the whole. That is what union means; that is what Pan-Africa means: when the child is born into the tribe the price of his growing up is to give over a part of his freedom to the tribe. This he soon learns or dies. When the tribe becomes a union of tribes, the individual tribe surrenders some part of its freedom to the paramount tribe.

When the nation arises, the constituent tribes, clans and groups must each yield power and much freedom to the demands of the nation or the nation dies before it is born. Your local tribal, much-loved languages must yield to the few world tongues which serve the largest numbers of people and promote understanding and world literature.

This is the great dilemma which faces Africa today; faces one and all: give up individual rights for the needs of the nation; give up tribal independence for the needs of Mother Africa. Forget nothing but set everything in its rightful place: the glory of the six Ashanti Wars against Britain; the wisdom of the Fanti Confederation; the unity of Nigeria; the song of the Songhay and Hausa; the rebellion of the Mahdi and the hands of Ethiopia; the greatness of the Basuto and the fighting of Chaka; the revenge of Mutessa, and many other happenings and men; but above all — Africa, Mother of Men. Your nearest friends and neighbors are the colored people of China and India, the rest of Asia, the Middle East and the sea isles, once close bound to the heart of Africa and now long severed by the greed of Europe. Your bond is no mere color of skin but the deeper experience of wage-slavery and contempt.

So too, your bond with the white world is closest to those like the Union of Soviet Socialist Republics, who support and defend China and help the slaves of Tibet and India, and not those who exploit the Middle East, the West Indies, and South America.

"Awake, awake, put on thy strength, O Zion"; reject the meekness of missionaries who teach neither love nor brotherhood, but emphasize the virtues of private profit from capital, stolen from your land and labor. Africa awake, put on the beautiful robes of Pan-African socialism.

You have nothing to lose but your chains!

You have a continent to regain!

You have freedom and human dignity to attain!

National Guardian, December 22, 1958.

34

HAIL HUMANKIND!

Dr. Du Bois celebrated his ninety-first birthday in Peking, China, where it was hailed in national festivities. On February 22, 1959, he spoke to all humanity, pleading especially for unity of China and Africa. His speech was broadcast from Peking to the world.

By courtesy of the government of the six hundred million people of the Chinese Republic, I am permitted on my ninety-first birthday to speak to the people of China and Africa and through them to the world. Hail, then, and farewell, dwelling places of the yellow and black races. Hail humankind!

I speak with no authority; no assumption of age nor rank; I hold no position, I have no wealth. One thing alone I own and that is my own soul. Ownership of that I have even while in my own country for near a century I have been nothing but a "nigger." On this basis and this alone I dare speak, I dare advise.

China after long centuries has arisen to her feet and leapt forward. Africa, arise, and stand straight, speak and think! Act! Turn from the West and your slavery and humiliation for the last five hundred years and face the rising sun.

Behold a people, the most populous nation on this ancient earth, which has burst its shackles, not by boasting and strutting, not by lying about its history and its conquests, but by patience and long suffering, by blind struggle, moved up and on toward the crimson sky. She aims to "make men holy; to make men free."

But what men? Not simply the mandarins but including the mandarins; not simply the rich, but not excluding the rich. Not simply the learned, but led by knowledge to the end that no man shall be poor, nor sick, nor ignorant; but that the humblest worker as well as the sons of emperors shall be fed and taught and healed and that there emerge on earth a single unified people, free, well and educated.

You have been told, my Africa: my Africa in Africa and all your children's children overseas; you have been told and the telling so beaten into you by rods and whips, that you believe it yourselves, that this is impossible; that mankind can rise only by walking on men; by cheating them and killing them; that only on a doormat of the despised and dying, the dead and rotten, can a British aristocracy, a French cultural elite or an American millionaire be nurtured and grown.

This is a lie. It is an ancient lie spread by church and state, spread by priest and historian, and believed in by fools and cowards, as well as by the downtrodden and the children of despair.

Speak, China, and tell your truth to Africa and the world. What people have been despised as you have? Who more than you have been rejected of men? Recall when lordly Britishers threw the rickshaw money on the ground to avoid touching a filthy hand. Forget not the time when in Shanghai no Chinese man dare set foot in a park which he paid for. Tell this to Africa, for today Africa stands on new feet, with new eyesight, with new brains and asks: Where am I and why?

The Western sirens answer: Britain wheedles; France cajoles; while America, my America, where my ancestors and descendants for eight generations have lived and toiled; America loudest of all, yells and promises freedom. If only Africa allows American investment!

Beware Africa, America bargains for your soul. America would have you believe that they freed your grandchildren; that Afro-Americans are full American citizens, treated like equals, paid fair wages as workers, promoted for desert and free to learn and travel across the world.

This is not true. Some are near freedom; some approach

equality with whites; some have achieved education; but the price for this has too often been slavery of mind, distortion of truth and oppression of our own people.

Of eighteen million Afro-Americans, twelve million are still second-class citizens of the United States, serfs in farming, low-paid laborers in industry, and repressed members of union labor. Most American Negroes do not vote. Even the rising six million are liable to insult and discrimination at any time.

But this, Africa, relates to your descendants, not to you. Once I thought of you Africans as children, whom we educated Afro-Americans would lead to liberty. I was wrong. We could not even lead ourselves, much less you. Today I see you rising under your own leadership, guided by your own brains.

Africa does not ask alms from China nor from the Soviet Union nor France, Britain, nor the United States. It asks friendship and sympathy and no nation better than China can offer this to the Dark Continent. Let it be freely given and generously. Let Chinese visit Africa, send their scientists there and their artists and writers. Let Africa send its students to China and its seekers after knowledge. It will not find on earth a richer goal, a more promising mine of information.

On the other hand, watch the West. The British West Indian Federation is not a form of democratic progress but a cunning attempt to reduce these islands to the control of British and American investors. Haiti is dying under rich Haitian investors who with American money are enslaving the peasantry. Cuba is showing what the West Indies, Central and South America are suffering under American big business.[1]

The American worker himself does not always realize this. He has high wages and many comforts. Rather than lose these, he keeps in office by his vote the servants of industrial exploitation so long as they maintain his wage. His labor leaders represent exploitation and not the fight against the exploitation of labor by private capital. These two sets of exploiters fall out only when one demands too large a share of the loot.

This China knows. This Africa must learn. This the

American Negro has failed so far to learn. I am frightened by the so-called friends who are flocking to Africa. Negro Americans trying to make money from your toil, white Americans who seek by investment and high interest to bind you in serfdom to business as the Near East is bound and as South America is struggling with. For this America is tempting your leaders, bribing your young scholars, and arming your soldiers. What shall you do?

First, understand! Realize that the great mass of mankind is freeing itself from wage slavery, while private capital in Britain, France, and now in America, is still trying to maintain civilization and comfort for a few on the toil, disease and ignorance of the mass of men. Understand this, and understanding comes from direct knowledge. You know America and France, and Britain to your sorrow. Now know the Soviet Union, but particularly know China.

China is flesh of your flesh, and blood of your blood. China is colored and knows to what a colored skin in this modern world subjects its owner. But China knows more, much more than this: she knows what to do about it. She can take the insults of the United States and still hold her head high. She can make her own machines, when America refuses to sell her American manufactures, even though it hurts American industry, and throws her workers out of jobs. China does not need American nor British missionaries to teach her religion and scare her with tales of hell. China has been in hell too long, not to believe in a heaven of her own making. This she is doing.

Come to China, Africa, and look around. Invite Africa to come, China, and see what you can teach by just pointing. Yonder old woman is working on the street. But she is happy. She has no fear. Her children are in school and a good school. If she is ill, there is a hospital where she is cared for free of charge. She has a vacation with pay each year. She can die and be buried without taxing her family to make some undertaker rich.

Africa can answer: but some of this we have done; our tribes undertake public service like this. Very well, let your tribes continue and expand this work. What Africa must realize is what China knows; that it is worse than stupid to allow a people's education to be under the control of those who seek not the progess of the people but their use as means of making themselves rich and powerful. It is wrong for the University of London to control the University of Ghana. It is wrong for the Catholic Church to direct the education of the black Congolese. It was wrong for Protestant churches supported by British and American wealth to control higher education in China.

The Soviet Union is surpassing the world in popular and higher education, because from the beginning it started its own complete education system. The essence of the revolution in the Soviet Union and China and in all the "iron curtain" nations, is not the violence that accompanied the change; no more than starvation at Valley Forge was the essence of the American revolution against Britain. The real revolution is the acceptance on the part of the nation of the fact that hereafter the main object of the nation is the welfare of the mass of the people and not of the lucky few.

Government is for the people's progress and not for the comfort of an aristocracy. The object of industry is the welfare of the workers and not the wealth of the owners. The object of civilization is the cultural progress of the mass of workers and not merely of an intellectual elite. And in return for all this, Communist lands believe that the cultivation of the mass of people will discover more talent and genius to serve the state than any closed aristocracy ever furnished. This belief the current history of the Soviet Union and China is proving true each day. Therefore don't let the West invest when you can avoid it. Don't buy capital from Britain, France and the United States if you can get it on reasonable terms from the Soviet Union and China. This is not politics; it is common sense. It is learning from experience. It is trusting your friends and watching your enemies. Refuse to be cajoled or to change your way of life so as to make a few of your fellows rich at the expense of a mass of workers growing poor and sick and remaining without schools so that a few black men can have automobiles.

Africa, here is a real danger which you must avoid or return to the slavery from which you are emerging. All I ask from you is the courage to know; to look about you and see what is happening in this old and tired world; to realize the extent and depth of its rebirth and the promise which glows on your hills.

Visit the Soviet Union and visit China. Let your youth learn the Russian and Chinese languages. Stand together in this new world and let the old world perish in its greed or be born again in new hope and promise. Listen to the Hebrew prophet of communism:

Ho! every one that thirsteth; come ye to the waters; come, buy and eat, without money and price!

Again, China and Africa, hail and farewell!

The Autobiography of W. E. B. Du Bois, pp. 405-08.

35

ENCYCLOPEDIA AFRICANA

In 1961 Dr. Du Bois was invited by President Nkrumah to come to Ghana, to live and work, and draw upon his great store of erudition and experience in planning an Encyclopedia Africana. *Du Bois took up residence in Ghana and in 1963 became a citizen of that country. On December 15, 1962, in what was his last public speech, he addressed a conference on the* Encyclopedia Africana *at the University of Ghana.*

I wish to express my sincere thanks to those of you here who have accepted the invitation of our Secretariat to participate in this conference and thus assist us in the preparatory work which we have undertaken for the creation of an *Encyclopedia Africana.*

Had there been any doubts in your minds of the importance of African Studies, I am sure the papers and discussions of the past week have dispelled them. The wide attendance at the First International Congress of Africanists attests to the almost feverish interest throughout the world in the hitherto "Dark Continent."

It remains, therefore, for me only to lay before you the importance of an *Encyclopedia Africana* based in *Africa* and compiled by *Africans.*

You have noted from letters cited in our Information Report, the most gratifying endorsement from scholars in all sections of the world of the general aims of this work. Some of you, however, ask if an *Encyclopedia Africana* at this time is not premature. Is this not a too ambitious undertaking for African scholars to attempt? Is there enough scientifically proven information ready for publication? Our answer is that an *Encyclopedia Africana* is long overdue. Yet, it is logical that such a work had to wait for independent Africans to carry it out.

We know that there does exist much scientific knowledge of Africa which has never been brought together. We have the little known works of African scholars of the past in North Africa, in the Sudan, in Egypt. Al Azhar University and the Islamic University of Sankore made large collections; *Presence Africaine* has already brought to light much material written in the French language. We can, therefore, begin, remembering always that an encyclopedia is never a finished or complete body of information. Research and study must be long and continuous. We can collect, organize and publish knowledge as it emerges. The encyclopedia must be seen as a living effort which will grow and change—which will expand through the years as more and more material is gathered from all parts of Africa.

It is true that scientific written records do not exist in most parts of this vast continent. But the time is *now* for beginning. The encyclopedia hopes to eliminate the artificial boundaries created on this continent by colonial masters. Designations such as "British Africa," "French Africa," "Black Africa," "Islamic Africa" too often serve to keep alive differences which in large part have been imposed on Africans by outsiders. The encyclopedia must have research units throughout West Africa, North Africa, East, Central and South Africa which will gather and record information for these geographical sections of the continent. The encyclopedia is concerned with Africa as a whole.

It is true that there are not now enough trained African scholars available for this gigantic task. In the early stages we have need of the technical skills in research which have been highly developed in other parts of the world. We have already asked for and to a most gratifying degree been granted the unstinted cooperation and assistance of the leading Institutes of African Studies outside Africa. Many of you who have gathered here from

distant lands can, and I believe will, make valuable contributions to this undertaking. And you can assist us in
finding capable African men and women who can carry
the responsibilities of this work in their own country and
to their people. For it is African scholars themselves who
will create the ultimate *Encyclopedia Africana.*

My interest in this enterprise goes back to 1909 when I
first attempted to launch an *Encyclopedia Africana* while
still teaching at Atlanta University in Georgia, U.S.A.
Though a number of distinguished scholars in the United
States and various European countries consented to serve
as sponsors, the more practical need of securing financial
backing for the projected encyclopedia was not solved
and the project had to be abandoned.

Again, in 1931, a group of American scholars met at
Howard University and agreed upon the necessity of preparing an *Encyclopedia of the Negro*—using this term in
its broadest sense. There was much organization work
and research done in the preparation, but once again,
the undertaking could not be carried through because
money could not be secured. Educational foundations had
doubts about a work of this kind being accomplished
under the editorship of Negroes. We are deeply grateful to
the President of Ghana and to the government of this
independent African state for inviting us to undertake this
important task here where the necessary funds for beginning this colossal work are provided. After all, this is
where the work should be done—in Africa, sponsored by
Africans, for Africa. *This encyclopedia will be carried
through.*

Much has happened in Africa and the world in the last
twenty years. Yet, something of what I wrote in the Preparatory Volume of the *Encyclopedia of the Negro,* which
was published in 1945, will bear repeating now:

"Present thought and action are all too often guided by
old and discarded theories of race and heredity, by misleading emphasis and silence of former histories. These
conceptions are passed on to younger generations of students by current textbooks, popular histories and even
public discussion. Our knowledge of Africa today is not,
of course, entirely complete; there are many gaps where

further information and more careful study is needed; but this is the case in almost every branch of knowledge. Knowledge is never complete, and in few subjects does a time arrive when an encyclopedia is demanded because no further information is expected. Indeed, the need for an encyclopedia is greatest when a stage is reached where there is a distinct opportunity to bring together and set down a clear and orderly statement of the facts already known and agreed upon, for the sake of establishing a base for further advance and further study."

For these reasons and under these circumstances it would seem that an *Encyclopedia Africana* is of vital importance to Africa as a whole and to the world at large.

Freedomways, Winter 1963, pp. 28-30.

36

LAST MESSAGE TO THE WORLD

Dr. Du Bois's last message was dated June 26, 1957, and was given to keeping of his wife, Shirley Graham Du Bois. As Dr. Du Bois was buried in Accra, Ghana, at a state funeral, it was read:

It is much more difficult in theory than actually to say the last good-bye to one's loved ones and friends and to all familiar things of this life.

I am going to take a long, deep and endless sleep. This is not a punishment but a privilege to which I looked forward for years.

I have loved my work, I have loved people and my play, but always I have been uplifted by the thought that what I have done well will live long and justify my life; that what I have done ill or never finished can now be handed on to others for endless days to be finished, perhaps better than I could have done.

And that peace will be my applause.

One thing alone I charge you. As you live, believe in life! Always human beings will live and progress to greater, broader and fuller life.

The only possible death is to lose belief in this truth simply because the great end comes slowly, because time is long.

Good-bye.

Encyclopedia Africana Secretariat Information Report No. 6, September 1963.

TRIBUTE TO W.E.B. Du Bois

By Dr. Kwame Nkrumah

The following message was broadcast to the people of Ghana by President Nkrumah following the funeral of Dr. Du Bois on August 29, 1963.

We mourn the death of Dr. William Edward Burghardt Du Bois, a great son of Africa.

Dr. Du Bois, in a long life-span of ninety-six years, achieved distinction as a poet, historian and sociologist. He was an undaunted fighter for the emancipation of colonial and oppressed people, and pursued this objective throughout his life.

The fields of literature and science were enriched by his profound and searching scholarship, a brilliant literary talent, and a keen and penetrating mind. The essential quality of Dr. Du Bois's life and achievement can be summed up in a single phrase: "intellectual honesty and integrity."

Dr. Du Bois was a distinguished figure in the pioneering days of the Pan-African Movement in the Western World. He was the secretary of the first Pan-African Congress held in London in 1900. In 1919 he organized another Pan-African Congress in Paris which coincided with the Paris Peace Conference. When George Padmore and I organized the Fifth Pan-African Congress in 1945 at Manchester, we invited Dr. Du Bois, then already seventy-eight years of age, to chair that Congress. I knew him in the United States and even spoke on the same platform with him. It was however at this Conference in Manchester that I was drawn closely to him. Since then he has been personally a real friend and father to me.

Dr. Du Bois was a lifelong fighter against all forms of racial inequality, discrimination and injustice. He helped to establish the National Association for the Advancement of Colored People, and was first editor of its fighting organ, *The Crisis.* Concerning the struggle for the improvement of the status of the Negro in America, he once said: "We will not be satisfied to take one jot or tittle less than our full manhood rights. We claim for ourselves every single right that belongs to a free-born American: political, civil and social; and until we get these rights, we will never cease to protest and assail the ears of America. The battle we wage is not for ourselves alone, but all true Americans."

It was the late George Padmore who described Dr. Du Bois as the greatest scholar the Negro race has produced, and one who always upheld the right of Africans to govern themselves.

I asked Dr. Du Bois to come to Ghana to pass the evening of his life with us and also to spend his remaining years in compiling an *Encyclopedia Africana*, a project which is part of his whole intellectual life.

We mourn his death. May he live in our memory not only as a distinguished scholar but a great African Patriot. Dr. Du Bois is a phenomenon. May he rest in peace.

Encyclopedia Africana Secretariat Information Report, No. 6, September 1963.

NOTES

1. On Being Black

1. Queen Nefertari, a black woman, was the wife of Ahmose I and co-founder of the Eighteenth Dynasty in Egypt.

Sonni Ali, "The Liberator," shook off Malian domination of Songhay in West Africa in 1465 and ruled the Songhay empire until 1492 when he was drowned while crossing the Niger River.

Askea Muhammed, who ruled Songhay from 1494 to 1538 and was known as Askea the Great, was the most famous ruler of the West African kingdoms.

2. On Marcus Garvey

The notes for this chapter are by Dr. Du Bois.

1. Of the fifteen names of his fellow officers in 1914 not a single one appears in 1918; of the eighteen names of officers published in 1918 only six survive in 1919; among the small list of principal officers published in 1920 I do not find a single name mentioned in 1919.

2. Mr. Garvey boasts February 14, 1920:
"This week I present you with the Black Star Line Steamship Corporation recapitalized at ten million dollars. They told us when we incorporated this corporation that we could not make it, but we are now gone from a $5,000,000 corporation to one of $10,000,000."

This sounds impressive, but means almost nothing. The fee for incorporating a $5,000,000 concern in Delaware is $350. *By paying $250 more the corporation may incorporate with $10,000,000 authorized capital without a cent of capital actually paid in!* Cf. *General Corporation Laws of the State of Delaware,* edition of 1917.

3. Technically the *Yarmouth* does not belong to the Black Star Line of Delaware, but to the "Black Star Line of Canada, Limited," incorporated in Canada, March 23, 1920, with one million dollars capital. This capital consists of $500 cash and $999,500 "assets."

Probably the Black Star Line of Delaware controls this corporation, but this is not known.

4. P. N. Gordon.

5. "The Universal Negro Improvement Association is raising a constructive loan of two million dollars from its members. Three hundred thousand dollars out of this two million has been allotted to the New York Local as its quota, and already the members in New York have started to subscribe to the loan, and in the *next seven days* the three hundred thousand dollars will be oversubscribed. The great divisions of Pittsburgh, Philadelphia, Boston, Chicago, Cleveland, Wilmington, Baltimore and Washington will also oversubscribe their quota to make up the two million dollars.

"Constructive work will be started in *January* 1921, when the first ship of the Black Star Line on the African trade will sail from New York with materials and workmen for this constructive work."

Eleven days later, November 6, the *Negro World* is still "raising the loan" but there is no report of the amount raised.

6. It might be argued that it is not absolutely necessary that the Black Star Line, etc. should pay financially. It is quite conceivable that Garvey should launch a business philanthropy, and that without expectation of return, colored people should contribute for a series of years to support Negro enterprise. But this is not Garvey's idea. He says plainly in a circular:

"The Black Star Line corporation presents to every Black Man, Woman and Child the opportunity to climb the great ladder of industrial and commercial progress. If you have ten dollars, one hundred dollars, or one or five thousand dollars to invest for profit, then take out shares in The Black Star Line, Inc. This corporation is chartered to trade on every sea and all waters. The Black Star Line will turn over large profits and dividends to stockholders, and operate to their interest even whilst they will be asleep."

7. He said in his "inaugural" address:

"The signal honor of being Provisional President of Africa is mine. It is a political job; it is a political calling for me to redeem Africa. It is like asking Napoleon to take the world. He took a certain portion of the world in his time. He failed and died at St. Helena. But may I not say that the lessons of Napoleon are but stepping stones by which we shall guide ourselves to African liberation?"

3. The Amenia Conference: An Historic Negro Gathering

1. This is the editorial Dr. Du Bois wrote in *The Crisis* shortly after the death of Booker T. Washington.

2. Actually, William Monroe Trotter, a leading figure in the Niagara Movement, refused to join the NAACP.

The reference to William English Walling, a socialist and a founder of the NAACP, is to his article, "Race War in the South," published in *The Independent* after the Springfield riots of August 1908.

3. The reference is to the so-called "Boston Riot" on June 30, 1905. Booker T. Washington had been invited to speak in the city by the Boston branch of the National Business League, but when he arose to address the audience, Trotter interrupted him with a series of questions directed towards forcing Washington to concede that he was advocating surrender of rights by the Negro people. Seized by the police, who had been alerted by Washington's agents, Trotter was arrested, fined fifty dollars and sentenced to thirty days in prison for disturbing the peace.

4. In January 1904, a conference of about fifty Negro leaders took place in New York's Carnegie Hall, called by Booker T. Washington, to "discuss all matters of interest to our race." A Committee of Twelve for the Advancement of the Interests of the Negro Race, dominated by Washington and financed by Andrew Carnegie, was established. Du Bois was a member of the Committee but soon resigned, not wishing to appear to be endorsing policies enunciated by Washington.

5. "Close Ranks" was also the title of an editorial Du Bois published in *The Crisis* in the summer of 1918 in which he supported the United States in World War I, and wrote: "Let us, while this war lasts, forget our special grievances and close ranks shoulder to shoulder with our own fellow citizens and the allied nations that are fighting for democracy. We make no ordinary sacrifice, but we make it gladly and willingly with our eyes lifted to the hills." (Vol. XVI, 1918, p. 111.) The editorial caused a good deal of criticism of Du Bois by radical black militants who accused him of surrendering the struggle for freedom and equality.

4. The Negro Citizen

1. In 1919 the NAACP published *Thirty Years of Lynching in the United States, 1889-1918*. Two years later, the Association held over 200 meetings in the United States, at many of which Dr. Du Bois spoke, to protest against lynchings. Dr. Du Bois filled the columns of *The Crisis* with facts about lynchings. On November 23, 1922, the Association placed full-page advertisements in the *New York Times* and other leading newspapers headed, "The Shame of America. . . . 3436 People Lynched 1889 to 1922."

2. After the defeat of the Dyer Anti-Lynching Bill, Negroes launched a campaign to assure that those congressmen responsible for its failure would not be reelected.

3. In 1816 the American Colonization Society was organized with Justice Bushrod Washington as president and Henry Clay as a prominent member. The object was to send free blacks to Africa, and the Society established Liberia as a Negro colony in Africa for this purpose. Many black and white Abolitionists attacked the Society for strengthening prejudice against free Negroes and the chains of slavery on those in bondage. Actually few Negroes left for Liberia.

5. The Denial of Economic Justice to Negroes

1. Dr. Du Bois is not entirely correct in his assertion. The Socialist Party at its founding convention in 1901 did take a strong stand in favor of the rights of Negroes and invited them to become members. However, not much was done to implement the resolution. The Socialist Party, at its sixteenth convention in 1928, adopted the following statement relating to the Negro:

"As a measure of protection for the oppressed, especially for our Negro fellow citizens, we propose:

"Enactment of the Berger anti-lynching bill making participation in lynching a felony."

Victor Berger was a Socialist congressman from Wisconsin.

6. Shall the Negro Be Encouraged to Seek Cultural Equality?

1. The Eighteenth or Prohibition Amendment barred alcoholic drinks; it was notoriously unenforced and was repealed in 1933.

7. Education and Work

1. These are excerpts from Booker T. Washington's famous Atlanta Exposition speech in 1895. Washington's actual words were ". . . separate as the five fingers, yet one as the hand in all things essential to material progress."

8. A Negro Nation Within the Nation

1. The Bull Moose Party was the popular name for the Progressive Party of 1912 led by Theodore Roosevelt. At the founding convention of the party which nominated Roosevelt for president, Du Bois attempted to get the movement to go on record against discrimination and for equal rights for Negroes, but Roosevelt, anxious to appease southern Progressives, rejected the proposal and privately informed Oswald Garrison Villard who headed a NAACP delegation that Du Bois was "a dangerous man."

2. Robert M. LaFollette (1855-1925), Progressive senator from Wisconsin, was the presidential candidate of the Progressive (Farmer-Labor) Party in 1924. He received a total of some five million votes.

3. Thaddeus Stevens's plan called for dividing the estates of the "leading rebels" into tracts of forty acres for each adult freedman. In this way, Stevens insisted, the freedmen would be adequately taken care of. These proposals were incorporated into a bill Stevens introduced into the House on March 1, 1867. Besides providing each head of a family with forty acres the bill would also appropriate $50 to each for a homestead. But the measure failed to pass the House.

4. The reference is to the New York City Draft Riots of July 1863, unleashed by opposition to the National Conscription Act. During five days, mobs burned and looted, and murdered and maimed Negroes.

5. James Weldon Johnson (1871-1938), noted Negro poet, was secretary of the NAACP, and opposed Du Bois's separatist program.

6. As early as 1852, Martin R. Delany in the appendix to his book, *The Condition, Elevation, Emigration and Destiny of the Colored People of the United States*, wrote: "We are a nation within a nation;— as the Poles in Russia, the Hungarians in Austria, the Welsh, Irish and Scotch in the British dominions." It is probable that Du Bois based his concept upon that of the man who is generally viewed to be the pioneer black nationalist in the United States.

9. What the Negro Has Done for the United States and Texas

1. The reference is to David Walker's revolutionary *Appeal to the Colored Citizens of the World* (1829-1830) in which he urged the slaves to revolt and overthrow their inhuman masters. The pamphlet has been reprinted with an introduction of its setting and meaning by Herbert Aptheker under the title, *One Continual Cry* (New York, 1965).

2. The reference is to *The Narrative of the Life of Frederick Douglass*, with introductions by William Lloyd Garrison and Wendell Phillips. It was published in May 1845, became a fast seller, was translated into French and German, and by January 1848 had gone through nine editions in English.

3. Twenty of these black congressmen sat in the House of Representatives between 1870 and 1901, all of them representing states in the South. When George H. White of North Carolina, the last of the post-Civil War congressmen, finished his term in 1901, he predicted, in his valedictory, that the Negro would return. But it took twenty-seven years for his prophecy to be fulfilled. In 1928 Oscar De Priest

of Chicago was elected to the first of three terms. De Priest lost his seat to Arthur Mitchell in 1934 who, during his eight years in Congress, seldom spoke up for Negro rights. Perhaps because of his refusal to take a position in behalf of his people, Du Bois did not mention Mitchell's name in referring to "one member at present."

11. Prospect of a World Without Racial Conflict

1. This is a quotation from Sidney and Beatrice Webb, *Communism: A New Civilization,* published in 1935. The Webbs visited the Soviet Union in 1932 and their book was an influential endorsement of Communism in operation.

12. Jacob and Esau

1. This is a quotation from Karl Marx's *Capital.* However, Du Bois in places has paraphrased Marx and interpolated his own words for those of the English translation of the work. The essential meaning, however, is not distorted. Since it is likely Du Bois used the translation of *Capital* by Samuel Moore and Edward Aveling (published by Charles H. Kerr and Co., Chicago, 1906) the reader can compare Du Bois's rendition with the original by consulting pp. 801-802, vol. I, of the Kerr edition of *Capital.*

2. *Ibid.,* pp. 823-826.

3. *Ibid.,* pp. 832-833.

4. Henry George, *Progress and Poverty,* New York, Robert Schalkenbach Foundation, 1939, pp. 3-4. This work, originally published in 1879, argued that the land belonged to society, which created its value and should properly tax that value, not improvements on the land. George's proposal for such a "Single Tax" gained many adherents.

5. *Ibid.,* pp. 5-6.

13. The Negro and Imperialism

1. Dr. Du Bois here is paraphrasing Chief Justice Roger B. Taney's opinion in the Dred Scott decision in which he declared that the tradition of the United States from its founding as British colonies justified the conclusion that Negroes "had no rights which the white man was bound to respect."

14. The Pan-African Movement

1. United States Marines occupied Haiti and dominated the life of the country from 1915 to 1934.

15. Human Rights for All Minorities

1. During the presidential election of 1928, Alfred E. Smith was the Democratic candidate. A powerful campaign of bigotry, aimed at the fact that he was a Roman Catholic, contributed to his defeat at the polls.

17. Behold the Land

1. James F. Byrnes, formerly a racist senator from South Carolina, was secretary of state under Franklin D. Roosevelt during and after World War II. He was bitterly anti-Soviet and a strong proponent of the Cold War.

John C. Calhoun (1783-1850), member of the House of Representatives and the Senate from South Carolina, U. S. secretary of war and secretary of state, was the most prominent defender of slavery on the floor of the Senate before the Civil War.

Wade Hampton (1818-1902), Confederate general and South Carolina political leader, led the forces which overthrew Congressional Reconstruction in South Carolina and instituted the era of white supremacy.

Benjamin R. Tillman (1847-1918), South Carolina governor and U. S. senator, was a leading foe of Negro rights and a champion of white supremacy.

2. Arna Bontemps, black poet and novelist, was born in Alexandria, Louisiana in 1902. He graduated from Pacific Union College in northern California, and moved to New York. He taught at a small Alabama college while writing children's books, and in 1936 published his novel about the revolt of Gabriel Prosser, *Black Thunder.*

18. An Appeal to the World

1. Many of these appeals for redress of grievances are published in Herbert Aptheker, ed., *A Documentary History of the Negro People in the United States*, with a preface by W. E. B. Du Bois, New York, 1951.

19. We Must Know the Truth

1. In 1961, Du Bois joined the Communist Party of the United States.

2. Henry Wallace had been forced to resign as President Truman's secretary of commerce late in 1946 after publicly rejecting the president's hostile policy toward the Soviet Union. In 1948, Wallace ran for president on the Progressive Party ticket, and was actively supported by Dr. Du Bois. In 1950 Du Bois ran for United States senator from New York on the same ticket.

22. America's Pressing Problems

1. For a full discussion by Du Bois of "The General Strike" during the Civil War, see *Black Reconstruction: An Essay toward a History of the Part which Black Folk Played in the Attempt to Reconstruct Democracy in America, 1860-1880* (New York, 1935), Chapter IV.

2. George Seldes was the editor of *In Fact*, called "An Antidote for Falsehood in the Daily Press," published weekly during the 1940s and early 1950s. His book *1000 Americans*, which Du Bois cites, exposed the "ruling families" in the United States and the financial and industrial empires they controlled.

23. I Take My Stand

1. General Douglas MacArthur was in command of the military operation in 1932 which resulted in the eviction of the "Bonus Marchers," World War I veterans who were encamped in Washington, D. C., demanding advance payment of their adjusted compensation insurance benefits. The veterans were driven out of their shanty town, which was then burned.

24. The Negro and the Warsaw Ghetto

1. "Gooks" was a derisive term used by racist American officers and soldiers to describe Koreans during the Korean War. It was revived and used to describe the Vietnamese people in the Vietnam War.

25. What Is Wrong with the United States?

1. Joseph McCarthy, senator from Wisconsin, was the notorious politician whose witch-hunting of Communists and progressives gave the word "McCarthyism" to the English language. Charlie McCarthy was a ventriloquist's dummy, famous on radio.

26. One Hundred Years of Negro Freedom

1. The reference is to the publication in 1944 of a two-volume, 1,500-page analysis of the Negro people in America by Gunnar Myrdal

entitled, *An American Dilemma: The Negro Problem and American Democracy.*

27. On the Future of the American Negro

1. In the original, this word is not fully clear.

28. Two Hundred Years of Segregated Schools

1. The reference is to Dr. Herbert Aptheker's *American Negro Slave Revolts* (New York, 1943).

2. This is a quotation from Dr. Du Bois's *Black Reconstruction in America.*

3. In the *Plessy v. Ferguson* decision of 1896, the Supreme Court established the "separate but equal" doctrine as constitutional.

4. On May 17, 1954, the Supreme Court in a unanimous decision (*Brown et al. v. Board of Education of Topeka et al.*) declared: "We conclude that in the field of public education the doctrine of 'separate but equal' has no place. Separate educational facilities are inherently unequal."

29. If Eugene Debs Returned

1. Debs was in prison when he received these votes, having been found guilty of violating the Espionage Act because of his speeches against American entrance into World War I which he denounced as an imperialist war.

2. The reference is to former Communists who testified for the government against members of the Communist Party in hearings before the McCarthy Committee and in the Smith Act trials of the Communist leaders.

3. Debs was released from prison in 1921 and died in 1926.

4. The reference is to Norman Thomas who during the first years of the Soviet Union was a supporter of the socialist revolution in that country but later became a bitter opponent. Debs was a staunch champion of the Bolshevik Revolution and the Soviet Union and publicly proclaimed himself a Bolshevik.

31. Tribute to Paul Robeson

1. In the middle of August 1949, People's Artists, Inc., a New York

theatrical group, announced a concert by Paul Robeson at the Lakeland Acres picnic grounds outside of Peekskill, New York. The concert which was scheduled for August 27 was never held. Paul Robeson came to the scene but he could not enter the grounds. A mob of vigilantes blocked the entrance, and the audience was attacked, stoned and mobbed. The police looked on and did nothing. On Sunday, September 4, Robeson returned and 25,000 heard him sing. Although the audience refused to be provoked by jeering mobs, when the concert was over, the vigilantes, again with police assistance, stoned hundreds of cars, seriously injuring many who had attended the concert.

2. In *A Pictorial History of the Negro in America* (New York, 1956) which he co-edited with Milton Meltzer, Langston Hughes did devote two sentences to Paul Robeson (p. 277).

32. The Negro and Socialism

1. In the summer of 1955 fourteen-year-old Emmett Till was kidnapped and lynched at Money, Mississippi, for allegedly whistling at a white storekeeper's wife.

2. The Smith Act of 1940 made it illegal for a person to advocate "overthrowing . . . any government in the United States by force," or to "affiliate" with groups teaching this doctrine. In July 1948, the justice department procured the indictment of Eugene Dennis and ten other high-ranking Communist leaders under the act. In October 1949, in the federal district court in New York, they were convicted and sentenced to heavy fines and jail terms. The United States Supreme Court, 6 to 2, upheld the convictions in June 1951.

34. Hail Humankind!

1. On January 1, 1959, nearly two months before Dr. Du Bois delivered this statement, the Cuban Revolution, led by Fidel Castro, had ousted the dictator Batista and initiated a new era in Cuban and Latin American history. It seems clear that Du Bois was referring to the Batista regime which was dominated by American imperialists.

SELECTED BIBLIOGRAPHY

Aptheker, Herbert, *A Documentary History of the Negro People in the United States,* New York, 1951.

Aptheker, Herbert, "The Washington-Du Bois Conference of 1904," *Science and Society*, XIII, Fall 1949, 344-51.

Aptheker, Herbert, "W. E. B. Du Bois: The First Eighty Years," *Phylon*, IX, First Quarter, 1948, 58-69.

Aptheker, Herbert, "W. E. B. Du Bois: Story of a half-century of service to humanity," *National Guardian,* February 8, 1950, 6-7.

Aptheker, Herbert, "On the Meaning of Dr. Du Bois," in *Soul of the Republic: The Negro Today,* New York, 1964, 1-8.

Aptheker, Herbert, "W. E. B. Du Bois: The Final Years," *Journal of Human Relations,* First Quarter, 1966, 149-55.

Bond, Horace M., "Negro Leadership Since Washington," *South Atlantic Quarterly,* XXIV, April 1925, 115-30.

Braithwaite, William Stanley, "A Tribute to W. E. Burghardt Du Bois, First Editor of *Phylon,*" *Phylon,* X, Fourth Quarter, 1949, 302-06.

Broderick, Francis L., *W. E. B. Du Bois: Negro Leader in a Time of Crisis,* Stanford, 1959.

Brotz, Howard, editor, *Negro Social and Political Thought, 1850-1920,* New York, 1966.

Cox, Oliver C., "The Leadership of Booker T. Washington," *Social Forces,* XXX, 1951, 91-97.

Franklin, John Hope, *From Slavery to Freedom: A History of American Negroes,* New York, 1967.

Frazier, E. Franklin, "The Du Bois Program in the Present Crisis," *Race,* I, 1935-36, 11-13.

Freedomways: W. E. B. Du Bois Memorial Issue, V, Winter 1965.

Golden, L. Hanga and Milikian, Ov., "William E. B. Du Bois: Scientist and Public Figure," *Journal of Human Relations,* XIV, First Quarter, 1966, 156-68.

Graham, Shirley, "Why Was Du Bois Fired?" *Masses and Mainstream,* I, November 1948, 15-26.

Harding, Vincent, "W. E. B. Du Bois and the Black Messianic Vision," *Freedomways,* IX, Winter 1969, 44-58.

Henderson, Lenneal J., Jr., "W. E. B. Du Bois," *The Black Scholar,* January-February 1970, 48-57.

Lovett, Robert Morss, "Du Bois," *Phylon,* II, Third Quarter, 1941, 214-17.

Meier, August, *Negro Thought in America, 1880-1915,* Ann Arbor, 1963.

Meier, August and Roderick, Francis L., editors, *Negro Protest Thought in the Twentieth Century,* Indianapolis, 1965.

Meier, August and Rudwick, Elliot M., *From Plantation to Ghetto,* New York, 1966.

Melish, William Howard, "One of 'The Great Companions,'" *Journal of Human Relations,* XIV, First Quarter, 1966, 169-70. This is an extract from the Memorial Service Address at Ghana, September 29, 1963.

Rudwick, Elliott M., *W. E. B Du Bois: A Study in Minority Group Leadership,* Philadelphia, 1960.

Rudwick, Elliott M., "The Niagara Movement," *Journal of Negro History,* XLIII, July 1957, 177-200.

Smythe, H. H., "The N.A.A.C.P. Petition on the Denial of Human Rights and the United Nations," *Journal of Negro Education,* XVII, 1948, 88-90.

Walden, Daniel, "W. E. B. Du Bois's Essential Years: The Link from Douglass to the Present," *Journal of Human Relations,* First Quarter, 1966, 115-27.

Walden, Daniel and Wylie, Kenneth, "W. E. B. Du Bois: Pan-Africanism's Intellectual Father," *Journal of Human Relations,* XIV, First Quarter, 1966, 28-41.

INDEX